Only in Holland, Only the Dutch

Marc Resch

Only in Holland, Only the Dutch

An in-depth look into the culture of
Holland and its people

ROZENBERG
Publishers

ISBN 90 5170 800 9

(Cover)-Illustrations: Chris P. Jones, New York
www. eye-candy.ws
Photos: Marc Resch, New Jersey
Cover design & DTP: Ingrid Bouws

First edition, November 2004
Second edition, May 2005

Rozenberg Publishers
Bloemgracht 82-hs
1015 TM Amsterdam
The Netherlands
Tel.: + 31 20 625 54 29 Fax: + 31 20 620 33 95
E-mail: info@rozenbergps.com
www.rozenbergps.com
www.onlyinholland.com

TABLE OF CONTENTS

Acknowledgements

Thank you Danielle Gradillas for your inspiration and patience in the early stages of this endeavor; your support made this book a possibility. Thank you Cindy Resch for your unbelievable attention to detail and for being my teammate throughout the course of this venture. Thank you Bill Vignes for unselfishly volunteering to proofread my manuscript and for teaching me invaluable lessons in writing. Thank you Chris P. Jones for your incredible artwork and for always delivering quality drawings under tight timelines. Thank you John "Johnny Modem" Jupp, the *original* International Man of Mystery, for your ambassador-like ways and for showing me the ropes in Holland. Special thanks to Rozenberg Publishers, and especially Sunny van der Berg, for establishing an incredibly amicable working relationship with me and for sharing such deep insights into the Dutch culture. As always, thank you Mom and Dad for your unwavering love and support and for being my safety net in life. Thank you Dave Oliver and Ken Frawley for your friendship and for your selfless assistance in helping me put the final touches upon this book and in helping me close out a significant chapter in my book of life. Finally, thanks to the Dutch for keeping me entertained, perplexed and always interested and for providing me with such a vast array of fascinating material for this book.

PREFACE

Year after year, millions of people visit Holland from all parts of the world for various reasons. Holland offers something for everyone, to include enthralling culture, tumultuous history, charm and an inimitable permissiveness unlike any place in the world. I was afforded the extraordinary opportunity of living and working in Holland and had the fortunate experience of interacting with the Dutch inhabitants on a daily basis. I was determined from the beginning of my journey to delve deeply into Dutch society in order to learn as much as I possibly could about the unique culture, history, people and even the numerous idiosyncrasies and stereotypes of the Dutch that have been perplexing people around the world for centuries. I lived and worked side by side with the Dutch and resolutely attempted to explore every facet of their interesting culture. I partook in the festivals, cheered on the local football teams, shopped at the local markets, consumed coffee and beer with the locals in the numerous cafés and attempted to become *as Dutch* as I possibly could. I felt that total immersion into Dutch society would be the only way to peel away the many complicated layers surrounding the Dutch people and their unique ways.

It didn't take long to appreciate that the Dutch were a unique breed of people. As time progressed, I became increasingly amazed with the peculiar behaviors that presented themselves within the Dutch borders. In addition to the obvious societal distinctiveness of the country, to include the infamous Red Light District and the numerous hash houses, just to name a few, I observed a deeper side to the Dutch than just the casual, nonchalant side that most tourists and outsiders saw. The homogeneity in their actions, mannerisms and overall demeanor piqued my interests of Dutch culture even further. Their work behaviors, cultural customs, manners of expression, social policies and even idiosyncrasies were all *so Dutch*. I had one interesting, frustrating and unimaginable adventure after another for the remaining time I spent in Holland in dealing with all of this *Dutchness*.

In today's ever-shrinking world, it's not very prudent to make broad, sweeping generalizations about a culture, nationality, race or religion, and I attempted to avoid making such generalities throughout this book. There is a profound and uncanny homogeneity and natural flow that permeates Dutch society, however, that makes it possible to analyze the Dutch as a collective whole and to formulate assertions based upon their tightly-woven cultural attributes that have stood the test of time. Even with Holland's diversity and high-regard for individuality, a remarkable, and even curious, societal uniformity and consistency can be conspicuously observed. The Dutch unfathomably seem to be all on the same page, acting in accordance to unwritten societal expectations and all reliably serving the same societal purpose. In an increasingly globalized world, it's refreshing to see that the Dutch have managed to preserve many of their time-honored cultural norms and traditions, no matter how peculiar they may be to outsiders.

Many years ago I read a quote by the great philosopher, Aristotle, which stated that every man should write a book in his lifetime, among a few other endeavors, in order to give something back to the world. Aristotle's statement had a profound impact on me and had been lingering in the back of my mind for quite some time, for I agreed with its philosophical assertion and knew that someday I would be up for such a challenge. Upon encountering the intriguing ways of the Dutch, I knew immediately what my book would be about. This book explores the Dutch culture, history, values and the uniqueness of Holland and its people.

Throughout this book I provide an insider's perspective into the fascinating tidbits of Dutch culture and history. I attempt to deliver an in-depth point of view into the various anomalies that exist throughout the land and to somehow explain the inexplicability that runs rampant throughout this fascinating country.

1. INTRODUCTION TO THIS INTRIGUING PLACE CALLED HOLLAND

Holland has been mystifying people throughout the world for centuries due to the inimitable nature of its inhabitants and the layout of its land. Holland and the Dutch are truly unique in this world and possess an aura of fascination and peculiarity that leaves visitors and expatriates both perplexed and stimulated. The word *Holland* itself triggers bewilderment and curiosity in the minds of even the most educated and well-traveled. Even in the 21st century, people throughout the world still envision Holland as this fairy-tale, idyllic place full of blossoming tulips, grazing cows, fresh cheese, happy-go-lucky Dutch people and, of course, windmills and wooden shoes. The author of the story about the famous two little children, Hans and Gretel, growing up in Holland, opens her 1899 classic, *Hans Brinker or the Silver Skates* by stating,

> *"Holland is one of the queerest countries under the sun. It should be called Odd-land or Contrary-land, for in nearly everything it is different from the other parts of the world."*[1]

In many ways, today's Holland is no different than 19th century Holland with its oddities and numerous peculiarities. Holland is still unlike any other landmass in the world and the Dutch still retain the uncanny ability of differentiating themselves with their unique customs and unusual cultural traits. So what could possibly make this tiny land so different and its inhabitants so distinct from the rest of the world? This book will attempt to elucidate the many mysteries surrounding Holland and its people and attempt to explain the incomprehensible nature of this intriguing country.

We will embark upon our journey of demystifying Holland and its inhabitants by peeling away at the many complicated layers surrounding the Dutch and their captivating homeland. In order to unravel the mysteries of Holland and to attempt to clarify many of its ambiguities, we must begin with a basic orientation of the country. To begin, there is no such place called Holland! Holland simply doesn't exist. It is not a country, a province nor even a city. Why, then, is this book titled *Only in Holland, Only the Dutch* and why do so many people refer to the Dutch homeland as Holland? The title is an attempt by the author to emphasize the perplexity and preposterousness of the Dutch and their unusual native soil. People refer to the Dutch homeland as Holland mainly because they've heard it being referred to in the past as Holland and assume it's correct. The Dutch exacerbate the confusion over this fictitious place called Holland by labeling their world-renowned products, such as Dutch Gouda and Edam cheese, tulips, Kettle One vodka, Heineken and Amstel Light, with "From Holland" or "Made in Holland," even though there is no such place.

So what exactly is Holland and how did this word become synonymous with the Dutch homeland? To set the record straight, the Kingdom of the Netherlands, formed in 1815 and populated with 16.2 million people, is the official name of the country in which the Dutch people reside. For comparison, the table below depicts various countries around the world and their current population statistics.

As can be seen from the table, the Netherlands is a rather minuscule nation when compared with many countries around the world. In fact, the population of the Netherlands is just 5.5% of that of the U.S. population and a mere 1.25% of China's population. Even though the Netherlands is tiny in size and population, the Dutch continue to significantly impact and spread their influence throughout the world, as we will discover when we delve deeper into the Dutch culture and their worldly prominence.

Country	Population
Austria	8.2 million
Belgium	10.3 million
Netherlands	16.2 million
U.K.	60.2 million
Germany	82.4 million
U.S.	292.4 million
India	1.06 billion
China	1.29 billion

Population by Country [2]

The word Holland is contained in two of the twelve provinces dispersed throughout the Netherlands – North Holland and South Holland. The other ten provinces are Drenthe, Friesland, Gelderland, Groningen, Limburg, North Brabant, Overijssel, Utrecht, Flevoland and Zeeland. Even though North Holland and South Holland are two distinct provinces and account for just a fraction of the overall country's provincial layout, there is no such province with the name Holland within the Netherlands, and once again contrary to popular belief, Holland is not the name of the country. Simply ask any Dutch person residing in any of the ten provinces outside of North Holland or South Holland if they're from Holland and you'll hear a resounding and rather cantankerous "No!" Dutch persons from other provinces detest being called Hollanders. Such an inaccurate categorization is analogous to calling an American southerner a Yankee, or in Germany, calling a Prussian a Bavarian – not a very smart *accusation* to make!

Amsterdam is the capital city of the Netherlands and situated in the province of North Holland. In the 17th century, commonly referred to as the Dutch Golden Age, Amsterdam was the world's economic juggernaut. With Amsterdam being the major trading power throughout the world and residing in the province of North Holland, the shortened name, Holland, became synonymous with the region and home to the industrious Dutch merchants and traders. This inaccurate classification of Holland as the Dutch homeland has endured for centuries and is still used incorrectly today. I've polled numerous people from different countries on this topic and it's absolutely astonishing hearing the varied responses. Typical responses to the question, "What is the name of the country where the Dutch reside?" include:

- Holland
- Amsterdam
- The Netherlands
- Benelux
- Germany
- Sweden
- Denmark
- Scandinavia
- The Kingdom of the Netherlands
- Dutch-land
- I don't know
- (Silence and blank stares)

Many of the people queried were even highly-educated and well-traveled. A general assertion states that geography isn't a very well-taught subject in many cultures throughout the world and that most people are ignorant when it comes to world geography. My little survey certainly lends credence to this.

What's even more startling, however, are the responses I received from the Dutch themselves. Upon asking the Dutch residents in and around Amsterdam the official name of their country, I almost invariably heard the response "Holland." In pointing out that their country's name is actually the Kingdom of the Netherlands, or even just the Netherlands, many of them became defensive and stated tersely that the Netherlands was just another name for Holland. With even the Dutch being confused about the official name of their country, there is no wonder why the inaccurate name Holland is still prevalently used today. Such Hollanders (persons living in either North or South Holland) with views that everything in life happens in Holland and nothing else really matters is analogous with the stereotypical New Yorker who feels that the only place west of the Hudson river is California and that that everything in between doesn't really matter.

The early settlers to this region of northern Europe encountered an exceptionally wooded terrain. Because of this wooded terrain, the early settlers called the region *Holt-land* (Wood-land), which eventually morphed into Holland.[3] *Aemstelredamme* originated in the year 1200 as a fishing village located on the Amstel River. *Dam* is the Dutch word for river, hence *Amstel-dam*, eventually becoming Amsterdam. The Netherlands, furthermore, is situated predominately below sea level and was originally called *Neder-land* (Low-land), eventually morphing into the Netherlands. As another example, the city of Rotterdam, which was founded upon the *Rotte* River, was originally called *Rotte-dam*, eventually morphing into Rotterdam. The place called *Benelux* further confuses many people around the world. Benelux is simply the region comprising the three neighboring countries in northwestern Europe – Belgium, the Netherlands and Luxembourg. The origins of Benelux date back to 1948 when the three neighboring countries joined an alliance in order to establish better business relations and to create a formal customs union.

The Dutch have always been, and remain, internationally focused and market their many products to virtually all corners of the globe. The Netherlands is the eighth largest exporter of goods and services in the world. The Dutch are the world's largest exporters of cheese, butter, powdered milk and mussels, and export a plethora of food, chemical and machinery products. Tourism also thrives in the Netherlands, with people from all parts of the world coming to this tiny country to enjoy the pleasantries of Holland. The Dutch exhibit their marketing genius by marketing their products, and even their country, by leveraging the name Holland. Even though it's somewhat of a mystery, the name Holland still conjures up images of wholesomeness and seems to represent all that is pure and good in life. The Dutch use this image to their advantage by continuing to promote their country as Holland for tourism purposes, and marketing all of their products as being from Holland. People would rather eat cheese and drink beer from Holland rather than from the Netherlands or Amsterdam. Amsterdam conjures up images in peoples' minds contrary to those untainted images of Holland. Initial impressions of Amsterdam are usually that of a liberal bastion of sex and drugs due to the infamous Red Light District and legalized marijuana. Furthermore, a family vacation to this traditional place called Holland sounds much more enticing and pleasing than one to the Kingdom of the Netherlands or to this salacious city called Amsterdam.

The name Holland is still as strong as ever and will continue to be used throughout the world as the name of the country where the Dutch people reside and flourish. With the Dutch international focus and their marketing prowess, the name Holland will continue bringing pleasant, and even mystifying, images and thoughts into the minds of those experiencing it. For these reasons, and to point out the paradoxical nature of the Dutch, the words Holland and the Netherlands will be used interchangeably throughout this book. It's been used that way in the past, it will continue to be used that way in the future, so in deference to this great country's ambiguity, it will be used that way here.

Of the 16.2 million residents in the Netherlands, approximately 80% are of Dutch origin, while the remaining 20% are of non-western origin, to include mainly Turks, Moroccans, Antilleans, Surinamese and Indonesians. Most of the foreign born residents of Holland reside in the larger cities; Rotterdam, for instance, encompasses a population that is approximately half foreign born. Dutch is the official language of the country, although Frisian is recognized and spoken in Friesland, the northern-most region of the country. The Kingdom of the Netherlands is located in Western Europe and is bordered by the North Sea, Belgium and Germany. The West Frisian Islands, off the coast of Northern Holland, are also a part of the Netherlands. The Kingdom, due to its colonial past, still includes the Netherlands Antilles (Bonaire, Curaçao, Saba, Saint Eustatius and Saint Maarten) and Aruba in the Caribbean.

The Kingdom of the Netherlands

CAPITAL CITY AMSTERDAM

According to Dutch legend, a damaged boat carrying a Norwegian prince, along with a Frisian fisherman and his dog, was blown into the reeds along the IJ river, where they founded Amsterdam.[4] Amsterdam is the capital of the Netherlands and is the most densely populated city in Europe. The city is a major European hub for trains, planes and ships, so it sees a multitude of visitors from all parts of the world. Europeans can travel to Amsterdam in just a few hours and even Americans can make it to the city in less than seven hours from New York. Visitors' first impressions of Holland are almost invariably that of Amsterdam, and these first impressions can certainly leave indelible marks. Amsterdam is a bustling city that has something to offer to everyone. The openness, tolerance, peculiarities and sheer outrageousness which surround Amsterdam and its people make this one of the greatest and most talked about cities in the world. Amsterdam retains its position as the tenth most livable city in the world, according to the latest "quality of life" report from the Mercer Human Resource Consulting agency. The results of this study are depicted in the table below.

2004 Ranking	2003 Ranking	City	Country
1	1	Zurich	Switzerland
1	2	Geneva	Switzerland
3	2	Vancouver	Canada
3	2	Vienna	Austria
5	5	Auckland	New Zealand
5	5	Bern	Switzerland
5	5	Copenhagen	Denmark
5	5	Frankfurt	Germany
5	5	Sydney	Australia
10	10	Amsterdam	The Netherlands
10	10	Munich	Germany

"Quality of Life" Top 10 Cities [5]

Visitors are usually besieged by Amsterdam's beauty and charm. The city is filled with well-maintained cobblestone streets, a profusion of picturesque trees, winding canals and quaint row houses. Amsterdam is Europe's greenest city; there are more trees per square kilometer than any other capital city in Europe.[6] Many of Amsterdam's beautiful gardens aren't visible from the street, but are neatly tucked away in the backyards of the buildings, forming row after row of lush vegetation. Holland is also world-renowned for their abundance of beautiful tulips. In fact, Holland has a yearly tulip festival that brings people from all over the world to enjoy the sights and smells of these delightful flowers. The Dutch are passionate about preserving the environment and find gardening to be one of the greatest pleasures of life.

The city's charming streets run parallel with the numerous canals and form half-concentric circles around the city center. The layout of the city can be compared to "ripples on a pond." The center of these ripples is Centraal Station and the further away from the center you go, the bigger the ripples become.

Aerial View of "Ripples on a Pond"[7]

23

Often times as tourists delight in the beauty and charm of the city, they find themselves completely lost as the ripples of the pond look very similar to one another. Furthermore, distinguishing one canal from another is a rather daunting task. People unfamiliar with the difficult Dutch language find it nearly impossible to navigate the city based upon the complicated and extremely hard-to-pronounce street names. Below are some examples of the complicated street names found throughout Amsterdam that certainly pose challenges for even the best of linguists:

- *Nieuwezijds Voorburgwal*
- *Oudezijds Voorburgwal*
- *Eerste Goudsbloemdwarsstraat*
- *Oudezijds Achterburgwal*
- *Cruquiusweg*
- *Kloveniersburgwal*
- *Egelantiersgracht*

Tourists usually rely on their senses of direction or focus on key landmarks for navigational purposes, as opposed to remembering such challenging street names.

Amsterdam is the quintessential international city where multiculturalism flourishes. With Holland's liberal immigration policies, the city has a significant portion of foreign-born residents. Additionally, only London, Paris and Rome attract more tourists than Amsterdam.[8] On any given day, and especially on the weekends, the city is swarming with people from all over the world speaking a multitude of languages. The English embark upon Amsterdam for weekend getaways, the Scots can be seen wearing their kilts during the many bachelor parties held in the city, and even tourists from as far away as Asia can be seen snapping pictures of the many sights throughout the city. Football matches held at Ajax stadium bring even more foreigners into the city fervently supporting their local teams. Even with the diverse cultures and rivaling sports fans continuously converging on the city, Amsterdam remains one of the cleanest and safest cities in the world.

Amsterdam – the Quintessential International City

The architecture of the row houses along the canals of Amsterdam is truly enchanting. The cobblestone streets and canals are lined with narrow, four to five storied buildings with contrasting facades and gabled tops. These breathtaking buildings lining the canals are the result of the incredible wealth that the Dutch accumulated during the Golden Age by trading lucrative items such as cocoa, cinnamon, tobacco, silk and even slaves. The architecture of Amsterdam is mainly residential; Amsterdam was built by citizens and businesses, not by governments. These narrow buildings align next to one another and each one has its own unique charm, but they all share certain foundational attributes. Large windowpanes, gables at the tops of the buildings, and extreme narrowness are found throughout the city. Additionally, most of these buildings have a slight forward slant, which adds to the eccentricity of the city.

There seems to be a logical explanation for everything the Dutch do, and their dwellings are no exception. Narrow buildings were necessary due to taxation. Taxes were levied based upon a property's square footage; therefore, the Dutch built narrow buildings to reduce the amount of taxes that they would have to pay. The smallest building in Amsterdam, remarkably, is a mere 2 meters wide and 6 meters deep – 12 square meters! The original inhabitant of this residence certainly didn't want to pay high taxes for his or her dwelling. This building can be found at Oude Hoogstraat 22, east of Dam Square. People who complain about the size of their homes or apartments really need to visit this abode.

Cramped Quarters

These narrow buildings with their slender, winding staircases, consequently, made it near impossible to transport furniture to the top floors. The pulleys at the tops of the gables of these dwellings allow for the furniture to be hoisted from the roof and to be brought into the buildings through the large windows. One problem with this system, however, was that the furniture kept banging into the building while being hoisted, damaging the façade and even breaking the windows. The Dutch, imaginatively, built these buildings intentionally leaning forward to avoid breaking windows or damaging the façade during the furniture hoisting process. Some of the buildings lean forward at such great angles that it appears they can topple over at any given minute. Often times, inexperienced tourists feel that the entire city is caving in on them, especially after visiting one of Amsterdam's famed Coffeeshops, i.e., marijuana house.

Beautiful 17ᵗʰ century architecture

Stoned tourist fearing the city is caving in on him

Even with all of its elegance, Amsterdam is a very unpretentious city. There are no modern skyscrapers extending into the skies, no intimidating castles glorifying its heroic past, no splendid statues of its heroes in all their glory, and only one unassuming war monument memorializing those who paid the ultimate sacrifice during World War II. Amsterdam's street names are rarely named after its heroes or people of prominence like in so many other countries. In the U.S. you can't go a few blocks in any city without running across a street, building or monument with the name George Washington, Abraham Lincoln, Martin Luther King Jr, or John F. Kennedy, just to name a few. In cities such as London, Berlin, Paris and Vienna, historical figures and monuments are proudly and prevalently displayed throughout the city neighborhoods. In many cases, due to the calamities of war, fire or other unfortunate events, many of these historical symbols have been completely destroyed. Many European cities have restored these symbols and buildings to their original glory, with the same look and feel, as opposed to building modern-looking structures. The Dutch simply don't exhibit such a penchant for past heroics and would rather their cities possess unassuming natures.

Even though the Dutch have 7,000 registered historical buildings, they don't show the typically European adulation and veneration for their past glories and triumphs with memorials. In fact, the second oldest church in Amsterdam, the beautiful, early 15th century *Nieuwe Kerk*, where the greatest Dutch naval hero, Admiral Michiel de Ruijter, and poets Joost van den Vondel and Pieter Cornelisz Hooft are buried, actually have commercial stores built *into* the beautiful old church! While admiring the architectural magnificence and appreciating the historical significance of this glorious church, one can pop right into the side of the old landmark and purchase a fruit smoothie or other types of merchandise!

One historical symbol that is displayed throughout the city that people simply can't overlook because of its prevalence is Amsterdam's coat of arms. The coat of arms comprises three St Andrew's crosses aligned vertically topped by the crown of Holy Roman Emperor Maximilian I. This symbol can be seen everywhere, especially on the thousands upon thousands of brown bollards (thick posts used on a ship for securing ropes), or *Amsterdammertjes*. The purpose of these *Amsterdammertjes* is to

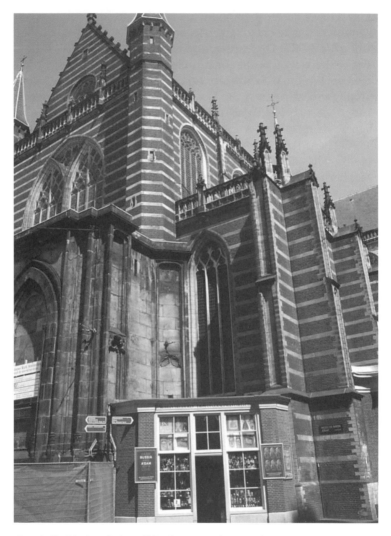

Store built right into the beautiful 15ᵗʰ century Nieuwe Kerk

keep cars from parking on the sidewalks. These posts, however, are rarely referred to as bollards or *Amsterdammertjes* due to the phallic looking attributes, and are commonly referred to by the numerous names that are associated with the phallus. Many visitors are incredulous with these odd-looking devices and question the Dutch motives and unusual fascination for placing such a profusion of phallic symbols throughout their city. These devices, compounded by the world famous Red Light District, leave many people suspecting that the Dutch have an overly-peculiar captivation with a certain human body part.

Suspicious looking Amsterdammertje

Dispersed throughout the City

CANALS, DIKES AND WINDMILLS

Mary Maples Dodge, in her classic book *Hans Brinker or the Silver Skates*, praises the Dutch fortitude and courage of living precariously in a land where waters could engulf them at any given moment:

> *"If we Americans, who after all are homeopathic preparations of Holland stock, can laugh at the Dutch, and call them human beavers and hint that their country may float off any day at high tide, we can also feel proud, and say they have proved themselves heroes and that their country will not float off while there is a Dutchman left to grapple it."* [9]

The Netherlands is, on average, fifteen feet below sea level. For centuries, the Dutch have been in a perpetual struggle to keep the grounds underneath them dry. The Netherlands is geographically very small, similar in size to the U.S. state of Connecticut. In order for the Dutch to keep their feet dry and even to expand their landmass, whether for population or agricultural reasons, they actually reclaimed land from the sea with creative irrigational methods. Much of the land in the Netherlands is a *polder*, or land that used to be at the bottom of the sea or lake. Such lands were reclaimed by building dikes across sea inlets or across rivers feeding lakes, and pumping the water out with the use of windmills and canals.

With people still commonly associating windmills to the Dutch and the fact that windmills played such a pivotal role to Dutch survival and expansion, no discussion on the Dutch would be complete without elaborating on these iconic devices. Dutch windmills are devices that run on the energy generated by wheels of adjustable blades rotated by the wind. The typical Dutch windmill has a huge tower of stone, brick or wood. At the top of the tower is a revolving apparatus to which usually four arms are attached. The arms are usually twenty to forty feet long and hold sails constructed of light wood or canvas to allow for movement.

A small fan serves as a rudder to keep the wheel facing the wind. At one point in Dutch history, there were over 10,000 of these incredibly engineered devices strewn across Holland's countryside.

Tenacious Dutchman repairing a leaking Dam

The Dutch even used these windmills for purposes other than irrigation. During World War II, the Dutch cleverly used their windmills to send secret messages back and forth to their neighbors. Certain positions and angles of the apparatuses had specific meanings that the Dutch could use as intelligence in their struggles against their German occupiers.

Although today the Dutch rely on more modern, mechanized ways for their irrigational needs, numerous windmills still abound the Dutch countryside and some are even still in use. Amsterdam alone still has eight of these remarkable devices strewn across the city. The following windmills, listed with other pertinent information, remain intact in Amsterdam and serve as wonderful visiting places for both tourists and locals alike.

Name	Address	Year	Location
De Otter	Gillis van Ledenberchstraat 78	1638	Amsterdam Center, just west of Jordaan area
De 1200 Roe	Haarlemmerweg 465	1632	Amsterdam West
De Bloem	Haarlemmerweg 701	1878	Amsterdam West (Harbor area)
De 1100 Roe	Herman Bonpad 6	1674	Amsterdam Osdorp (West)
Sloten Windmill	Akersluis 10	1847	Amsterdam West (Sloten)
Riekermolen	De Borcht 10	1636	Amsterdam South
De Gooyer	Funenkade 5	1814	Amsterdam Center/East
D'Admiraal	Kanaaldijk 21	1792	Amsterdam North

Windmills of Amsterdam[10]

In comparing old maps of the Netherlands with modern ones, one can easily observe the acquisition of new land over the years where water once was. A significant portion of the *Zuiderzee* (South Sea) is now surrounded by dikes and serves as flat,

Spectacular Dutch Windmill

fertile agricultural land. Additionally, the complete province of *Flevoland*, located northeast of Amsterdam, was once submerged under water but is now dry land. The Netherlands is an extremely flat country with very few spikes in elevation, which undoubtedly contributes to the remarkable land-retrieval capabilities of the

Dutch. A staggering sixty percent of all land in the Netherlands was once under sea or lake, but is now dry land used by the Dutch for a myriad of reasons. Ajax stadium, home to the world famous Ajax football team, is built on a former lake, and even Schiphol airport is located on an area where a naval battle once occurred.

The capital city Amsterdam is often referred to as the Venice of the North because of its numerous canals, bridges and islands. To illustrate the abundance of such water-related entities, the table below offers a side-by-side comparison of the two cities. These numbers, however, are moving targets due to the constant redistribution of land and water.

	Venice	Amsterdam
Islands	117	90
Canals	150	160
Bridges	400	1281

Venice and Amsterdam Comparison[11]

The profusion of canals in Amsterdam spans approximately 62 miles (100 kilometers) and beautiful stone bridges provide means for crossing them. These charming stone bridges are slightly arched to allow for small boat transportation through the canals. Some of the bridges are laden with lights that make for spectacular sights at night. The color of the lights that are dispersed along the bridges of the Red Light District is certainly no secret to anyone. Bridges are so plentiful in Amsterdam that pedestrians are almost always within eyesight of a multitude of bridges. In fact, standing on the Herengracht Bridge offers incredible views of eleven different bridges at one time! This spot, consequently, is referred to as "Eleven Bridges" and spans the Reguliersgracht and offers incredible picture opportunities for photographers and tourists.

Very low, bulky tourist cruise ships continuously meander throughout the city along the numerous canals. Transport barges carry their goods throughout various locations day and night. The Dutch even conduct their parades and festivities on the canals. On such celebratory occasions, barges carrying parade revelers float along the canals as far as the eye can see. The canals aren't used just for transporting, sightseeing or partying, but for living as well. Beginning with the 1950s housing shortages, houseboats began floating along the canals providing for alternative ways of living. Today, approximately 2,500 houseboats exist throughout Amsterdam accommodating about 6,000 people.[12] Until the 1980s, the canals doubled as sewers and had to be flushed daily. With all of the houseboats along the canal edges and the poor water quality of the canals, it's quite conceivable that they are inconspicuously still using these canals as sewers. Word of caution to tourists: No swimming! (in the canals, at least).

Waterfront Living!

The Dutch observe an age-old tradition of ice-skating along the canals with a remarkable event called the "Eleven cities ice-skating tour," or *Elfstedentocht*. This event takes place in Friesland and attracts thousands of Dutch to skate 200 kilometers, starting and finishing in Leeuwarden. Unfortunately there is one requirement for skating on frozen canals – cold weather. This event hasn't taken place in years due to the mild winters. With the Dutch intense passion for protecting the environment, many, undoubtedly, attribute the mild winters to the global warming phenomenon. Others just attribute the lack of freezing temperatures to the cyclical nature of global weather patterns. Whatever the reason, the Dutch have their skates sharpened and eagerly await the next blistery winter when they can take part in their Eleven cities ice-skating tour. I've been waiting over a decade now to lace up my skates and take part in this incredible event, but the weather just doesn't want to cooperate!

In addition to using canals, dikes and windmills to peacefully acquire new lands and to keep their feet dry, the Dutch amazingly used them in defending their small, but sacred land against foreign adversaries. Leave it to the Dutch to discover ways of repelling foreign invaders without the use of military force or weaponry, but with the use of their irrigational expertise. In the 16th century, William I, Stadholder of the Netherlands, opened the dikes against the invading Spanish fending off the attack with the onrush of water. William III, the great grandson of William I, remembering the ingenious tactic from his great grandfather, opened the dikes against the invading French army in the 18th century, yielding the same victorious results. Furthermore, Wilhelmina, Queen of the Netherlands in the 19th century, reportedly warned the Prussian Kaiser Wilhelm II, when he was flexing his military might, that she would open up the flood gates and drown his invading armies should he seek to invade her country. The Dutch miraculously and ingeniously repelled and deterred invading armies by unleashing the tremendous force of the immense bodies of waters lurking behind their sturdy dykes. Being cognizant of the powers of these pent up waters, we now know why that little boy, Hans Brinker, has become a hero in world literature. Without the bravery exhibited by that little boy by sticking his thumb into a crack of a leaking dike, the same dismal fate could have been bestowed upon the Dutch residents as that of its invading armies!

SPREEKT U NEDERLANDS?

The Dutch language is an extremely intimidating one for non-Dutch speakers. The guttural sounds and particularly long words can make even the best of linguists shudder. The Dutch language is a western-Germanic language spoken by about 25 million people worldwide.[13] The official name of the language is Nederlandic. Nederlandic is spoken in the Netherlands, northern Belgium, a tiny northwestern portion of France, Surinam in South America, the Dutch Antilles in the Caribbean, and to a lesser degree in Indonesia. The language of South Africa, Afrikaans, is a descendant of 18th century Nederlandic. The Nederlandic language being spoken in the various parts of the world substantiates the prowess of the colonial Dutch of the 17th century.

Frisian is officially recognized and protected as a minority language in the Netherlands and in parts of Germany. The Frisian language is Germanic in nature and was initially spoken by traders and raiders during the Viking era in northern Europe. The language was protected from competing languages due to the speakers residing mainly in marshy and island areas, which shielded them from foreign influences and even invasions. Today, there are 450,000 and 730,000 Frisian speakers in the Netherlands and Germany.[14]

The Dutch, typically, are capable of speaking four different languages – Nederlandic, German, English and French. Those living out in the rural areas may have more difficulty with these languages since they lack the exposure to foreigners. Many Dutch even speak Spanish and Indonesian. The Dutch have been multilingual for centuries due mainly to Amsterdam being a major port city welcoming foreigners from abroad and due to the Dutch always being prolific merchants on a global scale.

The Dutch are not averse to speaking the foreign tongues of their visitors. Most European countries, on the other hand, exhibit disdain for foreigners not attempting to speak the language of the host country. The Dutch, however, actually *prefer* that visitors speak their own languages rather than to practice and struggle with Nederlandic in order not to waste their precious time. Of course the gesture is greatly appreciated by the locals, but the efficient Dutch would rather just converse in a different language, or the universal English language, rather than deal with tourists struggling with the Dutch language.

My first exposure to the Dutch language was rather startling. Upon arriving to Amsterdam for the first time and speaking to my friendly cab driver, I was pleasantly surprised with the willingness and ease in which he spoke English. We conversed for quite awhile and then I started asking him for directions and advice on how to navigate around town. He proceeded to give me directions and periodically would let out a repulsive sound that came deep within his throat whenever mentioning the name of a canal. Whenever he spewed that dreadful Dutch word for canal, I expected him to roll down his window to properly dispose of whatever it was that he was trying to dislodge from his throat. Upon seeing my utter abhorrence of his throat peculiarities, he smiled slightly and told me to get used to hearing the word *gracht* because of the abundance of canals throughout the city. I quickly realized what he was talking about when I observed street signs along canals with names such as Herengracht, Prinsengracht, Keizersgracht, Elandsgracht and Rozengracht. In order to properly pronounce *gracht*, one is forced to trigger muscles in the throat and to make an unpleasant noise that is usually made only when one has a very bad upper-respiratory disorder and is trying to dispose of infectious phlegm. I was initially determined to learn the Dutch language, but upon hearing the guttural distinctiveness of this language, I quickly became skeptical of such a colossal feat.

Although skeptical of learning this rather difficult language, I felt that it would be appropriate since I was going to be living in Holland for an extended period of time. I embarked upon this endeavor by analyzing the written translations of American movies and sitcoms on television. The Dutch don't superimpose their language on English speaking television shows or movies, but use Dutch subtitles at the bottom of the screen. Other European nations, such as Germany and France, superimpose their languages on foreign speaking programs, as opposed to utilizing subtitles, to show there deference for their native tongues.

Watching the American cartoon sitcom *The Simpsons* in Germany is certainly a treat as Homer and Bart battle it out screaming German at one another. Although Homer's vintage "D'oh!" is untranslatable, the Germans attempt to translate all of the other quirky expressions of the characters on the show. The Germans even go as far to superimpose their language on foreign lustful movies, even though most of the discourse doesn't consist of meaningful dialogue. One has to wonder about the screening process and requirements for those particular language-translating jobs. The all-time classic voice superimposition movies, however, have to be the Japanese Godzilla movies where English (with really bad Japanese accents) was inserted over the Japanese and didn't come close to matching the lip movements of the Japanese actors. The Dutch, meanwhile, don't bother with the effort of inserting their native language over English speaking programs. Subtitles suffice in Holland.

After analyzing these Dutch subtitles in an effort to learn the language, I saw remarkable similarities to both the English and German languages. In fact, Nederlandic seemed to use an equal combination of both English and German and fell somewhere in the middle. In analyzing the Netherlands' geographical proximity to England and Germany, it made sense to me that the Dutch language would fall somewhere in the middle of these two languages. As ancient Germanic tribes migrated westward, they maintained their base language, but made slight modifications and even picked up influences from other languages as they migrated further westward. The table on the next page illustrates the similarities of the three languages and supports my initial supposition that Nederlandic seems to fall somewhere in between English and German.

English	Nederlandic	German
Brother	Broer	Bruder
Daughter	Dochter	Tochter
Father	Vader	Vater
Mother	Moeder	Mutter
Yes/no	Ja/nee	Ja/nein
Thank you	Dank U	Danke
Good Morning	Goedemorgen	Guten Morgen
Good Evening	Goedenavond	Guten Abend
Do you speak English?	Spreekt U Engels?	Sprechen Sie Englisch?
I speak a little Netherlandic	Ik spreek een beetje Nederlands	Ich spreche ein bisschen Niederländisch
Where are you from?	Waar komt U vandaan?	Woher kommen Sie?
I am from Belgium	Ik kom uit Belgie.	Ich komme aus Belgie
No smoking	Verboden te roken	Rauchen Verboten

Dutch Words – Half English and Half German

In discussing the similarities of the Nederlandic and German languages with many of my German colleagues, I've often heard them refer to the Dutch as actually being Germans with dyslexia because of the way they speak and write. Dyslexia is a learning disorder marked by impairment of the ability to recognize and comprehend written words. Such a stereotype certainly doesn't bode well with the Dutch, especially coming from their neighboring rivals, the Germans.

In an effort to kill two birds with one stone, I made the decision to learn German instead of Nederlandic, because I felt that by knowing both English and German, Nederlandic would follow easily since it seemed to fall somewhere in between the two languages. Once I knew German I figured I could then just extrapolate from the English and German languages to speak and understand Nederlandic. What I didn't realize at the time, however, was the disdain that the Dutch had for Germans. So, consequently, my Dutch colleagues didn't look favorably on me taking German lessons while living and working in their country. Additionally, my assertion that the Dutch language would be easy to grasp by learning German is a gross over-simplification and an insult to both languages, which both have their own unique characteristics and charm. Needless to say, my attempt to learn Dutch by learning German was a complete failure and not one of the smartest decisions I've ever made. Nevertheless, the Dutch language is truly a difficult one to master, but this should not deter those undaunted linguists striving to learn new and challenging languages.

RAIN, RAIN GO AWAY!

The weather in Holland is damp, unpredictable and very disheartening, especially for visitors from temperate climates. The sun shines only about 35% of the time, while the other 65% of the time the weather is rainy, misty or cloudy. A beautiful sunny morning with blue skies can change to a gray, misty morning with dark clouds and gusty winds in virtually no time at all. It's nearly impossible to dress appropriately for the Dutch weather since it changes so often and rapidly. Leaving for work on a beautiful, cloudless, sunny day doesn't mean that it's going bc that way by the time you get to work. Often times I'd walk onto my commuting train wearing sunglasses and a short-sleeved shirt only to walk off of the train wearing a jacket, hat and having to carry an umbrella. The only way to plan for Dutch weather is to always be prepared for the worst. I had an umbrella in my laptop bag everyday and used it regularly. Most of the Dutch don't even bother with umbrellas since they're so accustomed to the damp and misty weather. A common adage in Holland is that all four seasons can be experienced in a single day. The different seasons, furthermore, are upon you so fast that it's nearly impossible to fully prepare for them.

Holland doesn't get an inordinate amount of total rainfall per year compared to some other countries, but the rain and mist are persistent. Amsterdam receives approximately 33 inches (83.8 cm) of rainfall per year. New York, rather surprisingly, receives more rainfall than Amsterdam, at 44 inches (112 cm) annually. The rain in New York doesn't occur nearly as often as in Amsterdam, but when it does occur, torrential downpours can last for days accumulating vast amounts of rainfall in short periods of time. Amsterdam doesn't receive such torrential downpours, but receives more of a unrelenting light rain or mist. Walking the streets of Amsterdam is akin to walking through a low-lying cloud with all of the dampness and mistiness. The table below provides an annual rainfall comparison of some of the major cities throughout the world.

City	Annual Rainfall (inches)	Annual Rainfall (cm)
Las Vegas	4.5	11.4
Prague	20.8	52.8
Berlin	23.2	58.9
London	23.2	58.9
Amsterdam	33	83.8
Seattle	35.2	89.4
New York	44.4	112.8

Annual Rainfall around the World[15]

My friends and I often joked about a table situated on my back patio that always had a puddle of water on top of it, no matter how dry the weather. As soon as the puddle was about to completely evaporate, another rainfall or fine mist would come along to replenish the puddle. The table was continuously wet and had to be wiped down every time I sat down at it. For those who suffer from asthma or other respiratory problems, the misty air acts as a humidifier enabling those sufferers to breathe more easily. Others not accustomed to such damp environments, meanwhile, always seem to be fighting a cold or some other sickness. At the workplace, I could always tell who the expatriates or visa workers were by their constant coughing and sniffling. Dutch residents have built up a strong resistance to this moist environment over the centuries while those coming from more temperate climates constantly struggle just to remain healthy. One of my expatriate friends has lived in Holland for over eight years and he's been sick ever since!

The constant changing and moist climate of the Netherlands contributes to what I call the Dutch "low maintenance" lifestyles. With the Dutch always being wet, they don't make such a fuss over certain aspects of life such as fancy hairdos, elegant clothing, dainty shoes or graceful mannerisms. The Dutch strive for practicality and want to keep their feet and heads dry. It's common for the Dutch to wear hooded garments and reliable, dry shoes. A common stereotype about Dutch women is that they are unrefined and walk like farmers. The English especially like to reinforce this stereotype. In defense of the Dutch ladies, it's certainly hard to be refined and debonair while constantly stepping over puddles and struggling just to keep their feet and heads dry. My lady friends who visited me from the U.S. would become so frustrated with their hair frizzing out of control and their makeup running down their faces upon encountering Holland's capricious weather. Exacerbating the matter, it took them long periods of time (which seemed like hours to me) of dolling themselves up prior to going out. All of that work proved to be in vain as soon as that damp and misty weather was upon them.

It's common for Dutch girls to forego the makeup and simply place their hair in ponytails or pigtails. Furthermore, with the Dutch reliance on bicycles for their preferred mode of transportation, it's more practical to sacrifice the lavishness for the sensibleness. The low maintenance of the Dutch ladies can also be observed as they lift and carry their heavy bicycles on their shoulders up and down stairs, not asking for assistance from the men. I, on the other hand, had to frequently run up and down stairs in order to transport the bicycles of many of my American lady friends. I'm pretty sure that most of them were capable of carrying the bicycles themselves, but they're just accustomed to men performing the typical societal male roles for them. The Dutch low-maintenance lifestyles, however, dictate that women fend for themselves and forego the formalities and pleasantries of chivalry and focus primarily on the practicality of tending to your own affairs.

With all of the clouds and dampness, it's no wonder the Dutch scamper outdoors whenever there is glimpse of sunshine. On those rare beautiful sunny days (and these days are indeed delightful with incredible blue skies), the usually punctual Dutch take extra long lunch breaks, leave work early and truly delight in the sunshine and pleasant weather. During the summer months, the beaches are exceptionally crowded when the forecast calls for sunny weather. The beaches are normally crowded without such forecasts with the hope that the sun will make a few rare appearances during the day. If the Dutch can't make it to the beach to relish in the sun, they can usually be found soaking in the rays at the local parks. The Dutch have to be ready at a moment's notice in order to dash out and enjoy moments of non-rain and dampness. With the persistent rain, living below sea level, and constantly struggling with rising seas, it's no wonder that the patron saint to the *Oude Kerk* (Old Church) in the heart of Amsterdam is *St. Nicolaas*, the water saint.

The Dutch enjoying one of those rare moments of sun at the park

CONSTITUTIONAL MONARCHY

After millenniums of oppressive monarchies throughout Europe and countless revolts against these establishments, it's hard to believe that any monarchies still exist in Europe, especially ones that still have power. The Dutch Constitution states that the head of state of the Kingdom of the Netherlands is the ruling Monarch. The Dutch constitution refers to the head of state as 'the King,' even when the monarch is a woman, as the present Queen Beatrix. The Dutch Monarchs aren't just figureheads and national symbols, but play roles in the laws of the land. The Monarchy, however, is limited in its powers. The Dutch Monarchy is strictly regulated by the Constitution, certain acts of Parliament and even unwritten constitutional law. The Dutch have had their share of oppressive regimes throughout history and have, therefore, taken active measures to ensure that these oppressive regimes don't rear their ugly heads once again. The Dutch system of checks and balances ensures that the Dutch monarchy doesn't become too powerful and prevents them from becoming another one of those oppressive regimes that Europeans continuously contended with throughout history.

As a result of all of the vehement revolutions throughout Europe in 1848, the Dutch Constitution decreed that the King is inviolable (cannot be transgressed or dishonored), but that governmental ministers bear governmental responsibility and are answerable to parliament for all legislation. Such a decree ensures a solid system of checks and balances; not one single entity has too much power. Membership to the Royal House is limited to the head of state, the former head of state, the members of the royal family in line for the throne, and their spouses. The line for the throne is only for members of the family of the reigning monarch to the third degree of consanguinity. In other words, the title to the throne is only for those of blood relations with the reigning monarch to the third degree (children, brothers and sisters, grand children, great grandchildren, nephews and nieces). The chart below provides an illustration of consanguinity with the various degrees of relationship by blood. The highlighted boxes indicate blood relations to the third degree.

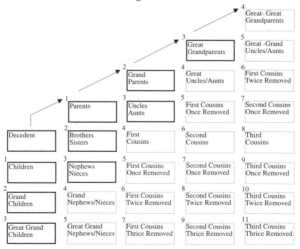

Degrees of Relationship by Blood

Being in line to be King or Queen of the Netherlands isn't as alluring as it may sound, it offers its share of hardships and restrictions as well. Members of the royal family, for instance, must receive the consent and permission of Parliament before getting married. Not only would a gentleman courting the Queen's daughter have to ask a *Queen* for her daughter's hand, but the entire House of Parliament. Talk about pressure! Members of the Royal House who fail to get Parliament's permission to marry certain individuals forfeit their membership to the Royal House. Furthermore, exclusion of membership from the Royal House also results in the loss of Dutch nationality. These rules aren't just scare tactics, as two of the queen's sisters, Irene and Christina, married without the official consent of the House of Parliament and are no longer in the line of succession to be queen. So much for Dutch tolerance!

The Queen is intimately involved in the formation of a new government after a general election. After the election, she consults the vice-president of the Council of State, the speakers of both houses of parliament, the leaders of the political parties represented in the Lower House and sometimes distinguished elder statesmen known as the ministers of state. The Queen then appoints formateurs and informateurs to form a new government on the basis of the election results. When the political parties reach agreement on the policies to be pursued by the new government, she appoints and swears in the ministers and state secretaries.

Even though the Queen acts as the political head and performs certain political acts in accordance with Dutch decree, she is still revered and venerated with all of the pomp and circumstance of monarchs of old. The Dutch truly adore their Queen, dearly respect her title and honor her in traditional, grandiose fashion. Every third Tuesday of September is known as *Prinsjesdag* (Prince's Day), a day in which the monarch addresses a joint sitting of the Lower House of Parliament and the Senate. The Queen departs her working palace in true splendor by riding in a horse-drawn golden coach. Of course, dignitaries and a military guard of honor accompany her on this magnificent thirty-minute journey. The military guard of honor fires salutes at one-minute intervals to let the public know that her majesty is approaching so that they can get a glimpse of the royal procession. When the Queen arrives to the historic Hall of Knights (*Ridderzaal*), the Dutch national anthem is ceremoniously played and the Queen salutes the flag from the steps of the ancient building which were built back in the 13th century. The Queen proceeds to deliver a thirty minute speech from her lofty throne and articulates the main points of government policy for the coming year.

March 20, 2004 was a very sad day for the Dutch as the Queen's mother, Princess Juliana, passed away at the remarkable age of 94. Juliana passed the crown to her daughter, Beatrix in 1980, after reigning as queen for 32 years from 1948. Reigning as Queen for so long, especially during the tumultuous post-war years, the Dutch had lost the country's symbolic mother with her passing. The Dutch truly esteemed Princess Juliana as she conducted her majestic affairs with the utmost humility and lived her life according to Dutch virtues. She never exhibited a royal arrogance, frequently shopped in the local villages without demanding preferential treatment, preferred to be called "Mrs" rather than "Your Majesty," sent her children to public school, rode her bicycle around town mingling with the locals, and even thoroughly enjoyed traditional pea soup in true Dutch fashion.[16] So, even with all of the glory and prestige that the Dutch bestow upon their reigning monarchs, they still expect the kings and queens to act with humility and in true Dutch form. The Dutch people adore them even more when they conduct their affairs in such a modest manner.

Many cultures throughout the world scoff at the concept of monarchies and royal families. The most notable royal family throughout the world, undoubtedly, is that of Britain's House of Windsor. The pomp and circumstance surrounding the Dutch royal family is pale in comparison to that of the British royal family. The adulation and sheer devotion to all of the affairs of the royal family is truly astonishing. This veneration and curiosity for majestic news and gossip is not only found in Britain, but in many other countries throughout the world. The Americans, for instance, have an insatiable appetite for the magnificence and grandeur surrounding the British monarchy. This insatiable appetite is evidenced with the British royal family and other royal figures around the world continuously gracing the covers of magazines, periodicals and newspapers. The prominent magazine *People*, for instance, for its thirtieth anniversary listed the top ten cover stories of all time and royal family members made the list an incredible five times. *People* magazine's top ten list is as follows:

Cover Story	Date
1. September 11, 2001	September 24th, 2001
2. Goodbye Diana	September 22, 1997
3. John F. Kennedy Jr.: Charmed Life, Tragic Death	August 2, 1999
4. John Lennon, 1940-1980: A Tribute	December 22, 1980
5. Princess Grace, 1929-1982: A Tribute	September 27, 1982
6. Fifth Anniversary Issue	March 5, 1979
7. Nice Work, Luv: Andy and Fergie Marry	August 4, 1986
8. Oh Boy! Diana Gives Birth to Prince William	July 5, 1982
9. Good Show! Royal Wedding of Prince Charles and Lady Diana	August 3, 1981
10. Olivia Newton-John: Greased Lightning	July 31, 1978

People magazine's top 10 Cover Stories[17]

If you count the Kennedy family as royalty, which many around the world do, then royal families comprise six of the top ten list. With this bizarre fascination for royalty and celebrity, it's no wonder that monarchies and royal families are still in existence and even flourish in this modern age.

TRADITIONAL DUTCH EATING AND DRINKING PLEASURES

An introduction into Holland and its culture wouldn't be complete without a discussion about Dutch cuisine. As portrayed in his famous *Potato Eaters* painting by Vincent van Gogh, the legendary Dutch painter, a staple ingredient in old-fashioned Dutch cuisine is potatoes. Dutch cuisine is often referred to as bland, but hearty, consisting mostly of potatoes and meat. Throughout the years as the industrious Dutch worked their windmills, constructed their dikes, plowed their fields, rode their bicycles and endured the harsh climate, they needed substantial meals. They needed meals that would replenish and warm their bodies. After a full day's work, the Dutch desired hearty meals that would stick to their ribs and provide comfort to them rather than that of any time-consuming, dainty, light meal. Pea soup, the quintessential Dutch food, is the ultimate comfort food and is still a Dutch staple on virtually all menus. The litmus test for exceptional and traditional Dutch pea soup is whether or not the spoon remains vertical after inserting it into the middle of the soup bowl and letting it go. If the spoon doesn't remain vertical, it's not good, traditional Dutch pea soup. If it does, be prepared for a true thick and hearty Dutch delicacy. Other popular Dutch dishes include ham, meatballs, eggs, smoked eel and pancakes. With Holland's colonial past and perpetual international orientation, influences from virtually all corners of the globe can be found in many of their recipes and meals. There is a myriad of international restaurants dispersed throughout the cities of Holland, to include Indonesian, Surinamese, Chinese, Thai, along with many others.

Dairy products play an important part in Dutch cooking. Milk, butter and, of course, cheese are consumed in large quantities. Throughout the world the Dutch are synonymous with cheese. Holland is the world's largest cheese exporter, and Dutch cheeses such as Gouda and Edam are savored in all parts of the world. Yearly, Holland produces over 630 million kilos (1.4 billion pounds) of cheese, of which 500 million kilos (1.1 billion pounds) is exported.[18] Not only are the Dutch the world's most prolific exporter of fine quality cheeses, but also the proud recipient of being the creators of the world's largest cheese, which weighed in at a mind-boggling 567 kilos (1,250 pounds)! In Alkmaar, north of Amsterdam, the Dutch produced this colossal Beemster cheese using 1,100 gallons of milk. (Numerous Dutch cows, incidentally, had a rather integral role in this marvelous creation). This particular piece of cheese had a diameter of 63 inches and stood 40 inches high. This chunk of cheese was bigger than a typical Dutch bathtub or even a tractor trailer tire. No wonder why this country has been referred to as *Odd-land* with such peculiar achievements.

The Dutch have an exceptionally long history of cheese. Throughout the history of time, the Dutch have been known as *cheese-heads* because of their propensity for making and eating vast quantities of cheese. In Dutch, coincidentally, the term *cheese-head* is also another word for the mold in which the cheese is made and shaped. It is rumored that in the middle ages, farmers in North Holland used these wooden molds as helmets when they had to turn in their plows for weapons.[19] Enemies of these Dutch farmers-turned-militia began referring to them as cheese-heads because of these distinctive helmets worn upon their heads. The reactions of the Dutch adversaries as they were being attacked by a horde of Dutchmen with cheese molds on their heads must certainly have been a sight to see. Such innovative warfare methods could have certainly served as scare tactics as well. Perhaps the Dutch learned something about psychological warfare from the ancient Celtic tribes, who engaged in battle completely naked and painted their entire bodies blue.

Modern day cheese-heads can actually be found in the United States. On any given Sunday during football season, maniacal cheese-heads can be found cavorting in stadiums wherever the Green Bay Packers are battling opponents. These loyal Packer fans wear giant cheese hats on their heads while cheering their team on to victory. Parenthetically, Green Bay, Wisconsin is home to a large Dutch ethnic contingent. Many of these modern day cheese-heads, although probably unbeknownst to them, are just carrying out the traditions of their ancient warrior forebears.

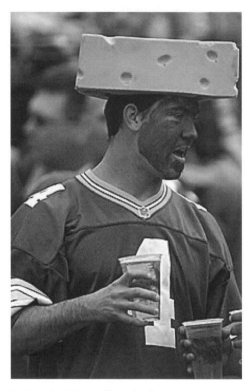

Modern day Warrior Cheese-head

Discoveries indicate that as early as two centuries B.C., cheese was being made in Holland. A widespread cheese trade centering around Holland has existed since the Middle Ages. In 1100, The Dutch bargemen and explorers even used cheese to pay their tolls in foreign city ports. Dutch cities such as Gouda, Edam and Alkmaar held dairy markets throughout the Middle Ages in order to promulgate their cheese. With all of these years of experience in cheese making, the Dutch certainly have mastered the fine art of making truly exceptional cheese. In fact, my family and friends are still thanking me and talking about how delectable the cheese was that I sent them from some of the many fine cheese makers of Holland. Note to tourists: Send home cheese!

The Dutch need to wash down all of this cheese and their hearty meals with something, and they do so with milk, coffee and beer. With the prosperous dairy industry of the Dutch, dairy products such as milk and cream are consumed in vast quantities. I was initially surprised to see most of my Dutch colleagues consuming multiple pints of milk during their lunch breaks. In the U.S., it's uncommon for adults to drink vast quantities of milk, especially with their lunchtime meals. The Dutch, however, truly savor this dairy beverage and drink it frequently throughout the day. They drink mainly whole milk, foregoing the fat-free, 2% or 1% versions that are consumed in those calorie-conscious cultures.

Coffee is a national passion in the Netherlands. On average, each Dutch person drinks 165 liters (43.6 gallons) of coffee every year. That's about 2½ cups a day per person. The Dutch demand freshness in every cup and won't settle for filtered coffee that's been sitting around for extended periods of time. All of their cups of coffee must be freshly and individually made using the traditional espresso pump which forces the hot water, utilizing intense pressure, through cup-sized filters. A cup of coffee isn't complete in Holland without the use of thick, Dutch cream and sugar. Coffee is such a craze in Holland that even one of its longest living natives, who lived to be an amazing 112 years old, directly attributed her health and longevity to coffee.[20] With the Dutch being such devoted coffee drinkers, one would think that the premier, global coffee multinational corporation, Starbucks, would be on practically every street corner. Surprisingly, there is not one Starbucks in the entire country of the Netherlands. This is just yet another example of the paradoxical nature of the Netherlands and the Dutch people. Even though Amsterdam ranked fourth on the list of "Most Favorable Cities in Europe in which to locate an International Business," and with more than 1,800 foreign companies based in the Amsterdam area, the Dutch somehow managed to keep the global entity Starbucks from creeping into their homeland and disrupting their coffee culture.[21]

Even fervent nationalists as the French and Austrians, where local coffee is a cherished national treasure with great cultural significance, allowed Starbucks to break ground into their countries. Below are just a few examples of the number of Starbucks in certain European countries.

Country	Number of Starbucks
The Netherlands	0
Italy	0
France	3
Austria	9
Germany	10
Spain	21
England	366
U.S.	Infinitesimal!

Number of Starbucks per Country[22]

With the Italians being perhaps the most ardent and passionate coffee drinkers in the world, it's no surprise that Italy hasn't succumbed to the Starbucks craze as well.

Even though there are no Starbucks stores in the Netherlands, their European headquarters, interestingly enough, recently relocated to Amsterdam to service Europe, the Middle East and Africa. In 2002, they moved their regional head office from London to Amsterdam because Amsterdam is more central to Europe and because the Dutch mentality fits perfectly with their corporate philosophy. Even with their regional headquarters located in Amsterdam and numerous store opening announcements, Starbucks has still been unable to establish a commercial beach-head in the Netherlands. It will be interesting to see how long the Dutch can hold out.

In addition to milk and coffee, the Dutch truly enjoy their local beers. Beer is an integral part of the Dutch culture and people go to relax by having a few good, cold beers. There is a wide variety of beer in the Netherlands, but the most common and preferred ones are of the pilsner and lager types. Pilsners and lagers are clear, crisp and golden in color. Such world-renown beers such as Heineken, Amstel and Grolsch are brewed and consumed in sizable quantities in Holland. There is a plethora of pubs dispersed throughout the country for the Dutch to go and enjoy their beer. In fact, in Amsterdam alone, there are over 1,200 beer cafés dispersed throughout the city. A Dutch person is never too far away from his or her favorite beer drinking establishment.

This introductory chapter into Holland and the Dutch illustrates, at a high-level, some of the oddities and unique characteristics that make both this land and its inhabitants so distinct from the rest of the world. As we delve deeper, even more surprising and fascinating Dutch attributes will be discovered. The next chapter, *Brief History of the Netherlands*, will explore the Dutch past and draw parallels between modern day Dutch cultural characteristics and Holland's intriguing past.

2. Brief History of the Netherlands

Introduction

Throughout history, the Netherlands has been surrounded on all sides by imperialistic powers who, at one time or another, attempted to absorb the small country of Holland into their dominions. Holland never provoked these imperialistic regimes nor did they pose an imminent threat to them. The business-oriented Dutch had transformed the small, marshy Lowlands into one of the most successful commercial and shipping areas in the world. Emperors, kings and dictators couldn't resist the temptation of attempting to engulf this prime, commercially prosperous territory. Attempts at subjugating the people of the Lowlands were made by numerous, militarily-strong regimes, including the Romans, Burgundians, Habsburgs, Spanish, English, French and Germans. Although most of these attempts were successful in the short term, the resilient Dutch always bounced back and regained their highly-desirous independence and self-governing lifestyles.

With the Dutch history of oppression and subjugation by the numerous tyrannical regimes, and with the Dutch proclivity towards self-governance, it's unfathomable to outsiders how the Dutch still maintain a Monarchy, albeit a Constitutional one. Not only is the Monarchy still in existence in Holland, but the present day queen and royal family are revered by the Dutch to the highest degree. Throughout history, the Dutch have turned to the royal House of Orange time and time again to bail them out of precarious situations with foreign adversaries. The royal House of Orange has always been there for the Dutch in their times of need. The Dutch and the royal House of Orange possess reciprocal respect for one another. As several of my Dutch colleagues have stated, "As long as the Queen supports the people of the country and doesn't do anything counter to our wishes, everything will be just fine." In analyzing the history of the Netherlands, it's understandable why such sentiments exist today amongst the Dutch, and why such a reciprocally respectful relationship exists between the monarchy and the people. It's been said that the past defines the present. The Dutch are no exception to this axiom as their tumultuous history has significantly shaped the modern day people of Holland and has influenced their cultural norms and traditions.

The Dutch perpetually struggling against hostile neighbors

IN THE BEGINNING...

Celtic and Germanic tribes started roaming the areas of the Lowlands of Northern Europe in search of food and areas to settle since the second century before Christ. These lands were first inhabited by the tribal groups the Batavi and the Frisii. The Batavi occupied the southern regions of the Netherlands while the Frisii settled in the northernmost areas. Encroachment by imperialistic powers started early in the history of the Netherlands. Julius Caesar and his Roman armies invaded in the first century and utilized the Lowlands as a strategic outpost for the next several centuries. Although the Romans weren't completely successful at imposing their culture on the Germanic tribes of the Lowlands, they did manage to Romanize the area to a certain degree. With Roman troops came technological sophistication as never seen before in these regions, such as the establishment of cities, the construction of roads, advanced plumbing and progressive weaponry. The Romans remained in the Lowlands of Europe until the fifth century, when westward tribal migrations intensified and the Roman Empire had begun its precipitous descent.

The "Wandering of the Nations" occurred when numerous and differing tribal groups throughout Europe migrated westward in search of food and habitable lands. The Wandering of Nations ascended to its peak between the third and fifth centuries. The Netherlands was greatly affected by these westward migrations, as mostly Germanic tribal groups such as the Saxons, Frisians, Goths, Angles and Franks swarmed into the region and began establishing permanent settlements. With the influx of these various Germanic tribes, the Romans were forced to surrender their northern outposts and head south in retreat to Rome. This period signified the end of Roman rule in the Netherlands. Over the next few centuries, the Netherlands became gradually Christianized as the Germanic tribes continued settling into the area and began accepting Christianity as their religion. Germanic culture soon began to flourish in the region and eventually replaced any remnants of Roman culture that had remained.

BURGUNDIAN RULE

As dukes, nobles and princes began sprouting up and wielding their power throughout most of Europe, the marshy wetlands of the Netherlands were mainly ignored. The French and German rulers paid little to no attention to the region for they saw little benefit in ruling over such uninviting terrain. During the twelfth century, however, trade and industry began to flourish in the Netherlands. Fishing, shipping, shipbuilding and textile manufacturing became integral industries in the Lowlands, and the hard-working inhabitants made these industries highly successful.

The Low Countries developed independently and free from autocratic or foreign rule for several centuries. By 1400, most of the regional states of the Low Countries were firmly established. Wealthy burghers held leadership positions in the Lowlands, rather than dictatorial monarchs, as in most regions throughout Europe. As trade in the Lowlands continued to flourish, the French and German kings suddenly, and for obvious reasons, became interested in the region. European rulers at the time were perpetually striving to acquire more land and riches in order to increase their power and spheres of influence. The powerful Burgundian princes ruled over parts of northwestern Europe for several centuries following the collapse of the Roman Empire. The Burgundi tribe conquered the Romans and occupied the fertile basins of present day France and Spain. As word spread about the thriving trading industries of the Low Countries, the Burgundian rulers began the process of absorbing these lands into their kingdom. From 1363-1472, the area was gradually assimilated by four generations of Dukes of Burgundy. The four generations of these dukes who ruled over the Netherlands, along with their rather odd nicknames, are as follows:

* Philippe le Hardi [Philip the Bold]
* Jean sans Peur [John the Fearless]
* Philippe le Bon [Philip the Good]
* Charles le Téméraire [Charles the Bold]

With nicknames like these, the reign of the Burgundians was doomed for oblivion.

Spanish Subjugation

Background into the Holy Roman Empire
One cannot fully comprehend the history of the Netherlands without a general background of the Holy Roman Empire. The Holy Roman Empire itself, however, is a rather unique institution in world history with historians still debating its precise definition. In general, the Holy Roman Empire was an establishment that covered a significant portion of Europe, centered mainly on Germanic lands and ruled by German emperors and princes, that lasted from 800 to 1806. In 800, the Pope bestowed upon Charlemagne the title of *Imperator Augustus* (Emperor), which was reminiscent of the title held by Roman Emperors, both in the glory days of Rome and in the Byzantium Empire of the time. After Charlemagne's death, his lands were divided between the east and the west. The eastern lands continued as the Kingdom of the Franks, or France, and the western lands continued as kingdoms of Germany. This simple delineation has been the catalyst for numerous conflicts between the French and Germans ever since.

The Holy Roman Empire continued to expand in these fragmented Germanic lands. The Empire grew into a confederation of territories that abided by the overarching rules on politics and religion, as mandated by the Holy Roman Emperor. These overarching rules, however, were loosely translated by the numerous factions, thus causing the proliferation of powerful and rivaling nation-states within the already fragmented Empire.

The Holy Roman Empire continued to exert its influence throughout much of Europe and expanded it territories to include modern day Germany; Austria; Slovenia; the Czech Republic; Switzerland; Belgium; Luxembourg; the Netherlands; and parts of France, Italy and Poland. At the end of the eighteenth century there were nearly four hundred entities within the Holy Roman Empire, differing widely in size, religion, ethnicity and power.

Voltaire, the French author and philosopher, in describing this loosely defined institution stated that the Holy Roman Empire is "neither Holy, nor Roman, nor an Empire." This assessment is not only witty, but accurate as well. Even though the Holy Roman Empire is rather ambiguous in meaning, its impact on history, and especially on the Netherlands, is indisputable.

The Habsburg Strategic Conquest of the Lowlands
The Habsburg royal family ruled the fragmented Holy Roman Empire far longer than any other royal line, beginning in 1273 when Rudolf I became the first of nineteen emperors and lasting until 1740. The imperial title eventually became regarded as a hereditary right, allowing the Habsburg dynasty to carry on as long as there were male heirs to fill the role. The Habsburgs were also able to systematically expand their powerbase throughout Europe with strategic marriage alliances with members from other royal families.

The Holy Roman Emperor and shrewd politician, Maximilian, systematically brought many regions of Europe under the Habsburg dominion through carefully arranged marriages. In 1477, Maximilian married Maria of Burgundy, while his son, Philip, married Juana of Castile, Spain. These strategic marriage alliances formally attached Spain and the Netherlands to the house of Habsburg. Although innocuous at first, these marriages triggered years of painful and bloody subjugation of the people of the Netherlands by foreign rule.

As a result of these carefully selected marriages, Maximilian's grandson Charles V (1519–56) inherited both the Imperial and Spanish crowns, as well as the Burgundian principalities, thus becoming Holy Roman Emperor, King of Spain and Lord of the Netherlands. The Habsburg dynasty continued the Burgundian policy of accumulating territories and centralizing authority. In 1548, Charles V absorbed all of the seventeen provinces of the Lowlands into the Hapsburg Empire and Spanish Kingdom. The Netherlands were now ruled by an even stronger and more influential imperial regime.

Protestant Reformation

As the Roman Catholic Habsburgs were gaining more territories and increasing their imperialistic powers, religious differences began to arise throughout much of northern Europe, mainly attributable to a German priest named Martin Luther. While serving in the priesthood, Martin Luther observed that many people in his congregation were not showing up for confession anymore. His once loyal congregation was now going into the cities to buy their indulgences, or in other words, to make monetary contributions to the church for the forgiveness of their sins and for the salvation of their souls. Martin Luther found such practices repugnant. The Peter Indulgence further exacerbated Luther's disgust for the hierarchy and bureaucracy of the Roman Catholic Church. The church was greedily using the monies received from the Peter Indulgence to finish construction of St Peter's Basilica in far away Rome.

Martin Luther's nailing of his famed Ninety-Five Theses to the door of the Wittenberg church was the catalyst for the Protestant Reformation that dramatically altered the political and religious composition of Europe. Luther's Ninety-Five Theses contained attacks on papal abuses and severe criticisms of the sale of indulgences by church leaders. Luther wanted the church to return to the pure and spiritual ways of the early church and to abandon its interest in power and wealth, which Luther felt was rapidly corrupting the once virtuous institution. He also wanted faith initiatives to be returned to the individual believer, as opposed to the hierarchy of the church. Luther also translated the Bible from Latin to German in order to allow the common people access to the word of God; thus, reducing their reliance on the church's interpretation. The church ex-communicated Martin Luther for his denigration of church leaders and practically declared him a heretic. While the church and its supporters wanted Luther to recant on all of his teachings, many Germanic princes supported Luther hoping that his message would weaken Rome's political power over the Germanic lands.

As the Lutheran movement began spreading across northern Germany and into Scandinavia, another branch of Protestantism was formulating in the Netherlands. This second phase of the Protestant Reformation was called Calvinism, after John Calvin, the French Protestant reformer. John Calvin's writings and influence first began to be felt in Switzerland, where the doctrine that he was preaching was independent of Luther's. Calvinism stressed the might of God as revealed in the Bible and treated humans as sinful creatures whose duty in life was sobriety and hard work. Calvinism also rejected church hierarchy and preached that people were not accountable to earthly rulers, but to God alone. Calvinism was destined from the start to cause great anguish amongst the traditional princely and priestly rulers who claimed to rule by divine rights. Soon the Calvinists began refusing to acknowledge the rule of any prince or religious ruler based solely upon divine right. Such religious dissent in the Netherlands caused great anguish amongst the Catholic Habsburgs. The king was determined to put an end to these religious uprisings and to restore Roman Catholicism to these lands.

The Habsburg Response
Even though a devout Catholic, Holy Roman Emperor Charles V was willing to accept a policy tolerating the Protestant Reformation in most of the principalities of the Empire, since most of them were self-ruling and sovereign. Charles knew that challenging the religious protesters in these principalities would be futile since he didn't wield much influence over them, even though he held the title of Holy Roman Emperor. But Charles' attitude towards Spain and the Netherlands was drastically different. His feelings towards Spain and the Netherlands were much more personal since he was also the King of Spain and Lord of the Netherlands, due to those shifty marriages of his forebears. Additionally, Charles V had been raised in the Low Countries, spoke Dutch and was originally sympathetic to the problems and traditions of the Dutch inhabitants. Since he considered these lands to be his home and under his direct authority, he was unwilling to tolerate religious movements that ran counter to Roman Catholicism.

Charles V had the power of the inquisition on his side to squelch any religious uprisings in his territories. The Inquisition started out as an institution of the Roman Catholic Church charged with the eradication of heresies. At the end of the 15th century in Spain, under the realm of Ferdinand and Isabel, the Spanish inquisition became independent of Rome and was brutally used for both political and religious reasons. Spain experienced centuries of tumultuous struggles between the various religions to include Catholicism, Islam, Protestantism and Judaism. Once the Christian Spaniards were successful in the re-conquest of their homeland following the Crusades, the Spanish leaders used the Inquisition to purify the people of Spain and to drive out Muslims, Jews, Protestants and other non-Roman Catholics. The legacy and brutality of the Spanish Inquisition was still fresh in the minds of those who opposed the Church and Charles V leveraged this powerful, yet sinister, institution.

In 1522, Charles V began sending Inquisitors to the Low Countries to ensure that Protestants would be dealt with according to the brutal methods of the Spanish Inquisition, which usually meant torture and death for the agitators. The Spanish Inquisitors immediately began sentencing Protestant heretics to be burned at the stake. Even though such drastic measures were imposed on the inhabitants of the Low Countries, the tenacious Protestant agitators continued to protest against the hierarchical and tyrannical methods of their religious and political oppressors.

With tensions intensifying, Charles V retired in 1555 and partitioned all of his possessions among his two sons, Ferdinand and Philip II. Ferdinand, who was raised in Vienna, inherited the Imperial crown and the Austrian lands, while his brother, Philip II, who was raised in Madrid, inherited Spain, the Italian possessions and the Low Countries. The immense and powerful empire of the Habsburgs was thus divided into Austrian and Spanish branches. This division of the Habsburg empire spelled trouble for the Netherlands, for Philip II was closely allied with the Pope and soon began organizing the church of the Netherlands, which further infringed upon the self-ruling nature of the Dutch inhabitants. Furthermore, King Philip II was now the ruler of the most powerful nation in the world at the time, with an abundance of wealth derived from the new world, to include Mexico and Peru. Philip II was more than eager to squander these riches on imperialistic and religious endeavors, which was disconcerting to the Dutch for their freedoms and liberties would, undoubtedly, be further infringed upon.

Increased tension...and then War
The Dutch inhabitants of the Low Countries were becoming increasingly frustrated with the king and the harsh manner in which the Spanish dealt with the new Protestant religion spreading throughout the region. Additionally, the economic-minded Dutch Burghers strongly opposed the centralized system of government by the Spanish, for it severely stifled their independent, commercially focused approach towards life. The Dutch had built a prosperous trading nation with self-governance and were very dismayed over this new autocratic system of government. Intensifying the friction between the Dutch and the Spanish king, Philip II appointed Spanish noblemen to high-ranking political posts within the Netherlands. The non-Dutch speaking King Philip II was considered a foreigner who wielded his power and influence from far away Spain. The Dutch considered the staunchly Catholic king to be out of touch with issues that were plaguing the Low Countries, especially since he never even visited any of the seventeen provinces.

The Dutch detested paying taxes to the Spanish king in order to help finance his foreign wars, which had no impact on the Netherlands. The Dutch were mainly focused on trade and no interest in such foreign wars. The Low Countries were an important source of tax revenues for the king because of the riches accrued from the numerous successful business ventures of the Dutch. The proverbial straw that broke the camel's back came when Philip II imposed new and even more burdensome taxes on the Dutch. The Dutch simply were fed up with paying taxes in order to finance wars they had no interests in and in order to support the lavishness of the Habsburgs. Revolution was looming in the air within the Netherlands.

In 1566, a group of Dutch radicals began their iconoclastic riots by roaming from city to city vandalizing churches, destroying paintings and statues and even murdering priests and Catholic sympathizers. These fanatic Calvinists were nicknamed *Geuzen* (Beggars). The name was originally established as a derogatory term, but the Dutch rebels soon took pride in this name as they continued their revolts against monarchical and religious oppression. The rebellion spread quickly throughout the provinces of the Netherlands. Calvinism's doctrine of strictness, discipline and sobriety offered a firm structure and organization for the insurrection.[1]

In 1567, Philip II resumed the crusade against Protestants and unleashed the merciless Spanish Duke Alva upon the Netherlands in order to destroy Calvinism. Alva soon became the most hated man in the Netherlands. The Spanish Duke instituted the Council of Troubles, which were responsible for the execution of thousands of Dutch rebels. Alva mainly succeeded in stamping out Protestants and restoring Roman Catholicism in the southern Netherlands (modern day Belgium). By cruel force of arms he returned the southern area to Catholicism, but in the process, destroyed the economic-social fabric of the region. This led to Antwerp's decline as a commercial superpower in the Netherlands. The Northern Netherlands of the Dutch, meanwhile, escaped Alva's cruel grip by undertaking drastic self-defense measures. In the process, they forged a small, powerful, independent mercantile nation, which would lead them to prominence during the Dutch Golden Age of the 1600s. With Alva's harsh and brutal policies, the Dutch, especially in the north, became even more united in their cause against Spanish subjugation.

In 1568, the harsh disagreements between Spain and the Netherlands erupted into a bloody rebellion known as the Dutch Revolt. William the Silent, Prince of Orange-Nassau, led the Dutch rebellion after he refused to swear a reformulated oath of allegiance to the king. The Dutch people, impressed with the Prince's defiance to the king, rallied behind him with the hopes that he could free the shackles of the Spanish oppressive regime. William set off to his sizable possessions in Nassau, from where he began a feud against the Spanish Netherlands. He staged three raids into the Spanish Netherlands in 1568, 1570 and 1572.

Between 1572 and 1576, the Dutch and Spanish fought numerous skirmishes throughout the Low Countries. The fighting eventually turned into a stalemate due to Spain's inability to conquer the northernmost portions of the provinces, mainly Holland and Zeeland, because of the logistical challenges, defiant resistance and marshy terrains. The Dutch rebels, conversely, were unable to conquer the higher grounds because of the superior Spanish Army.

On January 6, 1579, a significant break in the uprising occurred in the provinces of the Lowlands. The southern provinces founded the Union of Arras in which they abandoned the uprising and proclaimed their allegiance to the Spanish king. This southern area, what is now known as Belgium, was predominantly Catholic, French speaking and pro-Spanish, and included the provinces of Flanders, Antwerp, Hainault, Brabant, Namur, Liege, Limburg, and Luxembourg. This union of the southern regions proved to be pivotal in the future landscape of the Netherlands.

Meanwhile, just a few weeks later the majority of Dutch-speaking territories in the north established the Union of Utrecht, which formally declared their rebellion against the oppressive Spanish regime. This union marked the formal beginning of the Dutch Revolt. The Union of Utrecht is analogous to the American Declaration of Independence, where the American colonists declared their independence from Great Britain. The northern provinces that formed this alliance included Frisia, Groningen, Overijssel, Holland, Gelderland, Utrecht and Zeeland. These provinces eventually became known as the United Provinces of the Netherlands, or the Dutch Republic, and formed the origins of modern day Holland.

While the Dutch continued battling the Spanish for independence during the Eighty Years War, Spain was fighting in numerous other theaters throughout the world in order to sustain its imperialistic empire. With Spain engaging in battles on numerous fronts around the globe, the Dutch were better able to organize their defenses and focus on exploiting Spanish weaknesses. With tenacity and perseverance, the Dutch were successful in firmly securing the northern portion of the Netherlands from Spanish rule. The Spanish, however, continued to control the French-speaking, Catholic southern regions.

As the Low Countries were now clearly divided between the north and south, and with the war draining both sides economically and militarily, a peace treaty was signed in 1648. The Treaty of Munster marked the conclusion of the Eighty Years War and resulted with the Spanish king formally recognizing the Dutch Republic as a free and sovereign nation. The Holy Roman Emperor even acknowledged Dutch sovereignty. The Dutch had won their independence, were freed from the shackles of despotic rule and were now able to self-govern in their own homeland once again. The Netherlands were now entirely self-ruling, and their momentous victory over the Spanish marked the beginnings of numerous democratic movements throughout the European continent.

As for the Spanish, they continued to control the southern provinces of the Low Countries, which were to remain in Habsburg hands as the Spanish Netherlands until 1794. At the conclusion of the Eighty Years war with the Dutch, the Spanish were now no longer allowed to trade in the East or West Indies, which opened the door for the trade-oriented Dutch to fully exploit business opportunities in these regions. Leading merchants and a wealthy bourgeois quickly took control of the Dutch Republic and their economically driven outlook dictated the country's policies. The small, independent country of the Dutch Republic now became an international powerhouse and established highly-profitable trading posts throughout most of the known world. The Dutch soon established themselves as leaders on a global scale and became the wealthiest country in the world due to their remarkable commercial prowess.

THE DUTCH NATIONAL ANTHEM

The story of the valiant struggle against Spanish and religious oppression is immortalized in the Dutch National Anthem, the *Wilhelmus*. Prince William fought gallantly in order to free his country from tyranny and religious oppression. Even though his three invasions with mercenaries from the Holy Roman Empire failed to achieve their objectives, Prince William rallied his countrymen in the pursuit of liberty. Prince William is accredited with being the "Father of the Netherlands." The anthem commemorates Prince William's leadership and heroic struggle against the mighty Spanish regime.

In the *Wilhelmus*, the Prince of Orange addresses the oppressed people of the Low Countries in dramatic fashion. In his lofty speech, the Prince conveys his sincerity, determination and innermost motives for rising against the king of Spain. Prince William shows sympathy and empathy towards his followers, but also encourages them to join in the struggle against their oppressors. His speech is interrupted by a prayer in verses six and seven and he also reminds his loyal followers of their duty to obey the law of God.

The poem comprises fifteen verses. Only the first and sixth verses are usually sung on national occasions. The first verse is to this day misunderstood and controversial as it describes the Prince being loyal to the king of Spain -- *"to the king of Spain I've granted a lifelong loyalty."* People from other countries are befuddled when they hear the Dutch singing these words of allegiance to the king of Spain. After all, a national anthem is supposed to be patriotic and should honor its own country. Outsiders often ask themselves, "What's with the Dutch and their lifelong loyalty to the king of Spain?"

At the outset of the war, William of Orange-Nassau was elected *Stadhouder*, meaning he still represented the king's authority. Originally, William and the Dutch people had no misgivings with honoring the king, as long as the king let them self-govern and respected their autonomy. The Dutch originally felt that the King of Spain had good intentions, but was receiving bad counsel from his Spanish delegates, which, subsequently, resulted in the king formulating bad policies. The Dutch rebels did not withdrawal their loyalty to the king early on in the struggle. They only wished that their rights were honored and that they didn't have to be subservient to Spanish policies. For these reasons, the Dutch national anthem commences with the line "*to the king of Spain I've granted a lifelong loyalty.*" As the king dismissed such requests, however, the Dutch rebels eventually forfeited their loyalty to the Spanish monarch.

The poem is simply a work of genius. The song's style resembles that of the work of the *Rederijkers* (rhetoricians), sixteenth-century poets. The rhetoricians played an important role in contemporary society and had a great influence on the development of the modern day Dutch language. The first letters of the fifteen verses strung together brilliantly spell the name "William of Nassau." The text is also thematically symmetrical, in that verses one and fifteen resemble one another in meaning, as do verses two and fourteen, three and thirteen, etc., until they converge in the eighth verse, which is the heart of the song: "*Oh David, thou soughtest shelter/From King Saul's tyranny.*"

1. *William of Nassau, scion*
   Of a German and ancient line,
   I dedicate undying
   Faith to this land of mine.
   A prince I am, undaunted,
   Of Orange, ever free,
   To the king of Spain I've granted
   A lifelong loyalty.

2. *I 've ever tried to live in*
   The fear of God's command
   And therefore I've been driven,
   From people, home, and land,
   But God, I trust, will rate me
   His willing instrument
   And one day reinstate me
   Into my government.

3. *Let no despair betray you,*
   My subjects true and good.
   The Lord will surely stay you
   Though now you are pursued.
   He who would live devoutly
   Must pray God day and night
   To throw His power about me
   As champion of your right.

4. *Life and my all for others*
   I sacrificed, for you!
   And my illustrious brothers
   Proved their devotion too.
   Count Adolf, more's the pity,
   Fell in the Frisian fray,
   And in the eternal city
   Awaits the judgement day.

5. *I, nobly born, descended*
   From an imperial stock.
   An empire's prince, defended
   (Braving the battle's shock
   Heroically and fearless
   As pious Christian ought)
   With my life's blood the peerless
   Gospel of God our Lord.

6.   *A shield and my reliance,*
      O God, Thou ever wert.
      I'll trust unto Thy guidance.
      O leave me not ungirt.
      That I may stay a pious
      Servant of Thine for aye
      And drive the plagues that try us
      And tyranny away.

7.   *My God, I pray thee, save me*
      From all who do pursue
      And threaten to enslave me,
      Thy trusted servant true.
      O Father, do not sanction
      Their wicked, foul design,
      Don't let them wash their hands in
      This guiltless blood of mine.

8.   *O David, thou soughtest shelter*
      From King Saul's tyranny.
      Even so I fled this welter
      And many a lord with me.
      But God the Lord did save me
      From exile and its hell
      And, in His mercy, gave him
      A realm in Israel.

9.   *Fear not 't will rain sans ceasing*
      The clouds are bound to part.
      I bide that sight so pleasing
      Unto my princely heart,
      Which is that I with honor
      Encounter death in war,
      And meet in heaven my Donor,
      His faithful warrior.

10. Nothing so moves my pity
    As seeing through these lands,
    Field, village, town and city
    Pillaged by roving hands.
    O that the Spaniards rape thee,
    My Netherlands so sweet,
    The thought of that does grip me
    Causing my heart to bleed.

11. A stride on steed of mettle
    I've waited with my host
    The tyrant's call to battle,
    Who durst not do his boast.
    For, near Maastricht ensconced,
    He feared the force I wield.
    My horsemen saw one bounce it
    Bravely across the field.

12. Surely, if God had willed it,
    When that fierce tempest blew,
    My power would have stilled it,
    Or turned its blast from you
    But He who dwells in heaven,
    Whence all our blessings flow,
    For which aye praise be given,
    Did not desire it so.

13. Steadfast my heart remaineth
    In my adversity
    My princely courage straineth
    All nerves to live and be.
    I've prayed the Lord my Master
    With fervid heart and tense
    To save me from disaster
    And prove my innocence.

14. *Alas! my flock. To sever*
    Is hard on us. Farewell.
    Your Shepherd wakes, wherever
    Dispersed you may dwell,
    Pray God that He may ease you.
    His Gospel be your cure.
    Walk in the steps of Jesu
    This life will not endure.

15. *Unto the Lord His power*
    I do not confession make
    That ne'er at any hour
    Ill of the King I spake.
    But unto God, the greatest
    Of Majesties I owe
    Obedience first and latest,
    For Justice wills it so.

THE ANGLO WARS

With the Dutch burgeoning economy and vast worldly possessions during the Golden Age of the 1600s, neighboring England became embittered rivals, especially for control of the high-seas. The Dutch had always depended upon sea trade to keep their economy flourishing. The small size of the Netherlands and limited resources forced the Dutch to turn to the international arena for its economic pursuits. The economy of the Netherlands depended on maintaining dominance of international trading routes and remaining the strongest sea force in Europe. England, meanwhile, had a very powerful navy and had the same intentions as the Dutch and soon proved to be source of intense competition. England wanted the profitable sea routes for themselves. The Anglo-Dutch Wars were fought over the possession of the seas and the lucrative trade routes and lasted from 1652 to 1784.

In order to protect their position in North America and its shipping and trading businesses, the English Parliament passed the Navigation Acts, starting in the mid-seventeenth century. These acts mandated that all goods from England's American colonies must be carried by English ships. Additionally, these acts mandated that European goods were only to be imported to England by English ships or by ships from the country of origin. These acts were directed against Dutch trade and certainly didn't bode well for the Dutch merchants, who depended on many of these shipments for their economic success. In a period of growing competition on the international waters, the first English Navigation Act was the spark that ignited the Anglo-Dutch wars and led to a century of hostile naval engagements between the two countries across the globe.

The first Anglo-Dutch War was fought from 1652 to 1654, and resulted in a severely weakened Dutch economy and proved to be a blow to the once infallible Dutch business hegemony. The Dutch had always maintained success in controlling their trade routes and had been the center of trade for Europe for decades. When England was gaining the upper hand in this first Anglo-Dutch war, Europe as a whole began losing confidence in the Dutch economy. The Dutch, however, were able to regain control of the high-seas and to secure their profitable trading routes. At the war's conclusion, the commercial rivalry between England and the Netherlands was not resolved. Both countries had vast overseas empires that they were determined to protect and were resolute in expanding these empires even further. A second Anglo-Dutch War was inevitable.

Further naval skirmishes between the Dutch and English continued throughout the decade following the conclusion of the first Anglo-Dutch war. These hostilities, along with clashes over West African and North American trading posts, led to a declaration of war in 1665. Due to the lessons learned from the first Anglo-Dutch war, the Dutch were better prepared for hostilities as they significantly enhanced their naval capabilities. Even with Holland's stronger navy, the English immediately gained the advantage with the use of overwhelming naval offenses. Once again, Europe was threatened with the prospect of total English domination of the seas and once again confidence in Dutch businesses had lessened, precipitating a decline in the overall Dutch economy. By 1667, the Dutch were able to once again regain control of the waters, and the tide of war had turned in their favor. At about the same time of this turning point, the English were suffering in their homeland due to the outbreak of the Great Plague and the catastrophic affects of the Great Fire of London. England was forced to surrender and the ensuing peace treaty lessened the impact of the Navigation Acts, opening the sea routes once again to the ambitious Dutch merchants.

The third Anglo-Dutch War began in 1672 and ended in 1674. The English initially took control of the seas and the Dutch economy was once again greatly damaged for fears of English domination. In the face of immense military and economic defeat, the Dutch performed amazing naval campaigns in order to regain control of the seas and to ensure continued vitality of their economy. England was forced to quit the war in 1674 and the two countries returned to the status quo. Hostilities between the two major sea and economic powers dissipated substantially over the next century, although they still remained bitter rivals in the pursuit of international markets.

The fourth Anglo-Dutch war (1780-1784) proved economically disastrous for the Dutch. The Dutch supported the American Colonists in their rebellion against the English Imperialists, causing even more friction between Holland and England. Great Britain declared war on the Dutch in 1780, initially gained military advantage and, this time, did not relinquish that advantage. The English navy, the best in the world at the time, simply overpowered the Dutch and firmly established their supremacy on the high seas. At the end of the war, the Dutch overseas trade was paralyzed and their fleet completely destroyed. This British victory ended all Anglo-Dutch wars and was the impetus for the decline of Dutch world power.

REVOLUTION IN THE AIR ONCE AGAIN

Following their defeat of the fourth Anglo-Dutch war, Holland progressed into a severe economic slump. This economic downturn adversely affected all segments of Dutch society, to include Dutch patriotism and pride. For two centuries, the Dutch flexed their economic and military muscle throughout all parts of the world and reaped the benefits that came along with being a world superpower. The Dutch people of this tiny trading nation were proud, wealthy and envied throughout the world. With their defeat and loss of profitable trading routes, Dutch prosperity was now being replaced with poverty and despair. The Dutch populace became extremely frustrated with the dire economic conditions and sought to regain the glory it once possessed during the Golden Age.

With the collapse of their economic empire and with mounting dissatisfaction with the current state of affairs in their homeland, the Dutch people found the ruling Monarch to be the perfect scapegoat. Although revered for centuries, the Royal House of Orange was now under bitter attack for being the root of all of the problems within Dutch society. The disgruntled Dutch felt that Prince William V and his royal subjects had become complacent over the years and were responsible for allowing their country to decline into such a state of despair. Those determined to restore Dutch glory found that radical change was essential, and this change could only come with the overthrow of the ruling monarchy. Revolution was in the air once again in Holland, but this time it was internally focused.

The American Revolution that was in progress against British Imperialism added fuel to the rebellious fire in Holland. The Dutch were sympathetic to the cause of the American rebels in their pursuit to free themselves from Imperialistic chains. There were many similarities between the American rebellion against England and the Dutch revolt against Spain. The American War for Independence brought hope to those in Holland who were disgruntled with the royal establishment and were desirous for change. The Dutch felt that the once glorious House of Orange was now severely detrimental to the country and that new leadership was needed to be infused into the country.

A group of anti-Orange reformers began their rebellious movement in order to dissolve the autonomous power of Prince William V and to distribute power to a broader segment of society. By 1783, the Patriot movement had gained significant momentum and had even assembled an organized militia, called the Free Corps. In the ensuing years, Holland was on a brink of a civil war as the Patriot movement gained much more strength and the Dutch became more supportive of its cause.

In 1785, demands for a new constitution were made by the Patriots. The Leiden Draft was passed, which proposed a new constitution stipulating a bold new direction for the United Netherlands. The constitution emphasized self-evident natural rights over historical rights, insured popular sovereignty with elected officials responsible to the people, declared an end to inherited offices and called for the freedom of speech.[2] Very similar reforms were demanded by the American freedom seekers just a few years prior.

Hostilities between the Free Corps and troops loyal to the House of Orange intensified and became violent. In 1787, the Free Corps gained the upper hand and defeated military units of the Prince, forcing the Prince of Orange to flee the country. The Patriots now had control over the administration of the large cities of Amsterdam and Rotterdam. With control over the nation's capital and with the Prince being forced out of the country, the Patriots proceeded to denigrate the House of Orange in every conceivable way. Since the color of orange was used to symbolize the Royal House of Orange, the Patriots banned the use of the color orange throughout the country. They even went as far as decreeing that carrots could not be displayed in the marketplace unless only their green tops were visible.[3]

Total victory for the Dutch rebels was within sight, but a remarkable twist of events sealed their eventual defeat. The Dutch Prince's wife, Princess Wilhelmina, was of the House of Hohenzollern of Prussia. Upon her arrest by the Free Corps, the King of Prussia was infuriated and demanded her release. Further intensifying the King of Prussia's fury, the Patriots accepted money, war munitions and other support from Prussia's rival, France. These events convinced the King of Prussia that the Patriot revolution had to be squelched. The Prussian king quickly deployed twenty-thousand troops to the Netherlands and easily occupied Amsterdam. The Free Corps could only muster limited resistance and were forced to surrender in October, 1787, ending their uprising and enabling the restoration of the Monarchy.

This brief revolution certainly made a great impact in the Netherlands while it lasted, but the intensity of the rebels was not strong enough to sustain it or to oppose any formidable force. A comparison between a French Revolutionary and a Dutch Patriot, as described in Simon Schama's book "Patriots and Liberators," proclaims the following: "The French Patriot seizes his arms and flies to the place where he can use them on behalf of the cause of freedom; the Dutch Patriot, told that his redeemers are at hand on his frontier, stuffs his pipe full of tobacco and goes peacefully to his back parlor for a quiet smoke."[4] Although the Patriot revolution lasted only a short period of time and did not achieve its ultimate goals, it proved to be the initial spark that ignited future rebellions throughout Europe, especially in France.

AND NOW THE FRENCH...

The legendary French Revolution occurred from 1789 to 1799 and resulted in French rebels overthrowing the French monarchy and radical restructuring within Europe. The French revolutionaries exerted their influence throughout other parts of Europe and used military force in conquering many lands in order to overthrow the various monarchies permeating throughout the continent. French revolutionary troops invaded and occupied a large part of the Netherlands in 1795. The revolutionaries counted on and received great support from the Patriot leftovers who still were dissatisfied with the ruling classes. Revolutionary committees subsequently took over governmental affairs in the major cities of Holland. Prince William V of Orange was forced to flee to England once again, this time never to return. Prince William V certainly had a tough time in office.

The United Provinces of the Netherlands were reconstituted as the Batavian Republic in 1795 and was now under the auspices of the French revolutionaries. The Batavian and French republics signed the Treaty of Den Haag, which formed a defensive alliance between both states. In contrast to the tumultuous events that occurred in France during the French Revolution, revolutionary changes in Holland occurred comparatively peacefully. The guillotine was not necessary in Holland in order to instill fear amongst those who opposed the revolution. The Dutch felt that they had been governed by an ineffective political establishment lacking a clearly defined vision and sense of urgency for far too long. The newly constructed Batavian Republic marked the beginning of a more centralized and functional government, which the Dutch hoped would restore their country to its splendor and glory of the Golden Age.

In 1805, Napoleon Bonaparte, the French dictator turned Emperor, became frustrated with the Dutch in their unwillingness to oppose and boycott trade with his English adversary. Napoleon had established a continental blockade in opposition to English commerce. The Dutch, being first and foremost international traders and merchants, did not observe this blockade and continued carrying out trade with England. For this reason, Napoleon favored the introduction of autocratic rule in the Netherlands in order to better organize Dutch support in the struggle against England. In 1806, he transformed the Batavian Republic into the Kingdom of Holland and appointed his brother, Louis Bonaparte, as its new king. Once again, a foreign king was thrust upon the freedom-loving people of the Netherlands. The reception of Napoleon's brother as king, however, was not totally antagonistic, as it was with Spain's imposition of a king. Many of the Dutch citizens were actually relieved that the Batavian Republic had not been simply annexed into France, but was able to remain relatively autonomous as the Kingdom of Holland, although a French king was at the helm.

During Louis Napoleon's reign as King of Holland from 1806 to 1810, numerous initiatives were made that proved to be quite beneficial for the Dutch. The new centralized form of government gave the weakened Dutch state the much needed stimuli to revitalize its economy. Additionally, the new kingdom established a unified currency, improved health care and implemented educational reforms. A new penal law code was compiled, largely modeled on the French law, which greatly influenced society in all of its legal aspects. A system of communal registry offices was established which required that all births, deaths and marriages be recorded. Many Dutch families were now given names for the first time.[5] The Kingdom of Holland also introduced significant cultural initiatives, such as the Royal Museum for Dutch paintings, which served as a cultural landmark where the Dutch could preserve their national memories and magnificent past.

Napoleon Bonaparte endeavored to reform European lands within his empire and initiated political, economic and cultural improvements similar to the ones in the Kingdom of Holland. These intentions are reflected in Napoleon Bonaparte's own opinion of his career, on which he stated:

> *I closed the gulf of anarchy and brought order out of chaos. I rewarded merit regardless of birth or wealth, wherever I found it. I abolished feudalism and restored equality to all regardless of religion and before the law. I fought the decrepit monarchies of the Old Regime because the alternative was the destruction of all this. I purified the Revolution.*

This relative autonomy within the Kingdom of Holland, unfortunately for the Dutch, did not last very long. Napoleon was still not satisfied with the unwillingness of the Dutch to oppose the English and with their efforts to continue trading with them.

The Little Dictator just had to have a piece of Holland

Napoleon couldn't understand that the Dutch simply found it hard resisting their natural urges for trade and commerce. Additionally, Napoleon was also intent on increasing the size and power of his empire. On July 9th, 1810, Napoleon annexed the entire Kingdom of Holland to France. The worst fears of the Dutch had become a reality. Prior to the annexation, the Kingdom of Holland was merely under French supervision, but now the Dutch were fully subjugated once again. Napoleon didn't waste any time in showing that the former Kingdom of Holland was now a part of his Empire, and proclaimed Amsterdam to be the third capital of the French Empire.

ORANGE ONCE AGAIN

With Napoleon annexing the entire Kingdom of Holland, the Dutch were shackled to yet another foreign empire. The Dutch were now directly affected by all of the policies coming out of Paris. As was the case under the Habsburg regime, the Dutch were being adversely affected by all of the wars that France was fighting with other nations, although the Dutch had no interest for such wars. Further infuriating the Dutch, Napoleon stifled commerce and trade because he didn't want the Dutch conducting business with any of his rivals. International trade, the foundation for Dutch existence, was now virtually impossible. Furthermore, with the Dutch being fettered to the dictatorial rule of Napoleon and France, England started occupying Dutch colonies around the world with relative ease. The Dutch were rapidly losing control over their own destiny. Needless to say, anti-French sentiments began to run high within the Netherlands.

Although the Dutch weren't interested in any of France's foreign wars, Napoleon conscripted Dutch soldiers to accompany his army as it marched and fought throughout much of Europe. Dutch soldiers served under Napoleon in the brutal campaign against Russia, resulting in devastating losses. Dutch troops were also used in the massive clash that took place at Leipzig, which became known as the Battle of Nations because of its size and the sheer numbers of troops that took part. The army of France battled with Sweden, Russia, Austria and Prussia -- in all approximately 200,000 French army troops and allies, against almost 400,000 troops.

After Napoleon's brutal defeat at Leipzig in 1813, French troops retreated back to France. A provisional government was formed in Holland under the leadership of many former Patriots. Ironically, these Patriots, who previously despised the Royal House of Orange, called William of Orange, son of William V, to the liberated country and offered him the title of King. Once again the Dutch turned to the Royal House of Orange to save and restore order in their homeland. In November, 1813, William landed at Scheveningen beach, the same place where he had left the country with his father eighteen years previously. The following year, King William I gained sovereignty over the entire region of the Low Countries and united the seventeen provinces of the north and south, after a separation of over 225 years. The Dutch kicked Prince William V out of their country and then offered his son the title of King – a rather interesting stratagem as only the Dutch could do.

Belgium Secedes

Although the new constitution implemented by King William I was accepted in the north, it was not wholly accepted by the southern regions because the residents of the south felt that they were being under-represented. Once again friction arose between the northern and southern provinces of the Netherlands. King William I was reminiscent that weak leadership by his forebears severely debilitated his country, so he was determined to demonstrate strong authority in order to unite the disparate provinces. King William I introduced Dutch as the sole language of administration, which infuriated the French speaking southern regions. He also imposed the taxation system of the north into the southern regions, which resulted in drastic tax increases in the south. As history has proven time and time again, such tax increases can only spell trouble for those imposing such taxes. President George Bush Sr. of the U.S., for instance, made the grave mistake of raising taxes after proclaiming the infamous line, "Read my lips, no new taxes," which directly led to his re-election defeat.

King William I had revitalized the economy substantially in the Kingdom of the United Netherlands with numerous projects such as the construction of canals, trains and roads. He spearheaded many trade initiatives which brought wealth back into the country. His nickname, in fact, was King-Merchant due to his proclivity towards commerce. As the entire country became wealthier, however, most of the money was flowing into the hands of the Dutch speaking, northern provinces.

Religion played a pivotal role once again in the history of the Netherlands. King William I was a strong proponent of Protestantism, so he made the state religion the same. People in the southern provinces were Catholic and were incensed by such a mandate. The southern regions felt that the king was undeniably trying to obliterate Catholicism, along with the French language, from the entire country.

The southern provinces came to resent the rule of William I and were desirous to replace his arbitrary style of government with a constitutional monarchy. The southern citizens looked to France for guidance. In 1830, when France expelled the Bourbon Dynasty, revolution was in the air once again in the Netherlands. Mass riots broke out in the southern provinces as the citizens demanded a new independent state of Belgium. King William I sent troops to Belgium, but to no avail. The rebellion was much too strong and the differences between the north and south, mainly religion, culture and language, were much too stark. In 1839, King William I declared an end to the hostilities with the southern rebels and the United Kingdom of the Netherlands was disbanded and renamed the Kingdom of the Netherlands. The united Netherlands were no longer united. This split marked the last noteworthy change to the borders of the Kingdom of the Netherlands. As with his father, King William I certainly encountered some rough times while holding office.

WORLD WARS

In the late nineteenth century, Otto van Bismarck of Prussia had prophesized that, "Some damn foolish thing in the Balkans" would trigger the seemingly unavoidable European war. He could not have been more precise in his prophetic statement. In the early twentieth century, the Balkans comprised numerous ethnic groups and were breeding grounds for nationalistic fervor. The Habsburgs of Vienna ruled over these lands and struggled with keeping the Balkans under control. The Archduke Franz Ferdinand, heir to the Austrian throne, and his wife Sophie were assassinated in Sarajevo by a Serbian nationalist on June 28, 1914 on their fourteenth wedding anniversary. This event triggered the start of the first World War.

Since the re-establishment of the Dutch kingdom in 1815 after Napoleon's reign, Holland had declared perpetual neutrality. Holland was determined to maintain this state of neutrality during this new conflict and announced their intentions of doing so to the world. Holland miraculously avoided being dragged into the war, even with fierce fighting taking place just outside of its borders. Holland was focused on remaining a nation of trade and commerce and didn't want to be involved in yet more European disputes between emperors and empires. Focusing on what they did best, the Dutch were actually able to profit economically during the initial stages of the war. But as the war progressed and became bloodier and more protracted than originally expected, economies across Europe began to suffer, to include Holland's.

Although the Netherlands was never occupied during the war and the Dutch were spared from the devastating consequences of twentieth century warfare, they certainly experienced many of the spoils of war. Numerous trade embargoes were established and import restrictions were imposed by the Allies in order to ensure that German war supplies weren't being imported through Dutch ports. Factories were forced to close down throughout Holland due to the lack of raw products coming into their ports from abroad. Additionally, food shortages were abundant in Holland which caused starvation and numerous food riots in many of the Dutch cities.

The Dutch felt grateful that through their neutrality they were able to avoid the terrible loss of life and destruction which had occurred throughout much of Europe. The Dutch Queen Wilhelmina was so thankful that the warring Empires honored her country's neutrality that she granted Kaiser Wilhelm of Prussia asylum in Holland after the war had concluded. This neighborly gesture certainly didn't bode well for the Allied forces who would have rather seen the deposed Kaiser tried for war crimes.

On Sept. 1, 1939, the Nazi military machine, under the command of Adolf Hitler, struck decisively at Poland, in what was to become known as blitzkrieg, or lightning warfare. High-speed German panzers stormed across the Polish border and blasted huge holes in the Polish lines. From above, the Luftwaffe bombers destroyed the Polish air force, damaged communications lines, and prevented the Poles from moving reinforcements and supplies to the front lines. World War II had begun its bloody course and Great Britain and France declared war on Germany two days later. Once again, Holland found itself in a very precarious situation and was caught in the middle or warring superpowers.

At the outbreak of this massive war, the Dutch trading nation maintained its neutral posture and declared its neutrality with the hopes of avoiding another World War. Before the Reichstag in Berlin, Adolf Hitler proclaimed that Germany would not invade Holland and would honor its neutrality. Years prior, Adolf Hitler also proclaimed that he would, "contribute to assure the peace of Europe" and even signed a non-aggression pact with British Prime Minister Neville Chamberlain. Such actions by the Nazi leader immortalized Chamberlain's grossly miscalculated, optimistic statement, "Peace for our time." A year later Hitler derided the agreement as just a "scrap of paper" and invaded Poland. The same dismal fate awaited Holland.

Hitler sought to conquer and occupy the Low Countries of the Netherlands, Belgium, and Luxembourg to secure industrial resources and to establish advance bases for the coming assaults on France and Britain. With the Low Countries in his hands, Hitler could outflank the French defensive Maginot Line and then move into France across the unfortified Belgian border. On May 10, 1940, German troops attacked the Low Countries. Luxembourg, with no defensive forces, was occupied without any resistance. The Dutch and Belgians, however, boldly fought back. The Dutch received the brunt of the German offensives and attempted to thwart the invasion by mining bridges, blocking roads, and flooding large areas. On May 14th, the city of Rotterdam, even after having surrendered, was horrifically bombarded by the German Luftwaffe, where over forty percent of the city was destroyed. The Dutch lacked sufficient aircraft and tanks and had little allied support at the time, enabling the Nazi mechanized forces to overwhelm the Dutch within five days. The invasion ended over one hundred years of peace in Holland and the Royal House of Orange, led by Queen Wilhelmina, was forced to flee the country yet once again.

Slowly but surely, the Germans started transforming Holland into a totalitarian state. The Dutch Parliament and most of the nation's elected bodies were abolished. German justice replaced Dutch justice in the courts, meaning very little justice at all for the Dutch. The Nazi propaganda machine made its way into Holland as newspapers were subject to heavy censorship and all radio stations came under Nazi control. Dutch children were forced to learn German in the schools and new courses celebrating the Nazi regime were being introduced. The Nazis prohibited the displaying of Queen Wilhelmina's portrait and changed the street names that bore her name or the name of any living member of the Royal House of Orange.

Once again Holland's economic success was being exploited by a foreign invader and used to finance and support foreign wars, which, of course, were of no interest to the Dutch. Holland was forced to hand over much of its food, especially products form its thriving dairy industry, to Germany in order to feed troops fighting throughout Europe. As a result, food became scarce in the Netherlands. Not only did food become a scarcity, but consumer goods as well. All products that could be appropriated by the Nazis were used to support the German war effort. The Dutch even had to contend with Germans entering their homes and commandeering their personal possessions. Many Dutchmen were deported to Germany to work as forced laborers in the German economy, many of them never to make it back home.

Most of the Netherlands remained occupied until the end of the war, even though some portions were liberated by allied forces much earlier. The failure of the Battle at Arnhem in September, 1944, which is immortalized by the movie "A Bridge too Far" caused the northern parts of the Netherlands to become isolated. That winter, the German occupiers systematically starved the Dutch by preventing any food supplies into the area. The final phase of the war is referred to as the Hunger Winter and lasted until liberation in May, 1945. During the Hunger Winter many Dutch men, women and children died of starvation. The Dutch were forced to eat tulip bulbs and even their family pets just to stay alive. Before the War Holland had been one of the best fed and healthiest countries imaginable, but in five short years Holland became one of the most dismal places on the face of the earth.

As they have done for centuries, the Dutch pulled themselves out of the rubble of economic, military, and societal subjugation and propelled Holland back into eminence as a world industrial leader. With the assistance of the Marshall Plan, Holland quickly recovered from the hunger, homelessness, sickness, unemployment and overall catastrophic effects of the deadliest war in world history. In the post-war years, Holland took on a much more active role in international affairs and abandoned its traditional policy of neutrality. The Dutch view themselves as leaders in the world not only in the fields of trade and commerce, in which they've always been world leaders, but also in the crucial areas of world peace and social justice. The Dutch are actively taking leadership roles in organizations such as the United Nations, NATO and the European Union in order to help ensure peace and justice throughout the world. Additionally, Holland has been forthcoming with sending military personnel to troubled areas, such as Bosnia and Iraq, in order to do its part in restoring peace and demonstrating leadership on a global scale. Dutch resiliency and tenacity has ensured Holland's survival and prosperity throughout history. Their unrelenting pursuit for world peace and justice is currently thrusting them into the world spotlight as leaders on matters of international significance.

War Monument in the Dam Square

3.   DUTCH WORLDLY IMPACT

INTRODUCTION

Even though Holland is a mere speck on the world's total geographical landmass, the impact and influence of the Dutch is felt in virtually all corners of the globe. Beginning in the early 17th century, the Dutch have been prolific players in the international arena and have left indelible marks on both the eastern and western hemispheres. The impact that the Dutch had on the world throughout the centuries is still very tangible today in even the most remote places. The Dutch footprint on the world ranges from the substantial, to include language, architecture and culture, to the surreal, where the underlying Dutch influence is observable only with a keen eye and a discerning sense of world history. Courageous Dutch adventurers left the snugness of their Holland where *the tall tree catches the breeze* in order to satisfy their insatiable appetites for exploration and opportunities abroad. These Dutch seafarers continuously altered the landscape of the globe and ardently renamed newly-claimed territories for their Dutch homeland, forever changing the composition of the maps of the world.

Throughout history, the Dutch have been keenly focused on the international market for all of their business affairs and opportunities. The small landmass of Holland, especially with its marshy terrain, could only support the Dutch economically in a limited manner. The Dutch realized the importance of becoming proficient and astute international business entrepreneurs, and focused on the entire world, instead of just their European surroundings, as opportunities for trade and commerce. Remarkably, the Dutch achieved world prominence of a magnitude that has never been seen before in the 17th century and established numerous settlements without maintaining a powerful military force. The Dutch achieved such eminence mainly through economic incentives and cunning business deals. It's rather surprising that the Dutch were able to develop and sustain such an international economic empire without possessing military supremacy over their rivaling, and militarily strong, European neighbors. Additionally, the Dutch weren't dedicated to spreading their religious principles or converting masses of people to their own religious ideologies. The Dutch were business people first and their quest for new lands was always economically driven.

The pioneering Dutch were always on the vanguard of discovering and settling areas around the world with unlimited economic potential and huge growth opportunities. An old adage proclaims, *Follow the Artists* when striving to identify prime real estate and fruitful business opportunities. The premise of the adage is that amateur artists, commonly referred to as *starving artists*, will always be the impetus for the discovery and revitalization of impoverished or underdeveloped communities. As *starving artists* implies, they are usually struggling financially and are driven to find affordable areas in which to reside, which are normally destitute areas ridden with poverty, or areas that have been ignored for decades. As more artists move into such areas, these newly-formed artist communities become clean, trendy and prime real estate markets due to the tireless efforts of these new residents. Business opportunists then capitalize on these burgeoning markets by ravenously purchasing all of the land, resulting in skyrocketing prices. The onslaught of the business opportunists and the increasingly high prices, meanwhile, push the resilient starving artists out of the communities and back into other deprived areas where the cycle of "gentrification" begins once again.

The English have been business opportunists throughout the centuries and have been following and capitalizing on the trendsetting Dutch *starving artists* for purposes of expanding their imperialistic empire. The popular idiom, "The sun never sets on the British Empire" is largely attributable to the English riding the coattails of the Dutch and driving them out of their newly-developed territories, usually after the Dutch had already firmly established safe living communities and profitable trading posts. The Dutch, meanwhile, as with the starving artists, were continuously forced to regroup in order to find other prime opportunities around the world to maintain their economic stability and to compete with their European imperialistic neighbors.

Without a strong military backing for their economic pursuits, the Dutch were virtually powerless in defending their newly-formed territories against such an imperial force as Great Britain. The British capitalized on the trailblazing efforts of the Dutch in such far away places as Australia, New Zealand, South Africa, India and New York. Perhaps if the Dutch focused less on the economic motivators for world exploration, and focused more on the imperialistic nature of spreading Dutch power throughout the world, the old maxim would have been phrased, "The sun never sets on the Dutch empire."

LAND DISCOVERY AND COLONIZATION

In the 13th century, the famous Italian explorer, Marco Polo, traveled eastward through lands unbeknownst to Europeans, as far away as China and India. Marco Polo brought back to Europe stories of riches beyond even the wildest of imaginations, in addition to such revolutionary products as eye-glasses and spaghetti. Europeans were skeptical of the stories of the lavishness and richness of these far away lands. On his death bed, Marco Polo even exclaimed to a priest when questioned if he was telling the truth, "I did not tell half of what I saw, because no one would have believed me." For several centuries following Marco Polo's death, opportunistic and adventurous Europeans attempted to retrace the long and arduous routes that brought Marco Polo into these alleged lands of abundance and opulence. As Europeans began to successfully reach these Asian destinations, they found the wealth and profusion of highly sought after items such as silk, porcelain, tea and spices that Marco Polo described and documented. As word spread throughout Europe of the vast riches of India and China, validating Marco Polo's claims, the far eastern trade wars amongst European powers began in earnest and the far east soon developed into a fierce and competitive commercial marketplace.

The land routes into Asia and India were lengthy, onerous and dangerous. Europeans desirous for these riches soon turned to the sea as a means to journeying to these distant lands. The sea routes also proved to be quite demanding and treacherous, and resulted in a plethora of vessels at the bottom of the ocean. Attempts of early seafaring nations, to include mainly Spain, Portugal and Holland, at discovering an easier passageway into the Far East became an obsession and an embittered race. The Dutch leveraged their years of experience of sailing and trading along the vast coastal areas of Europe, even as far away as the Baltic region, in their audacious endeavors to establish trade routes throughout the Far Eastern region of the world. Due to their maritime prowess, the Dutch became very successful in not only establishing profitable trade routes, but in dominating the market of the entire Far Eastern region. By the mid-1600s, the Dutch had more than 700 ships at sea, more than the English, French and Scottish fleets combined.[1] Between the early part of the 17th century and the beginning of the 19th century, nearly half of all of the ships sailing in the Far East came from the ports of Holland.[2]

An Adventurous Dutchman off to the New World

THE EASTERN HEMISPHERE

Shipwrecks and piracy were prevalent on the high seas along the Far Eastern trading routes and proved quite costly for individual merchants. The loss of cargo and the costs of establishing foreign ports, storage houses and military fortresses were immense.

The Dutch merchants who were engaged in the profitable, yet daunting, East India trade business collaboratively formed a joint venture in order to alleviate the challenges inherent in such audacious adventures and to jointly capitalize on the immense economic opportunities. This new venture was called *the Vereenigde Oostindische Compagnie* (United East India Company), or V.O.C. The V.O.C. was given an official charter by the Dutch *Staaten Generaal*, granting it a monopoly for the entire East India trade market. The United East India Company established trading posts throughout all parts of the Far East, negotiated with local rulers on behalf of the Dutch government, built military fortresses for the protection of their trading monopoly and even raised local militias for further protection of their economic strongholds.

The V.O.C. was the world's first public Multi-National Corporation (MNC) where individual investors throughout Europe were able to invest in the company and share in the vast profits. The world's first stock exchange was established in Holland in order to publicly encourage investing in the Dutch East India Company. This newly formed company needed to raise money in order to successfully compete with other seafaring nations in the Far East and to finance the long and perilous journeys. The Portuguese, Spanish and English were all vying for dominance in this lucrative market. Shares of the company were feverishly bought and sold as the V.O.C. began recording phenomenal economic results. The New York Stock Exchange, and Stock Exchanges around the world, owe their existences to the capitalistic and innovative 17th century Dutch.

In an effort to facilitate raising money for the company's far away ventures, the Dutch opened the Bank of Amsterdam in 1609 which accepted all forms of currency from around the world. With the vast influx of differing world currencies, the bank of Amsterdam felt it necessary to establish a monetary standard in order to facilitate the numerous financial transactions that were occurring with the investments made into the East India Company. The Bank of Amsterdam soon minted standard gold florins and exchanged them based upon the value of silver or gold of the currencies of their customers and investors. These gold florins, or *gulden florijn*, became known as Dutch guilders and were used in financial transactions in virtually all parts of the world due to the extensive economic empire of the Dutch republic. The Dutch guilders have been the standard currency in Holland until the Euro came into existence and made the guilder obsolete in 2002.

The V.O.C. eventually became a monopolistic juggernaut in the highly-profitable Far East trade market. Thousands of investors from continental Europe contributed to the vitality and economic strength of this company. European competition was virtually eliminated and the publicly traded V.O.C. expanded its market to include regions as far away as Indonesia, Japan and Africa. The V.O.C. focused almost exclusively on only those markets that would give them the best economic returns and focused less on land discovery and colonization for nationalistic or religious purposes. Having monetary incentives and responsibilities to its shareholders, the V.O.C. was concerned with profitability, which led to territorial settlements in only those untapped areas where attractive economic potential existed.

The V.O.C. claimed sovereignty in numerous territories in the name of the Dutch Republic and established economic trading posts in these regions. Moluccas, or more commonly the Spice Islands, was a fountainhead of highly-profitable, high demand spices. An intense European demand existed for cloves and nutmeg, which were prodigious on the Spice Islands. Such products were valued as food preservatives and wealthy Europeans kept these spices in lockets around their necks in order to freshen their breaths easily, much like modern day breath mints. Additionally, Europeans enjoyed adding nutmeg to their food and drinks and even used these spices for medicinal purposes. The Dutch governed the fruitful Spice Islands between 1605 and 1945 and profitably distributed the indigenous spices to all regions of the world.

The headquarters of the V.O.C. empire was located in modern day Jakarta, Indonesia. Upon attacking and destroying this ancient city in order to establish a beachhead into this strategic location, the Dutch renamed it Batavia, in honor of an ancient Germanic tribe, *Batavi*, which occupied present day Holland preceding the Dutch civilization. The *Batavi* tribe valiantly fought for their freedom against the occupying Roman forces. This historic struggle remains to be a source of Dutch national mythology and pride. Batavia, Indonesia soon became a replica of a typical Dutch coastal town, with an abundance of canals, windmills and sea vessels. The V.O.C. also established a military fortress in order to protect the "nerve center" of its monopoly and the numerous storage facilities that were loaded with stockpiles of spices. The Dutch enslaved the local populace to more effectively acquire the sought after spices that the Europeans insatiably demanded. Even after the V.O.C.'s eventual collapse, the Dutch remained in Batavia until shortly after the second World War, since it remained as one of the most profitable territories for the Dutch.

A significant portion of the Eastern Hemisphere that the Dutch are credited with discovering includes the large land masses of New Zealand and Australia. The Dutch explorer, Abe Tasman, was the first European to set sights on New Zealand, with the original Dutch version being *Nieuw Zeeland*. The island of Tasmania, situated just off of the coast of Australia, was also discovered by the Dutchman and bears his name in his honor. The Tasman Sea, furthermore, also bears the name of the famous Dutch explorer, Abe Tasman. Without Tasman's discovery of these remote lands, the famed *Looney Toons* cartoon character and Bugs Bunny's pal, the Tasmanian Devil, would come by a different name or not even be in existence today. The Tasmanian Devil cartoon character, parenthetically, is a caricature of the real animal possessing the same name that is indigenous to the Tasmanian island. This animal was named the Tasmanian Devil by early European settlers because of the nocturnal nature of the animal, its ferocity and its eerie growl that reverberates throughout the night.

The Tasmanian Devil -- with Dutch roots

Abe Tasman and the Dutch are also credited with discovering modern day Australia. The island was originally named *Nieuw Holland* upon its discovery, laying Dutch claims to the massive landmass. Tasman, acting in accord with the Dutch East India Company, sought only those lands that would be of significant economic value to the Dutch and to the V.O.C. shareholders. Tasman found no immediate economic value or potential with inhabiting Australia and establishing a settlement and, therefore, made the hasty decision to bypass *Nieuw Holland*. In fact, the Dutch never set foot on the massive island but made detailed maps documenting the whereabouts of their discovery. The English rode the coattails of the Dutch and began sailing to this new found land upon hearing of the discovery. The English eventually claimed the territory as their own and dismissed the name *Nieuw Holland* in favor of Australia, even though the Dutch V.O.C. previously claimed the land for the Dutch republic. The English soon began sending their convicts and miscreants to this far away land in order to firmly establish a Far Eastern British colony. The British flag, the Union Jack, is still represented on the official flag of Australia.

International competition in the Far Eastern trade market became fierce as highly-profitable and high-demand products were continuously being discovered. World powers, such as England and France, began flooding the market with their merchants and navies. Nationalistic rivalries amongst the European nations were becoming even more intense. With Holland's diminutive size and limited population reserves compared to their European adversaries, it became increasingly difficult to maintain their trade monopoly and to compete in such a fierce market. The V.O.C. eventually declared bankruptcy in the late 1700s due to the increased competition and overwhelming nationalistic threats from rivaling European nations. The Multinational Company was dissolved and many of its former territories became official colonies of the Netherlands. Many shareholders, consequently, who didn't cash out during the economic high-times of the V.O.C., were left with nothing but regrets, similar to those who hung on too long during the Internet bubble of the 1990s that eventually burst.

Overall, the Dutch United East India Company established its dominance in a multitude of Eastern Hemisphere locations. The Dutch remained in many of these strategic locations for centuries and colonized many of them in order to continue to reap the benefits of the profitable resources. The V.O.C. and the Dutch either discovered or dominated the following Eastern Hemisphere locations and built their empires around the economic successes derived from them:

- Indonesia
- India
- Bangladesh
- Malaysia

- Sri Lanka
- Taiwan
- Japan
- Eastern Africa
    - Ghana
    - Mauritius
    - Nigeria
    - Senegal
    - Sierra Leone
- South Africa
- Australia
- New Zealand

THE WESTERN HEMISPHERE

While the Dutch maintained and enjoyed their economic hegemony over the Far Eastern trade market in the 17th century, they also set their sights on the western portion of the world to tap into even more of the world's profitable and sought after resources. The major catalyst for this westward exploration and expansion was for a natural resource that was an integral component to European civilization – salt. Salt, or *white gold*, as it was often referred to because of its tremendous economic value and high demand, provided a means for food preservation in the days before refrigeration. Additionally, salt added flavor to the bland foods that were consumed throughout much of northern Europe at that time. With the Dutch being voracious consumers of raw herring and being deeply entrenched in the lucrative herring trade business, they relied on vast quantities of *white gold* for the preservation of the fish, in addition to adding flavor to these little delicacies. Unfortunately for the Dutch, their adversaries, the Spanish, closed access to the Spanish saltpans where the Dutch had been acquiring the much needed salt to support their thriving herring business. Although other sources of salt were prevalent in other parts of Europe, such as Salzburg (Salt Castle), the Dutch were bordered by such military powerhouses as Prussia, Spain, and France, that their best chances of securing this precious mineral lied somewhere west of Holland, where their only restrictive border was the vast ocean.

The Dutch leveraged the maritime experience acquired from their Far Eastern trading endeavors and set sails westward over the treacherous seas in search of much needed salt. The *white gold* at the end of the proverbial rainbow was found as far west as the Caribbean Islands. With the Dutch discovery of their sought after food preservative and flavoring, the Caribbean now became the source for Dutch salt and soon became an integral part in the Dutch herring industry. The Dutch merchants, meanwhile, continued to explore the entire region of the Caribbean seeking out untapped economic potential. Similar to, and for the same reasons as the establishment of the Dutch East India Company, the Dutch merchants of the western trade routes formed a similar consortium in order to pool their resources to lessen the severe risks involved with long marine voyages and establishing far away trading posts. In 1621, the Dutch United West India Company (WIC) was established with Dutch authorities granting this newly formed company with the same monopolistic powers as the V.O.C., throughout the entire Western Hemisphere. The ruling powers of Holland also granted the W.I.C. with authorization to act on the behalf of the Dutch republic in colonizing lands. The government knew that the establishment of new colonies would bring even more treasures back to their homeland.

In addition to Dutch merchants sailing and dominating the Caribbean region, they now sailed to the Americas and even to western African countries. The Dutch strived to further expand their economic empire and to solidify their dominance over their European rivals on the international trading front. They established profitable trading businesses in the Western Hemisphere based mainly on sugar, tobacco, pearls and ivory. The Dutch hurriedly established settlements in order to quickly reap the benefits of indigenous resources and constructed military fortresses for the defense of their newly claimed territories. The Dutch officially established settlements which encompassed such far away lands as South America, North America and across the Atlantic Ocean to the western portion of continental Africa.

The Dutch West India Company dominated numerous Western Hemisphere locations. To this day, the Dutch still possess, as colonies, some of the territories that were established by the W.I.C. Former Dutch colonies within the Western Hemisphere are still a part of the Kingdom of the Netherlands, to include Curaçao, Bonaire, Aruba, St. Eustasius, Saba and the Dutch half of St. Maarten. The Dutch maintained establishments in the following Western Hemisphere locations:

- Brazil
- Venezuela
- Cape Horn
- Curaçao
- Bonaire
- Netherlands Antilles
- Aruba
- St. Eustasius
- St Maarten
- Saba
- Suriname
- Trinidad and Tobago
- Virgin Islands
- New York metropolitan area
- Western Africa
   - Elmina (Gold Coast)

Both the East and West India Companies eventually declared bankruptcy, but well after the Dutch had made an indelible mark on the world. With Holland being a small country with limited population reserves, the Dutch simply overextended themselves too far and too thin. Overextension is a classic military blunder that has been repeated by even the strongest of military powers throughout time. The Dutch overextension, however, was really a matter of economic intemperance rather than colonial conquests, although degrees of subjugation and maltreatment of indigenous populations certainly existed.

With the disinterest of the Dutch to forcefully impose religious or imperialistic ideologies upon indigenous populations, they were actually welcomed by the inhabitants in many regions, especially where the wrath of the colonial and missionary conquests of other European nations had already been encountered. The Spanish, for instance, sought to spread Christianity throughout the new world and did so rather successfully, although brutally, as evidenced by the predominance of Christianity and the Spanish language being spoken today throughout Central and South America. Neil Young, the legendary musical icon, sings about the brutality of the Spanish Conquistadors in their conquest of new lands in the song *Cortez the Killer*.

> *"He came dancing across the water*
> *With his galleons and guns*
> *Looking for the new world*
> *In that palace in the sun......*
>
> *He came dancing across the water*
> *Cortez, Cortez*
> *What a killer."*

After the brutality and oppression of the Spanish Conquistadors, the Dutch were a welcome relief from the cruelty and suffering that the native populations endured.

Nieuw Amsterdam – the Big Orange?

New York City, the most famous metropolis on the planet and the self-proclaimed "Capital City of the World" was originally overwhelmingly Dutch in the 17th and early 18th centuries. Early Dutch settlers and merchants established villages and trading posts throughout the entire New York metropolitan area beginning in the early 1600s in order to profit from the vast resources within the region. The Dutch are credited with negotiating the "Deal of the Millennium" with the purchase of the island of Manhattan from the Indians for, ostensibly, \$24. The borders of the Dutch territory claimed by the West India Company stretched as far from southern Delaware through New Jersey and east-central Pennsylvania, and into eastern and central New York, including Long Island. This Dutch region was originally called *Nieuw Nederland* and New York City was originally called *Nieuw Amsterdam*, both names paying homage to the Dutch motherland in Europe.

Still vigorously striving to find that elusive Northwest Passage into India and the Orient in order to shorten the lengthy and perilous voyage around the Cape of Good Hope, Africa, the Dutch East India Company hired the English sailor Henry Hudson to lead an expedition to find this desirous passageway. Henry Hudson was a famous sea captain who had previously established a fine reputation as an intrepid sailor in the frigid waters of the Arctic. Henry Hudson and his Dutch passengers set sail for the highly sought after Northwest Passage on the famous Dutch ship *De Halve Maen* (The Half Moon). After first attempting and failing to find the passage above Norway, Hudson strategically set sails westward across the Atlantic Ocean. Hudson eventually sailed into the mouth of a tremendous river, which bears his name today. Hudson and the Dutch crew of *De Halve Maen* ventured upstream of the Hudson River still seeking that elusive passage into the Orient. The crew sailed as far as present day Albany before realizing that the river would not provide them with such a passageway. Upon *De Halve Maen's* return to Europe, the entire Hudson River valley was officially claimed as a Dutch territory.

With the entire Hudson River valley's potential as a lucrative trading region and firmly established as a Dutch territory, Dutch merchants and potential settlers to the region soon began emigrating to these promising lands. The original Dutch settlers established an outpost on the Indian island of *Manna-hatta*, present day Manhattan. They formed business relationships with the local Indians and traded beads, clothing and other European products for beaver pelts and miscellaneous animal furs. The Indians, mainly Delawares and Mahicans, initially called these tall, white Dutchmen the *Great Mannitoos* or Supreme Beings.

Unfortunately for the Indians, as more of these *Great Mannitoos* arrived to the new world and began sailing up the Hudson river and venturing westward, the Indians were extricated from their homelands and forced westward. Additionally, the European settlers introduced more than just beads and clothing to the Indians, but smallpox, guns and booze which contributed to the eventual detriment of the Native Americans.

Deal of the millennium -- or was it?
Perhaps only the Dutch, with their notorious frugality and never-ending quests for tremendous bargains, could have purchased the island of *Manna-hatta* for a mere pittance. The commonly told story is that the Dutch purchased modern day Manhattan from the Indians for the now legendary price of 60 guilders, or a paltry $24. This legendary $24 came in the form of beads and other items that served little use to the Dutch, but were cherished by the Indians of the region. Once the purchase was finalized, the island was promptly named *Nieuw Amsterdam* and served as the hub for Dutch business transactions and logistical endeavors throughout the entire Hudson River valley. Incidentally, modern day Wall Street, the financial hub of the world, is the site where the original Dutch inhabitants built a wall for protection against Indian attacks. The Dutch have always been heralded as shrewd European businessmen due to their cunning negotiation for the purchase of Manhattan from the trusting Indians. A present day monument even exists in lower Manhattan depicting a Dutchman purchasing the island from an Indian for a mere $24 worth of beads.

As with much folklore, the story of the Dutch cleverly purchasing the island of Manhattan for a song and dance is more myth than reality. The Dutch actually purchased Manhattan for upwards to thousands of dollars worth of goods such as kettles, steel tools, knives, guns and blankets. They purchased the island, however, from the Indian tribe, the Canarsies, who didn't even live on the island of Manhattan, but lived in modern day Brooklyn. The Canarsies were a rival tribe of the Weckquaesgeeks, who actually lived on the island of Manhattan. The Weckquaesgeeks were obviously outraged that their homeland had been sold to the Europeans by a rival tribe and that their rival tribe benefited greatly with this deceitful transaction. The Dutch and the Canarsies, meanwhile, allied themselves in repressing the revolts of the Weckquaesgeeks in their attempts at defending their homeland, and nearly exterminated the entire tribe. The story of the Dutch purchasing Manhattan for $24 in a friendly transaction with amicable Indians is a much more pleasant story than what really transpired, which undoubtedly led to the story's propagation throughout the years.

A little more than $24, but still a great bargain!

With the key strategic location of Manhattan firmly in Dutch control, the Dutch sought to further expand their territories outside of Manhattan and establish villages and trading posts in unchartered territories. Such lines of thinking are analogous to modern day urban sprawl, which accounts for the mass migrations out of New York City and into the suburbs, and even further into the country. Regardless of such migrations, then and now, people always seem to gravitate back to the island of Manhattan where, as Frank Sinatra sang, *If you can make it there you can make it anywhere!* Manhattan was truly the foundation for most of the Dutch wealth in the Hudson River valley and the Dutch laid the foundation for Manhattan's prosperity for centuries to come.

Seeking to encourage colonization, the Dutch government authorized the title of patron to anyone who would settle a colony of over fifty people. A patron received a grant of land and was vested with all of the privileges of feudal lords. Another method of fostering settlement at this time was the issue of land patents, which were grants of land usually conditioned on payment similar to a rent or lease. Dutch settlers eventually began conducting brutal campaigns against the local Indian tribes in order to settle the areas and take full advantage of all of the natural resources that the land afforded them. The Dutch were successful in devastating the Indian tribes along the rivers, such as the Hudson and Delaware, in order to secure these valuable transportation sources. Intense suspicion and eventual hatred began to arise in both the Dutch settlers and Native Americans, which led to further hostilities and aggression.

The most notorious Dutch "Indian killer" was unquestionably Thomas Quick, who emigrated from Holland in 1733 and settled in the northwest section of *Nieuw Nederland*. In fact, in 1851 a book was written about this legendary Indian fighter, titled *Life and Adventures of Tom Quick, the Indian Slayer*, which starts out:

> *"Hero of many a wondrous tale,*
> *Full of his dev'lish cunning!*
> *Tom never flunked or turned pale,*
> *Following on the Indian's trail,*
> *Shooting as he was running."*

Legend has it that frontiersman Tom Quick slaughtered 99 Indian men, women and children, but lamented on his deathbed in 1796 that he didn't get to make it an even 100. The Dutchman swore revenge on the entire Indian nation after he saw Indians brutally kill and scalp his father in 1756. Quick spent the rest of his life avenging his father's death and was a local hero to the non-Indian, white population. In fact, a monument still exists today in Milford, Pennsylvania honoring the famed frontiersman with the inscription, *"Maddened by the death of his Father at the hands of the savages, Tom Quick never abated his hostility to them until the day of his death, a period of over forty years."* Native Americans and many activist groups are still outraged over this monument and have expressed their disapproval on several occasions, periodically desecrating the monument itself.

The British heavy-metal rock group, Iron Maiden, perhaps had the Dutch in mind, along with other numerous European expansionists, when they wrote the notorious song, *Run to the Hills*, which expressed the plight of the Native American at the hands of the European invaders.

> *"White man came across the sea*
> *He brought us pain and misery*
> *He killed our tribes, he killed our creed*
> *He took our game for his own need*
>
> *We fought him hard we fought him well*
> *Out on the plains we gave him hell*
> *But many came too much for cree*
> *Oh will we ever be set free?*
>
> *Riding through dust clouds and barren wastes*
> *Galloping hard on the plains*
> *Chasing the redskins back to their holes*
> *Fighting them at their own game*
> *Murder for freedom a stab in the back*
> *Women and children and cowards attack*
>
> *Run to the hills run for your lives*
> *Run to the hills run for your lives*
>
> *Soldier blue on the barren wastes*
> *Hunting and killing their game*
> *Raping the women and wasting the men*
> *The only good Indians are tame*
> *Selling them Whiskey and taking their gold*
> *Enslaving the young and destroying the old*
>
> *Run to the hills run for your lives"*

After benefiting from the immense resources of the region for several decades, the Dutch eventually lost *Nieuw Nederland* to the English in 1664. The English sent a naval fleet to the Dutch settlement with the intentions of a hostile takeover. The famed, peg-legged Dutch Director General Peter Stuyvesant did not possess an army or navy formidable enough to challenge such a European powerhouse and was forced to surrender the colony without any resistance. The ghost of Peter Stuyvesant is said to be still haunting St. Mark's church (the site of his burial) in New York City. The Dutch were able to salvage the small territory of Suriname in the Caribbean with the English takeover of *Nieuw Nederland*, although rather pale in comparison to the magnitude of wealth of their once *Nieuw Nederland* colony.

To this day, numerous cities and towns in the New York region possess their original Dutch names, with minor Anglicization. Once again the English rode the Dutch coattails by waiting for the Dutch to firmly establish safe living quarters and profitable trading posts before driving the Dutch out of their settlements and taking advantage of the region's prosperity. Much like the *starving artists* of modern times, the Dutch were forced out of their newly established community by business opportunists ready to exploit the riches of the lands. As usual, the Dutch were concerned primarily with economic vitality and profitable trading than with employing overwhelming military force, even in defense of their newly established territories. The English acquired the metropolis of the world with little Dutch resistance. Perhaps today New York City would be referred to as the "Big Orange," instead of the "Big Apple" if the Dutch were able to provide formidable resistance and to persevere against British aggression.

The Dutch impact in the Hudson River valley was immense, although their formal occupation lasted only 55 years. Dutch merchants and explorers established numerous towns, trading posts and military fortresses all along the lengthy Hudson River from Fort Orange (present day Albany) to *Nieuw Amsterdam* (present day New York City). The impact that the Dutch had on

Could have been the "Big Orange" instead of the "Big Apple"

the region is still tangible today with many of the cities, towns and regions deriving their names from the original Dutch names crafted by the early frontiersmen. The table on the next pages illustrates just a few of the many towns and cities that exist in the New York metropolitan area that still possess their original Dutch names, with minor Anglicization. The purpose of this table is to illustrate the dominance that the Dutch once maintained over the New York region and the subtle influences that they still have on the Big Apple and surrounding areas.

Modern-day Anglicized Name	Original Dutch Name	Origins of the Name	Current Claim to Fame
Harlem	*Haarlem*	Town in Holland	Home to the world famous Harlem Globetrotters Basketball team and Apollo Theater
Brooklyn	*Breukelen*	Town in Holland	Home to the legendary Brooklyn Bridge, the world's first suspension bridge
The Bowery	*De bouwerij*	Translation "the farm"	Gritty east side artistic area of Manhattan
The Bronx	*Bronck*	Jonas Bronck owned a farm north of Manhattan and people traveling to this area spoke of "going to the Broncks"	Home to the legendary New York Yankees
Cape May	*May*	First Governor of New Netherlands Cornelis Jacobsz May	Beautiful New Jersey ocean front town with a famous lighthouse
The Catskills	*Kaatskill*	Translation: cat's stream	Mountain retreat for wealthy New Yorkers and backdrop for the movie "Dirty Dancing"
Coney Island	*Conyne Eylandt*	Translation: Rabbit Island	Home to Nathan's famous hot dog eating contest
Fishkill	*Vischers Kill*	Translation: Fisher's stream	New York City suburb
Greenwich	*Greenwyck*	Pine area	Home of the New York City "counter-culture" and famed musicians as Mick Jagger and Iggy Pop
Hell's Gate	*Helle Gadt*	Dangerous Tidal Currents	Area of the East River between the Bronx and Queens

Hoboken	*Hoboken*	Town in Northern Belgium (formerly of the United Provinces)	Birthplace of Frank Sinatra and site of the first baseball game ever played
Sandy Hook	*Sant Hoek*	Sand Hook	New Jersey beach and fishing areas, and home to one of the few nude beaches in the U.S.
Staten Island	*Staaten Eylandt*	Dutch States-General (government)	Home to the Fresh Kills Land Fill, one of the largest rubbish dumps in the world
Wall Street	*Vaal Straat*	Protective wall against the Indians	The wealthiest street in the world and the center of the financial universe
Yonkers	*Jonker*	Translation: The propertied gentleman, after Adriaen Van der Donck	Neighbor to New York City and 4th largest city in New York
Gramercy	*Kromme Zee*	Crooked sea/lake	Birthplace to Teddy Roosevelt in NYC
Flushing	*Vlissingen*	Town in Holland	Home to the New York Mets, 1964 World's Fair and U.S. Open tennis tournament

Dutch Influence throughout the New York Region[3]

The current New Jersey state flag pays homage to the region's early Dutch settlers. The flag displays the New Jersey state seal emblazoned in dark blue on a brilliant buff background. These colors represent the colors of the uniforms worn by the soldiers of the Continental Army from the colonies of New Jersey and New York. General George Washington selected these colors for the soldiers residing in the former *Nieuw Nederland* region because of the substantial Dutch population and the fact that the colors of dark blue and buff were the colors of Holland's insignia. Incidentally, only the New Jersey and New York soldiers had such colored uniforms; the rest of the Continental Army had different colored uniforms. Additionally, since General Washington was headquartered in New Jersey for the majority of the war, his uniform, as well as his officers' uniforms, were also dark blue and buff, showing deference to the large Dutch contingent in the vicinity.

Retribution that Backfired
With the Dutch resenting that they lost control of one of the greatest economic and strategic locations throughout the world to the English, they provided assistance to the American colonies during their War for Independence against imperialistic Great Britain. The Dutch actually professed neutrality, but clandestinely bypassed the British naval blockade of America and sent the colonies weapons and ammunition in support of their war efforts. In true Dutch form, the Dutch merchants wanted to tap into that burgeoning American market, and in order to do so, they needed the colonists to defeat the British imperialists. Additionally, the Dutch had always been the bastion of freedom, tolerance and independence, so they were sympathetic towards the ideals of the American Revolution. The cause of the American colonists was similar to that of the Dutch revolt against imperialistic Spain. At the near conclusion of the American Revolution, the prominent American, John Adams, facilitated the signing of the Treaty of Amity and Trust with the Dutch which laid the foundations for a strong partnership between the two countries. The Dutch provided the new and struggling country with its first international loan of five million guilders to assist in getting the newly formed nation off the ground.

Even though the colonists displayed unbelievable resolve in defeating the mighty British, the U.K. was still a power to be reckoned with. Since the Dutch supported the colonists in their rebellion against the British, the British declared war on the Dutch republic and deployed naval blockades off of the Dutch coast impeding what the Dutch did best – international trade. Furthermore, the British continued riding the Dutch coattails and systematically overtook numerous Dutch trading posts around the world, capitalizing on stable and profitable economic hubs founded and developed by the Dutch. Directly attributable to the hostile actions of the British, the West India Company folded in 1791 and the East India Company went under in 1800, just years after America gained its independence in 1783.

DUTCH ORANGE AROUND THE WORLD

On any festive occasion in Holland, the color of orange is unequivocally the most conspicuous and glaring feature blanketing the city streets. On such occasions, Dutch revelers cover themselves from head-to-toe with orange attire, waving orange flags and blowing orange whistles. The stores, restaurants and pubs are all strewn with orange banners and decorations. Football stadiums are filled to capacity with orange-clad fans when the Dutch national team battles it out on the fields of friendly strife. The numerous souvenir shops throughout Holland are all loaded with orange colored trinkets and merchandise. The Dutch are world renowned for their association with, and passion for, the color of orange. The Empire State building in New York City, in fact, brightly displays colors of orange along its apex once a year commemorating the Queen's Day celebration in Holland.

The Dutch have always been fanatical about the color orange and are even responsible for the carrot being its current color of orange. During the Dutch Golden Age, Dutch farmers bred and cultivated carrots using mutant seeds in order to produce these world famous orange colored vegetables, which were originally purple and white. Leave it to the Dutch and their peculiar ways to genetically alter a vegetable in order to produce a color honoring their country. The Dutch passion for the color orange is directly attributable to the Dutch royal family, which derives from the House of Orange. The royal House of Orange has even had lasting effects on other parts of the world, and upon religion itself.

During the tumultuous 17th century, national and religious rivalries ran rampant throughout Europe. The French, Dutch and English were constantly at odds with one another, and to exacerbate matters, sparring religious factions were interspersed throughout each of the nations. The most intense of these religious rivalries was between the Catholics and the Protestants. To make matters even more precarious, members of various European royal houses comprised differing religious affiliations; therefore, resulting in divided support from the masses. The King of England, Charles II, was a secret Catholic and formed a secret alliance with the Catholic King of France, Louis XIV, much to the chagrin of the English Protestants. Meanwhile, Dutch Prince William III of the House of Orange, the Protestant great-grandson of William the Silent, the "Father" of the Dutch homeland, married the King of England's Protestant niece, Mary Stuart.

Although European nations could be warring rivals, the European royal families weren't deterred from marrying royal family members from nations with which they were battling. The Habsburgs exemplified such marriages and greatly expanded their territories with such strategic marriage alliances. The Habsburg Empire nearly doubled with the marriages of Habsburg males to the heiresses of Burgundy and Spain. Meanwhile, the marriage between the Dutch Prince William III and the English Mary Tudor may not have started out as a marriage of convenience, but certainly proved to be one of the most pivotal and strategic alliances throughout history.

When the King of England, Charles II, died in 1685, his brother, James II, assumed the royal crown. James II, incidentally, was the Dutch Prince Williams' father-in-law. James was a fervent Catholic and ardently resolved to bring Catholicism back to England. The English Protestants feared that this would result in Protestant subjugation, for the memories of the brutal rule of the Catholic Mary Tudor, or *Bloody Mary*, was still fresh in their minds. The Protestants had some comfort knowing that the next in line for the throne was Mary, the Protestant oldest daughter of King James. King James, however, gave birth to a son and made it abundantly clear that he wished his son to supersede Mary in succession to the throne. A Catholic dynasty, consequently, appeared imminent in England.

The English, French and Dutch continued warring for monetary and colonial supremacy. Since the French monarchy was Catholic, the influential Protestant members within England felt that the only hope to deter a Catholic dynasty was to show support for the Dutch Protestant Prince William. The English Protestants vowed their allegiance to William and promised their support should a Dutch army invade England. William and his Dutch army did indeed invade England in 1688 and easily drove James II and his Catholic army out of the country. This invasion is referred to as the "Glorious Revolution" for the ease in which it succeeded and with the removal of the Catholic king from the throne of England.

To make the already blurred lineage lines of European royal families even more blurred, Prince William was the grandson of England's King Charles I, on his mother's side. For this reason, William and his wife Mary were considered to have equal lineage claims to the throne of England. Now that is what you call a marriage of convenience! King William III and Queen Mary II established the only dual monarchy in English history. The Dutchman William was now king and ruler over England, Scotland, Ireland, Wales and the Netherlands and was declared the "Defender of the Protestant Faith."

Meanwhile, the Catholic ex-King James II fled to Ireland with intentions of establishing his authority and seizing Protestant lands. Numerous conflicts between the Catholics and Protestants resulted from the former King's ambitious endeavors. Many high-ranking Protestants were forced to flee to England in order to avoid James' attempts to subjugate them. The Catholics laid siege to many Irish cities, resulting in the Dutch King William and his armies embarking on an invasion of the northern part of Ireland to squelch the Catholic uprisings. King William was able to defeat the Catholics in Derry, which established a solid base of Protestant support in Northern Ireland, which has lasted to this day. The Battle of the Boyne is perhaps the most significant and famous battle that occurred in Ireland. The Protestant victory at this battle is still celebrated annually by Protestants in Northern Ireland and Scotland.

The Protestants in Northern Ireland and Scotland adopted William's heraldic color of Orange as their own, paying homage to their defender of the faith and to the Dutch royal House of Orange. The color orange has continued to this day to symbolize Irish and Scottish Protestants. Even in the Irish Republic (southern Ireland – separate from the United Kingdom and predominantly Catholic) one stripe of the Irish flag remains orange. Ironically, there is no orange in the official flag of the Kingdom of the Netherlands – yet another way in which the Dutch perplex the world community. This Dutch Prince, who became the King of England, Scotland, Ireland, Wales and the Netherlands, had such an impact upon history and religion that the color of his royal family is still revered and celebrated in all parts of the world. When Scottish and Irish Protestants emigrated to America, they brought with them their Protestant flags and firmly established territories around these flags, as evidenced in the numerous cities, towns and counties possessing the name Orange, or some derivative of Orange, throughout the United States. There is an abundance of such Orange names throughout the U.S., to include Orangetown, Orangeburg, Orangeville, South Orange, West Orange, and so forth, all paying homage to the Dutch royal House of Orange.

Several other towns and cities throughout the world, and even universities, are named in honor of the Dutch Prince of Orange and the Protestant faith, but without the word orange in their names. Princeton, home to the prestigious Ivy League college, bears its name from the original *Prince-town*, in honor of Prince William of Orange. The College of William and Mary was chartered in 1693 by King William and Queen Mary themselves. The name has endured for centuries and William and Mary still remains the second oldest college in America. Syracuse University, furthermore, desired to show their allegiance to the Protestant color of orange and named their mascot "The Orangeman" and their sports teams are known as the Syracuse Orangemen.

King William and Queen Mary did not produce any offspring, so the throne was passed to Mary's sister, Anne. If the royal couple had produced an offspring, perhaps today the English royal family would still be that of the Dutch House of Orange. Three hundred years of continuing a specific blood line may seem like an unreasonably long period of time, but the bloodlines of the Dutch House of Orange residing over the Netherlands has remained intact and has lasted for over 500 years! Incidentally, when Queen Anne of England was unable to produce any offspring able to live long enough to ascend to the throne, the English Royal House shifted from the Stuarts to that of the German Hanovers. George I of Hanover, who was the German grandson of King James I, did not even speak English upon acquiring the English throne!

The Dutch King William was able to bring strength and unity to what is now the United Kingdom, but, ironically, was unable to preserve and expand the greatness of 17th century Holland. England was able to economically and militarily surpass the Dutch more easily as an ally to the Dutch under William's reign than as an enemy to the Dutch under Charles II. With William's new found glory as King, he was so preoccupied with his regality and fending off the French, that he neglected his Dutch homeland. Despite its economic stature among European nations for nearly a century, Holland quickly lost its prestige as one of the leading nations of the world, even though the Dutch William of Orange was King of the most powerful nation in the world at the time.

HUMAN EXPLOITATION

Slavery
Slavery has deep and far-reaching roots, stretching back to the beginnings of historical and biblical times. This sinister institution contributed significantly to the expansion and prominence of powerful empires in virtually all parts of the world.

Although a rather objectionable topic of conversation in modern times, most industrialized and advanced countries throughout the world owe much of their prominence to the exploitation of human capital. The Dutch are no exception. In addition to trading sugar, spices, tobacco, pearls and ivory in both Eastern and Western Hemispheres, the Dutch also played an active role in the human slave trade. The Dutch East and West India Trade companies, as well as Holland itself, profited generously from the purchasing and selling of human slave labor.

For centuries, the Dutch have been credited with breaking into new, revolutionary ground and being the pioneers in numerous aspects of life, with modern times being no exception with many of Holland's progressive, yet controversial, social policies. The Dutch, obviously, didn't invent the institution of slavery, nor were they one of the early adapters of the human slave trade. They were, however, responsible for transporting and selling the first African slaves to the continent of North America. In 1619, even before the Pilgrims arrived in America on the Mayflower, Dutch and English ships jointly ransacked a Spanish slave ship in the true spirit of pirating and buccaneering, a common practice on the high seas during the 17th century. The Dutch returned to the Jamestown, Virginia area and promptly sold the captured Africans into servitude for needed supplies. Although the Spanish had been transporting and selling slaves in the present day Dominican Republic since the early 1500s, the transatlantic slave trade in America began in earnest with the Dutch sale of captured Africans to wealthy residents of present day Virginia.

With tobacco being a highly-profitable crop throughout America's southland and with the need for cheap labor to harvest the numerous tobacco plantations dispersed throughout the area, the slave trade burgeoned. The Dutch, English, Portuguese and French all played active roles in this lucrative business. The Dutch West India Company not only participated in the African slave trade, but controlled numerous plantations in the Americas. With the Dutch penchant for capitalizing on lucrative trade markets, they even dominated the transatlantic slave trade and controlled approximately half of this profitable, yet contentious, business during the first half of the 17th century.[4] The Dutch were responsible for selling approximately 70,000 slaves into servitude between 1626 and 1650 alone.[5] Slavery became the third largest source of revenue for the WIC, slightly behind gold and ivory.[6] The Dutch conducted their international business affairs in the transatlantic slave trade industry as efficiently as all of their other business transactions.

Clear on the other side of the world in the Eastern Hemisphere, the Dutch were also deeply involved in the human slave trade. Although not very well documented in the historical annals, the Dutch played a significant role in the slave trade in the East Indies in support of their commercial spice trade and numerous territorial establishments. With the Dutch East India Company dominating the entire Eastern Hemisphere trade market, they had little resistance tapping into and establishing dominance in the Indian Ocean slave trade as well.

The Dutch certainly weren't the only Europeans profiting off of the slave trade. They were, however, the last Europeans to terminate their involvement in the slave trade. The trade-oriented Dutch simply found this industry too profitable to abolish – a fact that the modern day Dutch certainly aren't particularly proud of. The Dutch perpetual desire for maintaining the status quo with their *not sticking their heads above the tall grass or it will be chopped off* mentality, undoubtedly, played a significant factor in the prolongation of their involvement in the human slave trade.

Apartheid
The Dutch established the first European settlement in South Africa on the Cape of Good Hope in 1652 in order to provide replenishment and a respite from the harsh journey as sailors of the V.O.C. journeyed to Asia. The journey from Holland to their eastern settlements could take up to six months, with the Dutch sailors consuming mainly just cheese, biscuits and water. The Dutch Cape Town, or *Kaapstad*, was founded and provided the necessary nutrition for the scurvy-plagued sailors. Scurvy, a

disease caused by deficiency of vitamin C and characterized by bleeding gums, bleeding under the skin and extreme weakness, was prevalent among many of the European explorers and merchants having to endure long sea voyages with a limited amount of fruits and vegetables, if any at all. In fact, the English sailors, and Dutch rivals, relied on lemon and lime juice on their long sea voyages in order to prevent the dreaded disease of scurvy. The English reliance on lemon and lime juice was so well-known that their European rivals soon began referring to them as "Limeys." Even today the term Limey is used throughout the world, mostly in a derisive manner, when referring the English. The Dutch, meanwhile, used the newly established southern tip of Africa to supply fresh fruits, vegetables and meat to their sea-weary, scurvy-ridden crews.

The early Dutch settlers into this South African region were referred to as Africkaaners, and also as Boers (farmers). The dialect that they spoke soon became known as "Cape Dutch" and remained a Dutch dialect until the early 20th century when the Africkaaner language began to be widely recognized as a distinct language. In addition to bringing a new identity and language to the southern tip of Africa, the Dutch also brought with them the notion of apartheid. Apartheid is an Africkaans word meaning aparthood or separation. The separation that this word referred to was that between the white European settlers and the indigenous blacks. As recent as the latter part of the 20th century, South Africa was synonymous with apartheid. With the enactment of apartheid laws in 1948, racial discrimination was institutionalized. Race laws touched every aspect of social life, including a prohibition of marriage between non-whites and whites, and the sanctioning of "white-only" jobs. It was only abolished after the first non-racial elections were held in 1994, which resulted in Nelson Mandela being elected as president, after serving decades in prison.

The Dutch gradually expanded their presence in the southern tip of Africa and in the process, displaced or enslaved the original inhabitants. Additionally, the Dutch refused to recognize the traditional grazing and hunting rights of the indigenous populations. The Dutch also forbade the marriage between European settlers and the original African inhabitants. As tensions increased between the European settlers and the indigenous populations, hostilities began breaking out resulting with the militarily advantaged Dutch gaining victories and even further solidifying their dominance in the region.

With the foundations of apartheid being firmly established, South Africa remained a bastion of hostilities between the people of white European descent and the original, black inhabitants. The legendary Shaka Zulu led the Zulu nation in battle against the Africkaaners. The Boer war, which pitted the British against the Boers of the Orange Free State (obvious indication of the Africkaaners' allegiance to Holland) led to British victory and eventual collapse of Africkaaner independence. Once again the British rode the coattails of the Dutch and eventually defeated them and claimed the original Dutch territorial establishment as their own.

Other interesting Dutch World Influences

Dutch Mascots
The most illustrious and heralded American football team throughout the world is undeniably the Fighting Irish of Notre Dame. Notre Dame's mascot, the Fightin' Irishman, is recognizable worldwide and the Fighting Irish of Notre Dame have a loyal fan base that is analogous to that of the fanatical fans of the New York Yankees, Manchester United or Bayern Munchen. Unbeknownst to many, meanwhile, is that there are several American universities that have a Dutch related icon as their mascot. Such universities and their Dutch related mascots include the following:

- Union College *Dutchmen* (Schenectady, New York)
- Central College *Dutch* (Pella, Iowa)
- Hofstra University *Flying Dutchmen* (Hempstead, NY)
- Hope College *Flying Dutchmen* (Holland, Michigan)
- Lebanon Valley College *Flying Dutchmen* (Annville, Pennsylvania)

Although these Dutch-related colleges and sports teams certainly don't have the history and pageantry of the Fightin' Irish or other big name teams throughout the world, the Dutch have more American college teams named after them than any other European country. There is only one Irish team represented and no French, German, Italian or Spanish related teams in the U.S. The number of Dutch mascots, however, is a far cry from the number of mascots that refer to Native Americans, or Indians. Native American mascots such as the Indians, Seminoles, Chiefs, Braves, Redskins, etc, dominate the American college mascot names. The number of these Indian names, however, has been diminishing with the overt political correctness that is running rampant in modern times. The St. John's Redmen, for instance, are now called the St. John's Red Storm because of the alleged insensitivities towards Native Americans and the color of their skin with the name *Redmen*.

So what exactly is the infamous Flying Dutchman? Nearly everyone has heard of the term before, but few can decipher its meaning. Other than being a very cool and hip name for a college mascot, what does the term "Flying Dutchman" connote? The legend surrounding the Flying Dutchman is as mysterious as the name itself. The Flying Dutchman is, ostensibly, a ghost ship that people for centuries believe has been lurking in the perilous waters off the Cape of Good Hope in South Africa. This ghost ship has been terrifying seamen throughout the ages with its blood-red sails and skeleton crew members. Sailors of the high seas believed that the mere sight of this specter ship guaranteed a watery grave. In addition to having to endure harsh climates, rough winds, violent tides and the loneliness of the sea, these sea-weary sailors also had to contend with the fears that this deadly Dutch ghost ship was prowling around the sea seeking to cause the demise of any ship in its path.

The notorious Flying Dutchman prowling the seas

The legend of the Flying Dutchman proclaims that the Dutch captain of this vessel was condemned to sail forever around the Cape of Good Hope on account of his blasphemous vow to round the Cape even if he had to fight God and the devil until doomsday. There are differing accounts of the sea captain's name - Vanderdecken, Van Demien, Van Straaten, Van der Decken - but with the *Van* present in all of the alleged names, the apparition is undoubtedly a Dutchman. The renowned German composer, Richard Wagner, even composed an opera depicting the dramatic events of the Flying Dutchman in his opera *Der fliedende Hollander* (the Flying Dutchman).

The Cape of Good Hope, incidentally, possesses extreme weather conditions and is home to one of the largest marine graveyards in the world with thousands of sunken ships strewn across the bottom of the sea. The extreme natural conditions played a direct role in the demise of all of the sunken ships, but the legend of the Flying Dutchman still continues to this day. Much like the saga of the Bermuda Triangle where ships, and even airplanes, have mysteriously disappeared into the forbidding waters, the Flying Dutchman is still believed to be roaming the seas around the Cape of Good Hope preying on unsuspecting victims.

The Dutch Masters – and not just Cheap Cigars
The Dutch Masters were renowned artists from Holland during the age of Enlightenment who have left a legacy of artistic brilliance and creative wonderment throughout the world. The age of Enlightenment brought forth new ideas and approaches to old institutions. These Dutch Masters were exceptionally creative in their own unique ways, but ingeniously expressed the underlying theme of typical Dutch life in many of their masterpieces. Such expressions of typical Dutch life include picturesque windmills, blissful family dinners and intricate self-portraits. The most notable Dutch Masters include Vincent van Gogh, Rembrandt van Rijn and Jan Vermeer. The esteem held for these Dutch Masters is evident today with the enormous popularity of museums displaying the works of these gifted artists, to include the van Gogh Museum, the Rijksmuseum and the Rembrandt house, just to name a few. Even further immortalizing the Dutch Masters, although somewhat dubiously, are the popular American cigars, *Dutch Masters*, that are relatively inexpensive and possess mass appeal. The pictures on these cigar boxes, furthermore, display men in typical Dutch garb of yesteryear, with striking resemblance to the Dutchmen found in many of Rembrandt's paintings.

Rembrandt van Rijn is the Dutch Master most notable for his use of color and mastery of light and shadow. Rembrandt's life was a continuous struggle, as tragedy and trouble continuously plagued him. Rembrandt is so well known that he is usually referred to by only his first name. Rembrandt's most notable works include the following:

- Anatomy Lesson of Dr. Tulp (1632)
- Angel Leaving Tobit and Tobias (1637)
- The Company of Captain Frans and Banning Cocq and Lieutenant Willem van Ruytenburch (Commonly known as The Night Watch – 1642)

Jan Vermeer was a Dutch artist cast into obscurity during his lifetime, only to be rediscovered for his brilliance nearly 200 years after his death. Contributing to his obscurity was the fact that he used three different names during his lifetime, to include Johannes van der Meer, Jan Vermeer and Jan Vermeer van Delft. Vermeer's work is admired for its optical precision, which was far ahead of its time. This Dutch Master's most notable works include the following:

- The Music Lesson (1665)
- Allegory of the Art of Painting (1665)
- Girl with a Pearl Earring (1665)

Vincent van Gogh was the eccentric Dutch painter, who is remembered for, in addition to his works of art, the chopping off of his own ear. Vincent van Gogh struggled throughout life with health and mental issues, and eventually shot himself in 1890. Vincent van Gogh's major accomplishments include the following:

- Self-Portrait with a Gray Hat (1877)
- The Potato Eaters (1885)
- Starry Night (1889)
- Self Portrait (1889)
- Crows in the Wheatfields (1890)
- Numerous self portraits, still-lifes and cityscapes

Presidential Dutch Boy Haircut

Former President of the United States, Ronald Reagan, is considered to have been one of the most powerful Presidents in world history and responsible for the demise of the Soviet Union bringing about the end to the cold war. President Reagan was also renowned for his charismatic charm, good looks and perpetual optimism. What may be surprising to some, meanwhile, is that Ronald Reagan had a nickname that originated in his youth and lasted the duration of his life. President Reagan's nickname was *Dutch*. In fact, the only authorized biography detailing Ronald Reagan's life is an 896 page book by Edmund Morris titled *Dutch: A Memoir of Ronald Reagan*. Ironically, Ronald Reagan has no ancestry dating back to Holland and doesn't even possess an ounce of Dutch blood.

The nickname *Dutch* was first applied to Ronald Reagan by his father in Reagan's early years as a child. It is purported that Reagan's father exclaimed that his newly born son looked like a "fat little Dutchman." Reagan is also reported as saying that the nickname *Dutch* lasted because of the "Dutch boy" haircut that he supported as a child. The Dutch boy haircut was once popular for little boys and is characterized by long bangs and the complete covering of the ears. Popular icons supported the Dutch boy haircut include the Beatles in the early 60s and Sonny of the legendary musical couple, Sonny and Cher. In Holland, however, the Dutch refer to such a haircut as *pagekoppie*, or page boy cut. Immortalizing the Dutch boy haircut and even personifying a stereotypical cute little Dutch boy, is the American paint company, Dutch Boy, which has as its logo a blonde haired boy with the Dutch boy haircut, overalls, cap and, of course, wooden shoes.

Dutchman's Breeches and Pipe

The term *Knickerbocker* is used to refer to the original Dutch settlers to the New York region and to the baggy, pantaloons that they wore. The term *knickers* is used today to refer to such baggy pants that are tapered off just below the knee. The legendary Dutch pants of yesteryear still have a lasting legacy not only in the clothing industry, but in the field of botany as well. A popular perennial American plant herb that grows predominantly in the northeastern region of North America is called Dutchman's Breeches (britches), because of its peculiar double-spurred flowers, which remarkable resemble the pantaloons of the early Dutch settlers.

Dutchman's Breeches – resembling Dutch Knickers

The Dutch have been known for centuries as voracious tobacco users, especially with smoking the tobacco with the use of pipes. Because of the Dutch reputation for being such ardent pipe smokers, a plant is named in honor of the highly-cherished pipe that the Dutch used to derive hours upon hours of tobacco pleasures. Such a plant is called the *Dutchman's Pipe*, and is indigenous to central and eastern North America. The plant resembles the elaborate pipes that were popular in Holland and in the newly settled lands by the Dutch in the 17th and 18th centuries.

Dutchman's Pipe – Resembling the popular Dutch pipe

First Highway
The Dutch are also credited with building the first commercial road on the North American continent. The Old Mine Road was built in the mid 17th century and extended approximately 140 miles. The road was built in order to transport ore from the numerous copper mines located along the Delaware River to present day Kingston, New York, located on the Hudson River. The Dutch would then ship the ore from Kingston to Holland for smelting and then distribution. With the Dutch being first and foremost merchants and traders, their actions were driven mainly by economics. The Dutch West India Company instructed its employees to seek sources of natural minerals and to establish mining as a profitable business.

With the discovery of copper mines in *Nieuw Nederland*, the Dutch hastily established a commercial trading business with the minerals that were extracted from these mines. In order to expedite the distribution of these minerals, the Dutch built the first paved road in North America which proved much more efficient than the old Indian trails. The Old Mine Road paved the way for the construction of future roads throughout the Dutch settlement and even throughout the rest of North America. The Old Mine Road is still in existence today and travelers revel in its antiquity and historic charm. Being more than 350 years old, the road has had is share of notable travelers, to include Presidents and Generals, and many of the original houses, barns and inns are still enchantingly scattered along the historic road.

DUTCH PATRIOTISM (OR LACK THEREOF)

The Dutch have undeniably left a huge footprint on the world that rivals even the mightiest of European imperialistic powers. Their legacy as trailblazing international merchants and explorers remains intact as cultures throughout the world still feel the reverberations of the Dutch impact and influence. One might think that the Netherlands would be full of patriotic, and even nationalistic, zealots with the innumerable contributions that the Dutch have made around the world and all of their notable achievements. This couldn't be further from the truth. The Dutch, as a whole, display very little nationalistic pride and are ambivalent about their historical contributions made around the world. They do, in fact, border on passion for their *lack* of patriotism and seem to consciously avert themselves from any nationalistic feelings. Such humble sentiments towards their homeland is a stark contrast to their bordering European neighbors, France and Germany, where nationalistic pride runs rampant and is paramount to their cultures.

The Dutch show disdain for overt patriotism and don't rely on historical achievements for their outlooks towards life. They are much more concerned with the present than with the past, as is evidenced with their shockingly limited interest, and even knowledge, of Dutch historical events. The only nationalistic pride permeating throughout Holland is the noticeable lack of pride in their own national identity and history. When the Euro replaced the Dutch guilder in 2002, the Dutch merely brushed aside the national significance that the guilder maintained for centuries and went on with business as usual. The Dutch did not put forth the bitter resistance towards the monetary conversion as did many other countries. The English, in fact, still haven't conformed to the European standard and are still using the cherished Pound as their unit of currency. The Dutch, meanwhile, stated, "good-bye and good-riddance" to their historical guilder and instead of feeling any resentment they just felt that they were simply making a step in the right direction for Europe's future.

A fairly accurate indicator of national pride is evidenced in the demeanors of people during the singing of their national anthems. People from many nations display intense national pride during such occasions by standing at attention, placing their hands over their hearts and proudly singing the verses of their sacred anthems. Such pride can be observed in the football stadiums around the world in the countries where national identity and pride runs supreme. In Holland, however, it's almost amusing watching the Dutch during the singing of their national anthem. They certainly don't display the intense national pride that so many other countries display, and they even seem perturbed by the whole affair and just want it to end as quickly as possibly. In football matches, such behavior can be observed both in the stands and on the field, as fans and players impatiently await for their national anthem to end so they can get on with the match. Many Dutch fans and players don't even know the verses to their national anthem, as is evidenced with the looks of confusion as some of them try to mutter the words.

The Dutch somehow always seem to come up with *Dutch* solutions for many of their issues and concerns. Since most of the Dutch don't know all of the words to their national anthem, which can be rather disconcerting when being viewed on a global scale, the Dutch created patriotic, bright orange shirts with the verses of the Dutch national anthem displayed all over them. With the Dutch fans wearing these rather odd-looking shirts, they not only appear to be patriotic, but are able to use them as "cheat-sheets" during the playing of their national anthem. When the Dutch forget the words to the song, they can simply glance at the shirts of the people standing in front of them and read the verses directly from the backs of their shirts.

Dutch "Cheat Sheet"

Many Americans aren't much better when it comes to memorizing their national anthem. The American national anthem, the Star Spangled Banner, can be a rather challenging song to memorize with its complex prose. Famous singers and pop icons have resorted to lip-synching the national anthem before popular sporting events fearing that they would forget the words or botch the lyrics. The popular comedic movie *The Naked Gun*, satirizes the difficulty that many people possess with the memorization of the national anthem. In the movie, actor Leslie Nielsen attempts to sing the song before a baseball game and terribly messes up the lines. While attempting to sing the Star Spangled Banner, Mr. Nielsen made the following egregious mistakes, which, unfortunately, occur way to often in real life in American society:

Actual verse: What so proudly we hail'd at the twilight's last gleaming?
Leslie's verse: *What so proudly we hailed at the dah dah daah daah daaaah?*

Actual verse: Whose broad stripes and bright stars
Leslie's verse: *Whose bright stripes and broad stars*

Actual verse: And the rockets' red glare, the bombs bursting in air
Leslie's verse: *And the rocket's red glare, a bunch of bombs in the air*

Actual verse: Gave proof thro' the night that our flag was still there
Leslie's verse: *Gave proof through the night that we still had our flag*

Actual verse: O'er the land of the free and the home of the brave?
Leslie's verse: *Over the home of the land and the land of the free*

This scene was hilarious to so many people because nearly everyone has committed similar mistakes in one form or another. Ok, so the Dutch aren't the only ones who struggle with their national anthem!

The Dutch still view themselves as world travelers and traders living in an open society where numerous cultures mingle. Their homeland is merely a mediating place between neighbors and a launching point for excursions throughout the world. The Dutch remain internationally focused, as corporations view the entire world as huge market opportunities and the Dutch citizens view the world as fantastic vacationing opportunities. When the Dutch travel on holidays, they don't simply go to their local beaches, but travel to far away exotic parts in order to fully take advantage of the many opportunities that the world presents. A popular aphorism proclaims, *"The world is my oyster,"* which means that the world is full of incredible opportunities. Parenthetically, the quote is derived from the Shakespearean play "the Merry Wives of Windsor" and states *"Why, then the world's mine oyster, Which I with sword will open."* The Dutch do indeed view the world as their oyster, and it tastes too good to them to be preoccupied with just nationalistic tendencies. The Dutch today eschew nationalist fervor for farther reaching, international perspectives, as their forebears did in centuries past.

4. THE LAND OF THE GENTLE GIANTS

INTRODUCTION

Visitors arriving to the Netherlands are immediately awestruck with the enormity of the inhabitants roaming these lands. The Dutch, on average, are the tallest people on earth. In numerous studies and reports around the world, the Dutch unanimously come out on top in attaining the towering distinction of being the tallest people on the face of the earth. Actual statistics vary slightly in these reports, but the average height of Dutch men soars to just over 6 feet (184 centimeters) and the average height for Dutch women ascends to slightly over 5 feet 7 inches (170.8 centimeters). Scandinavian countries follow a short second behind the Dutch with their men reaching approximately 5 foot 11 inches (180.7 centimeters), while the British men average approximately 5 foot 10 inches (177.8 centimeters). Arriving into Schiphol airport or Centraal Train Station, visitors immediately feel the impact of the Dutch vertical dimensions as they find themselves feeling rather diminutive amongst these immense people. Additionally, visitors find it disconcerting always having to strain their necks looking upwards in order to ask for directions or to carry on other forms of communications with the Dutch. With Holland lacking in geographical size, they certainly compensate with the enormity of its inhabitants. No wonder why the American Indians called the Dutch the Great *Mannitoos*, or Supreme Beings!

Numerous explanations abound as to why the Dutch are so tall. Many theories suggest that their tallness is derived from their socialist policies whereby all members of society receive public health benefits, even including the poor and jobless. Another postulation is that their tallness is due mainly to the Dutch economic prosperity and vitality, which encompasses all segments of society. Other theories suggest that their protein-rich diets, with plenty of milk and cheese, contribute to their immense height. Another, rather unusual theory, suggests that the Dutch liberal education provides students with a psycho-sexual stimulus that promotes human growth. This last supposition may be a little far-fetched, but then again with the Dutch anything is possible.

I would suggest that their tallness is directly attributable to generation after generation maintaining high protein-rich diets and constantly enduring the harsh northern European climate. The tenets of survival of the fittest, undoubtedly, contributed significantly to the Dutch modern day tallness, since only the strongest members of Dutch society would be able to survive such a damp environment below sea level. Regardless of which theory is correct, or most correct, the Dutch consistently rise to the top of the measuring stick above all others throughout the world, even though they comprise just .003% of the world's population.

Embarking upon this land and interacting with the towering Dutch can be a rather daunting and intimidating experience for first time visitors. As visitors begin to meld into Dutch society and mingle more with the Dutch citizens, they perceive a mild mannerism of the Dutch people that pervades throughout the country. Visitors soon realize that Dutch people are calm, reserved and possess an aura of gentleness, which can yield great relief for those apprehensive first-time visitors intimidated by their size. Hardly anyone seems to get disturbed or irritated in Dutch society; they contend with all issues, regardless of the severity, with composure and calmness. There are exceptions to all rules, of course, but the overall Dutch populace seems to go through life serenely and rarely developing states of agitation.

Even when debating contentious issues, a favorite pastime of the Dutch, they discuss the issues rather than argue them. Such a manner of debate is drastically different than other cultures throughout the world where exaggerated body language and yelling of discussion points are paramount. The Italians, for instance, are legendary for their vivacious body language and vociferous shouts during even the most pleasant of conversations. Even first and second generation Italian-Americans carry on this age-old tradition of exaggerated gestures during communications. Anyone unfamiliar with this Italian tradition would be mortified playing cards for the first time with a group of Italian card players. The Dutch, meanwhile, show much more reservation in tone and body language than the Italians, as well as many of their other European neighbors.

Even members of the Dutch counter-culture maintain this mysterious aura of gentleness. On a recent visit to Arnhem to survey the historical events that transpired during World War II, a friend and I happened to stumble upon a heavy-metal rock n' roll motorcycle bar. We were in the midst of gigantic, tattooed, biker men dressed in black leather and wearing biker boots. For sure I thought I was finally going to see an angst-ridden, aggressive side of the Dutch that I've been unable to find. In striking up conversations with these ruffian looking Dutchmen, it turned out they were as pleasant and mild-mannered as the rest of the Dutch. We talked politics, religion, marriage – all of the things you're not supposed to talk about in mixed company – and the towering men didn't take a definitive stand on any of the issues and discussed the topics in such a mild manner as if they were talking about gardening in the springtime.

For these reasons, I've dubbed the Netherlands the *Land of the Gentle Giants.*

There are numerous contributing factors to the gentleness and laidback nature that permeates Dutch culture. The Dutch constant pursuit of *Gezelligheid* certainly plays a significant role. Striving for coziness, snugness and content requires the Dutch to

The Land of the Gentle Giants

consciously disavow such opposing forces as agitation and hostility. Additionally, the ethos of Calvinism guided the Dutch throughout the years to be humble and to avoid any form of ostentation. Calvinism preaches that god is a vengeful god, which influences many of the Dutch to avoid extremes and to live humble lives. Other Dutch cultural norms such as *act normal that's weird enough* and *don't be better than average* also contribute to the Dutch unobtrusive, unassuming manner.

With the Dutch being so *normal,* one might think that the Netherlands is a mundane country and that the Dutch are dull and uninteresting. This couldn't be further from the truth. In fact, people from around the world often describe the Dutch as weird, perplexing and even bizarre. The Dutch being perceived in such a manner, even though they strive to be average and inconspicuous, is just one of the many dichotomies that exist in Dutch culture. The recent movie *Austin Powers Goldmember* satirizes Dutch society by portraying the character, Goldmember, as an eccentric Dutchman who frolics around on golden wooden-shoe roller skates and offers his guests pancakes, cigarettes, blintzes and bongs. Goldmember even pokes fun at himself by stating, "I'm from Holland, isn't that weird" in an exaggerated Dutch accent. Goldmember is even referred to as *Perv-boy* and a *freaky-deaky Dutch bastard.* The capstone of the Dutch mockery has to be, however, when Michael Caine states, "There are only two things that I hate in this world, one – intolerant people, and two – the Dutch." Perhaps Mike Myers, the creator of the movie, is frustrated with the Dutch because he can't decipher their peculiar and bewildering ways, as with so many other people from around the world.

Dutch stereotypes are not a recent phenomenon, but have been widespread throughout the centuries, especially during the Dutch Golden Age of the 17th century. Dutch prosperity and prudent business practices, along with many of their peculiar customs, elicited gloomy stereotypes from their European brethren. Such Dutch mannerisms and unique customs include their insatiable quest to acquire land from the sea and their incessant desire for cleanliness. With the Netherlands being land primarily acquired from the sea, Europeans, especially the English, took liberties in calling the Dutch "usurpers that deprive fish of their dwelling places." [1] Additionally, adversaries claimed that a Dutch sovereignty could not be built upon silt and unclearly defined borders. In 1651, an English poem undermines Holland's claim to substance due to the country's sedimentary nature:

> *Holland, that scarce deserves the name of land,*
> *As but th'off-scouring of the British sand...*
> *This indigested vomit of the sea*
> *Fell to the Dutch by just propriety* [2]

Other stereotypes of the Dutch refer to them as pigs that wallow deep down in the dirt and grime and as frogs, or croaking people. The frog stereotype undoubtedly derives from the Dutch living in marshy environments and their guttural manners of speaking. The English even went as far as referring to frogs as Dutch nightingales. As can be deduced from past stereotypes, the Dutch always had an uncanny ability of raising the ire of those who encounter their inexplicable temperament and customs. It's truly amazing that such a small country is able to elicit such stereotypes from numerous people from around the world.

So what is it that makes people think that the Dutch are so weird? How can the Dutch elicit such sentiments and make people from around the world view them as odd and bewildering? After all, the Dutch aren't walking around in wooden shoes anymore. (Actually, I've personally witnessed Gentle Giants prancing around proudly in wooden shoes at home football games, which was certainly a sight for sore eyes). So occasionally the Dutch do brush the dust off of their clogs and strut around in order to show their *Dutchness*. It's also not uncommon for the Dutch to wear their wooden clogs while gardening in order to keep their feet dry. For the most part, however, wooden shoes only contribute slightly to all of the Dutch stereotypes. The Dutch are full of unique and peculiar mannerisms which cause people to be befuddled and incredulous. It's common for expatriates and long-term visitors to the Netherlands to describe certain individuals as being *so Dutch*. Many expatriates will frustratingly beseech certain individuals to stop being *so Dutch*. So what is it that makes the inhabitants of the Netherlands *so Dutch*? This chapter will explore some of the Dutch customs that leave visitors in utter awe, but to the Dutch they are merely ordinary, commonplace, day-to-day rituals. This chapter will explore many of the interesting segments of Dutch culture that make the Dutch *so Dutch*. Additionally, this chapter will delve into those areas of life where the Gentle Giants actually display passionate and vivacious behavior, which is truly a rarity for the usually mild-mannered Dutch.

A CYCLING SOCIETY

Holland is one of the most bicycle-friendly countries in the world with the Dutch being the most fervent bike riders. The pulse of the country can be found on its many bike paths, or *fietspads*. In Amsterdam alone there are 4,500 miles (10,000 km) of bike paths dispersed throughout the city dedicated solely for cyclists. These bike paths are not to be used for any other reasons other than cycling. Cycling is the preferred mode of transportation for the majority of residents and is even encouraged by the government. The Dutch tax system entitles people to a yearly tax deduction just by biking to and from work a minimum of ten kilometers and three days a week. Such incentives are aimed at reducing pollution, gridlock, automobile casualties, parking issues and other problems associated with automobile congestion. An ancillary benefit of having a cycling society is the positive health impact to the Dutch cyclists, which undeniably reduces the demands placed upon the Dutch socialistic healthcare system. The obesity problems found in other parts of the world, to include the U.S., are simply not found in the Netherlands, due to a large part with their cycling oriented approach, and, of course, their *everything in moderation* mentality. (The Dutch MTV generation, however, isn't riding as much as their elders, undoubtedly due to MTV, video games and the Internet, causing some concern as these youngsters are packing away a few extra pounds.) Perhaps all of the exercise and fresh air they receive while cycling is another contributing factor to their extreme tallness.

The Dutch, with their penchant for unambiguous signs and markers, clearly identify the bike paths by painting large symbols of bicycles in the centers of them in order to thwart disorientated pedestrians from wandering onto them. Additionally, the Dutch paint "No Pedestrians" symbols (symbol of a person in a circle with a big line going through it) all along the paths for further emphasis for pedestrians to stay off of the *fietspads*. Even with all of these conspicuous indicators, people from other cultures always seem to be drifting carelessly into the sacred *fietspads*, disrupting the natural flow of Dutch society. As cycling Gentle Giants approach such careless pedestrians, they are eager to let the pedestrians know that they have wandered into a *verboden* zone and need to depart immediately. Without showing any signs of agitation, true to Dutch form, they simply ring the bells that are attached to virtually all bicycles in Holland. Many tourists, however, take awhile to fully grasp the concept of bicycle paths meandering alongside busy city streets and don't heed the call of the first ring of the bell. When this occurs, the Dutch seem to release all of their vent up emotions through their bell-ringing fingers as they unrelentingly ring their bells which causes unsuspecting pedestrians to frighteningly scamper off of the bike paths. Once this happens, tourists then walk around Amsterdam with trepidation for fear of being run down by more speeding cyclists.

Dutch bicycles are almost as unique as their owners. These bikes can be described as ugly, heavy, durable and reliable. These *no frills* devices serve the sole purpose of getting their riders from point A to point B. Bicycles are so prevalent in Dutch society that one cannot walk more than a couple of steps without seeing one locked up to a lamp post or some other stationary fixture. There are approximately 550,000 of such devices in Amsterdam alone, and 10,000 of them are in the canals! When a bicycle reaches the end of its lifecycle, it's convenient for the Dutch to simply dispose of it in one of the numerous canals, much to the frustration of the workers who have to periodically cleanout the canals.

Dutch parking lot – a common sight in Holland

The Dutch are so adept at riding bicycles that they are capable of multitasking while on their bikes. It's quite common to see a cyclist smoking a cigarette, talking on a cell phone and holding an umbrella while traversing through town – all at once! The Dutch rely on these bikes for practically all facets of their lives, to include traveling to and from work, the grocery store, church and school. They are even able to return from food shopping with their bikes loaded with bags of groceries. Regardless of the weather, business professionals can be seen commuting to and from work on their bicycles. Formal suits for men or even short skirts for ladies won't deter the resolute Dutch cyclists from cycling to and from work. Dutch teenagers will even pick their dates up on their bikes, with the girl usually sitting side-straddle on the bike-rack. Dutch senior citizens rely on their bikes for transportation just as the younger generations of society. A family bicycle ride, a.k.a. Dutch style, is certainly a site to see for visitors to the Land of the Gentle Giants. Dutch families are known to go for bike rides, with all family members on one bike! I've personally seen, on several occasions, a father riding a bike with his wife sitting on the bike-rack with a child on her lap and another child sitting on the handlebars. And some families are even audacious enough to put the family dog in the bike-basket!

A family bike ride in the park – Dutch style

The much sought after Dutch conformity and harmony doesn't always exist on the dedicated bike paths. All members of Dutch society must carry out their societal duties in order for the Dutch system to function properly. Conforming to the rules on the *fietspads* is no exception. When a cyclist becomes careless or when a pedestrian defies all of the warnings to stay off of the *fietspads*, complete pandemonium ensues. With the Dutch proclivity for timeliness, cyclists are usually zipping around town at accelerated speeds. Crashes do occur on the *fietspads* and they can be pretty brutal. I've seen bodies strewn and bicycles mangled following such crashes. For mild crashes, the unremitting Dutch quickly regain their composure and immediately proceed with their affairs. For the more severe ones, especially when one party committed a glaring breach of *fietspads* etiquette, the usually mild mannered Dutch may actually exchange some quick unpleasantries, but will once again immediately tend to their affairs at hand and get back on their bikes.

Bicycles are truly an integral part of the Dutch culture. It is quite fascinating to observe the natural flow of Dutch society with the thousands of cyclists going about their business all at once. A cycling-oriented society is quite foreign to many cultures throughout the world. In many countries, most people after their teenage years never even get back onto a bicycle, let alone rely on one for their daily affairs. Most countries never planned for cycling-oriented societies, as evidenced in the lack of bike paths around the major cities. Many people around the world are forced to rely on their automobiles because of the lack of planning from government officials for adequate bike paths, even though these people would opt for cycling safely through town as opposed to driving. The Dutch, meanwhile, undoubtedly executed intense planning sessions when determining the infrastructure of their country. Dutch citizens ensured that they would not be denied the time-honored tradition of riding their bicycles, even through the busy streets of their major cities.

My advice to first-time visitors to Holland – don't wander onto the *fietspads* unless you plan on getting run down by zealous cyclists. If you want to get on those *fietspads*, rent a bike and do as the Dutch do – just make sure you follow the rules of the road.

Dutch Frugality

Everyone has heard of the phrases *going Dutch* or *Dutch treat*. Members of the fairer sex usually don't like *going Dutch* on dates for it requires them to split the bill with their tightfisted, male companions. *Going Dutch* and *Dutch treat* refer to the concept that everybody pays their fair share of the total bill, even on intimate dates. Leave it to the Dutch to somehow enabling to allow their heritage to become synonymous with frugality on a global scale. I had to satisfy my curiosity and find out if the Dutch truly deserve to be associated with the dubious phrase *Dutch treat*. I discussed the *Dutch treat* concept with one of my married colleagues and asked him if guys and gals really do *go Dutch* while on dates. A smile came across my colleague's face and he proceeded to tell me a story. To paraphrase my colleague, the story went as follows:

> *"Oh yes, I remember my dating days well. I would pick my date up at her house, usually bringing her some small, inexpensive flowers. I would compliment her on her looks and attire. I would open and close the car door for her and drive her to a romantic, little restaurant. I would pull her chair out for her like a true gentleman. I would then sit down and give her another nice, little compliment. When the menus came I would say, "Honey, order what you want. Order the best, this is our special evening out. But remember honey (as he held up his forefinger) you're paying for your portion so make sure you order what you can afford."*

I nearly fell off of my chair with laughter when I heard this story. So the Dutch really do *go Dutch*. The Dutch are indeed world renown for their financial prudence. As they enjoy debating politics, religion and any other social topic, they also enjoy finding bargains and bartering over just about everything. Weekly flea markets are hotbeds for Dutch bargain hunting and bartering. The Dutch seem to take pride in their tightfisted behavior; they relish in their uncanny abilities to always find good bargains and to somehow always get the better end of the deal. The English brought this Dutch characteristic to the forefront centuries ago by developing the terms *going Dutch* and *Dutch treat*. With the English and Dutch being great seafaring nations and rivals on the world's oceans during the tumultuous 17th and 18th centuries, the dry-witted English derided the Dutch by poking fun at their frugality and peculiar ways with money.

A young couple Going Dutch – One thing on their minds!

Nothing is free in the Netherlands, which further exacerbates the Dutch reputation for frugality. Visitors to Holland are astounded with the parsimonious behavior of the Dutch. In many restaurants, for instance, items such as ketchup, mustard and steak sauce are not free, but show up as fixed-priced items on the menus and bills. Asking for an extra napkin can even yield a disapproving look from a waiter or waitress. Requiring an extra napkin is a waste and a sign of irresponsibility. When the Dutch go grocery shopping they even bring their own bags with them.

If they forget to bring their own bags, they'll have to pay for new ones at the counter. In the U.S., not only do grocery shoppers expect free bags to be provided for them, but also expect that the grocery clerks pack all of the groceries in those free bags and sometimes even carry the groceries out to their cars. In Holland you don't get something for nothing – you bag your own groceries with your own bags.

Even many restrooms in public places, such as train stations, restaurants and pubs, require a couple of Euros to utilize the facilities. This can be very disconcerting for visitors as there is usually a lady present in the restroom to collect the money, and often times with a wide-open view of the personal activities transpiring within! Even Dutch auctions are rather unique, and very *Dutch*. If you go to such an auction you certainly don't want to be the first person to bid for an item for you may end up buying that item on that first bid. At a Dutch auction, the prices start high and progressively drop until someone makes a purchase bid. One bid and the transaction is over. In other words, the Dutch don't waste their time by starting low and having multiple parties bid on items forcing the price to go up, they simply start high and then drop the price until someone offers a purchase bid for the item.

Some theories suggest that Dutch frugality is mainly attributable to the tulip bulb market crash of the 1600s. When tulips were selling like wildfire throughout the world, the Dutch started buying and selling on mere speculation; they took it for granted that the tulips would just be there. Lo and behold, one year during the 17th century the tulips weren't as plentiful as everyone hoped and expected, which led to the tulip bulb market crash similar to the New York stock market crash of the 1920s. Many of the Dutch went bankrupt because of the crash. Never again, so it is said, will the Dutch speculate when it comes to their money. In Dutch society, nobody gets something for nothing. Equality is a cherished trait and nobody should ever have an unfair advantage. When it comes to money, the Dutch use their resources wisely and by *going Dutch* they merely ensure that equality is maintained and everyone is playing on a level playing field.

THOSE GERMANS!

Even the mild-mannered Gentle Giants can't suppress their indignation when it comes to their neighboring Germans. The Dutch possess a deep aversion to all things German, especially the people. Such hostilities, undoubtedly, are attributable to the German invasion and subsequent occupation of the Netherlands during the Second World War. The total devastation of Rotterdam by the Germans in an attempt to stifle Dutch resistance, invariably, only exacerbated the Dutch resentment of the Germans. For centuries leading up to the invasion, the Netherlands was immune from the atrocities of war and the Dutch lived a relatively peaceful existence in their homeland. Even during World War I the Dutch were somehow able to maintain their neutrality. The evils that World War II brought to the Dutch homeland are not forgotten to this day and the perpetrators are not forgiven. Germans are even cognizant of this resentment and usually tread carefully when in the Netherlands. Even though the Dutch are fluent in German, the Germans will speak English to the Dutch because most of the Dutch citizens won't even acknowledge German speakers. Even German restaurants are absent on the Dutch homeland. In the New York metropolitan area, I can think of at least twenty German restaurants off the top of my head, and NY is 4,000 miles away from Germany. In Amsterdam, which is practically a stone's throw away from Germany and where there is a plethora of ethnic restaurants, not one German restaurant can be found.

In addition to the violence and subjugation that the Dutch endured during World War II, they were deeply distraught over the fact that the Germans stole all of their bicycles and used the parts and material to support the war effort. As stated previously, the pulse of Holland can be found on its *fietspads*; by taking all of the Dutch bicycles, the Germans crushed a deeply cherished attribute of Dutch culture. Even to this day, the Dutch convey their contempt for such thievery by demanding that the Germans give them back their bicycles. During football matches against German teams, Dutch fans hold up signs and sing chants stating that they want their bicycles back. Even when vacationing Germans ask the

Dutch for directions the usual response is, "I'll give you directions when you return my grandfather's bicycle."

Dutch-German football matches stir up excitement and patriotism in the Dutch perhaps more than anything else. When the Dutch beat the Germans 2-1 in a 1988 semi-final match in Hanover, Germany, Holland became one massive party scene. The Dutch partied in the streets for days, shooting off fireworks, drinking and celebrating the stupendous victory over their rival Germans. Revenge was theirs. This match was much more than just a football game, it was payback for the hardships that the Dutch endured during the war. The victory tasted sweet for the entire Dutch populace.

The resentment towards Germans became even worse on the football pitch in the year following this momentous victory when it was reported that Dutch football star Ronald Koeman admitted he had used, as toilet paper, the shirt he had swapped with his own with Olaf Thon of the German team.[3] Swapping shirts with members of the opposing team is a football tradition done as a sign of respect. Mr. Koeman made it clear that there was no respect for his German rival. When Holland played Germany in Rotterdam that same year, a Dutch banner was displayed comparing Lothar Matthaus, a star of the German team, to Adolf Hitler.[4] In 1990 during the World Cup, the Dutch football star Frank Rijkaard demonstrated Dutch contempt for the Germans when he spat at German player Rudi Voller.[5] The Gentle Giants certainly lose their composure and mild demeanors when it comes to the Germans. Over the years there have even been numerous border clashes between the Dutch and Germans over a myriad of reasons. Dutch authorities are cognizant of such anti-German sentiments and have been trying to moderate such feelings over the past few years.

The Germans still invade the Netherlands from time-to-time, but in a much more peaceful manner. As soon as there is a glimmer of sunshine, the Germans, en masse, swarm to the Dutch beaches. Since the sun rarely shines in Northern Europe, beach moments are absolutely cherished. When the forecast calls for a weekend of sun, the roads leading to Dutch beaches, such as Zandvoort, are besieged with Germans seeking refuge from the usually grey and rainy weather and looking to enjoy the beaches of the North Sea. The Dutch, of course, resent these modern day Teutonic invasions. Once the Germans get together en masse, their German identity crisis is no longer threatened and they speak, act, drink and eat German. There are so many Germans present at these beach towns during the summer that street signs and advertisements are written in German. In Zandvoort and other beach towns during the summer months, German food is devoured and German beer is consumed as if it was a typical town in *Deutschland*. The usually anti-German Dutch waiters and waitresses succumb to the shear numbers and resort to speaking German during these Germanic invasions.

The Dutch also detest some of the German idiosyncratic beach behavior. The Dutch loathe the peculiar and bizarre Germanic desires for man-made boundaries. Germans have a strange fascination with digging holes and creating boundaries at the beach. It is quite common to see a middle-aged German man waist deep in the sand with a giant shovel digging away in order to form a moat of sorts around his turf. Additionally, the Germans designate one representative from their clan to wake up early in order to claim their turf at the beach. That designated person wakes up around 0600 hours, heads down to the beach with a multitude of towels and places all of them on beach chairs at the optimal beach location. That person then goes back to sleep and then when the entire clan is ready to head down to the beach, after a hearty breakfast and coffee, their chairs and towels are waiting for them at the most ideal beach location. The Dutch relish the opportunities to ridicule German beach behavior, especially to a crowd of expatriates and visitors unfamiliar to such odd customs.

The overt detestation of the Germans may actually exist because of a more profound and deeper basis other than the German invasion and occupation during World War II. A common theory suggests that the overt enmity exhibited towards the Germans may actually be a defense mechanism utilized by the Dutch in order to deal with their collective, repressed guilt over the actions of their forebears during that horrific time period during the war. Nazi corroboration was rampant and the Dutch resistance, although valiant in its cause, wasn't very ubiquitous. Whatever the reason for this modern day aggression, history must never be ignored or repressed. The old adage is true – *those who don't study history are doomed to repeat it.* If the world wants to avoid another catastrophic war, the events leading to, during and following the Second World War must be meticulously scrutinized in order to identify those trigger points that brought about all of those years of calamity.

As usual with the Dutch, a glaring paradox exists with their overt animosity towards the Germans. The Dutch original founding father and revered hero for repelling the Spanish during the Inquisition, William I, was a German. William I was the Prince of Orange, and derives from Germany. Even the first two lines of the Dutch national anthem celebrates William's Germanic lineage:

> *Wilhelmus van Nassouwe*
> *Ben ik van Duitsen bloed*

> William of Nassau am I,
> of Germanic descent

Often times the word *Duitsen*, or the older version *Duytschen*, is translated to mean 'Dutch' instead of 'German' in an attempt to make the anthem more Dutch-centric and patriotic. These two words are similar to the German word *Deutsch*, which have been confusing people throughout the ages. In fact, the legendary Pennsylvania Dutch of the U.S. aren't even Dutch at all, they're German. The early German settlers to Pennsylvania were commonly referred to as Pennsylvania *Deutsch*. Over the years the term had morphed into Pennsylvania Dutch due mainly of the ease of English speakers saying the word Dutch instead of *Deutsch*.

In 1787, the German King of Prussia's sister, Wilhelmina married the Dutch Prince William V. Princess Juliana, the mother of the current queen, was also married to a German, Bernhard von Lippe-Biesterveld. More recently, in 1966, the Crown Princess Beatrix married the German diplomat Claus von Amsberg, who had even served in the Hitler Youth and German *Wehrmacht*. Numerous protests occurred during the wedding celebration of this Dutch-German couple. Loyal Dutch citizens ignited smoke bombs as the wedding procession traversed through Amsterdam and one protestor even threw a live chicken at the royal coach. And of course, loud chants of "give back our bicycles" reverberated throughout the city. True to Dutch form and showing their penchant for tolerance, the Dutch eventually came to adore the German diplomat and welcomed him into their country.

BARING IT ALL

The Dutch despise any kind of behavior that may be construed as secretive or concealing. They view themselves as free and open members of society with nothing to hide. The Dutch take this free and open mentality, however, to new levels with their propensity for public nudity. The Dutch feel that their openness toward nudity is a sign of a healthy society that has no secrets. The Dutch postulate that this openness toward nudity has therapeutic value for individuals and Dutch culture as a whole. Public nudity may indeed be signs of a healthy society with some kind of therapeutic value for its inhabitants, but can be culture shock for those visiting Holland. I, for one, nearly fell off of my bike the first few times I stumbled upon half-naked women sunbathing in parks and even in front of windmills. The Dutch are certainly more open with their bodies and sexuality than most societies around the world, which can certainly lead to anxiety and uneasiness amongst visitors to Holland.

More bare skin can be seen at Dutch beaches than most beaches throughout the world. Nude beaches are plentiful along the shores of the Netherlands for both men and women to really bare it all. For the regular beaches, as with many other European countries, the women prance around topless. This rather commonplace European behavior is way too risqué for people from conservative cultures. Dutch children can even be seen at the beaches wearing nothing but playful smiles and life preservers around their arms. Teenage girls bare their breasts at the beaches and even frolic around topless with their male classmates. True to Dutch form, the teenagers seem to be just as relaxed and comfortable with each other as if they were fully clothed. I can say with certainty that teenagers from the more conservative cultures, to include the U.S., would not be so comfortable in such situations. This is not to imply that the American youth are more prone to sexual yearnings or perversions, just that as a culture America is not as open with their bodies, especially with regard to public nudity.

The halftime show at the U.S. 2004 Superbowl created tremendous controversy when musical icon Janet Jackson exposed one of her breasts. American newspapers, talk shows, political commentators discussed the "breast incident" unremittingly for weeks after the occurrence. People were utterly mortified with Miss Jackson's gratuitous exposure of her breast during the biggest television event of the year. Unfortunately, Miss Jackson's right breast received more public attention than the actual football game, which happened to be one of the best Superbowl games ever played. The Dutch, meanwhile, probably would not have made such a ruckus over the infamous breast incident, but probably would have disparaged Janet Jackson for her disgraceful attempt for public attention. In fact, the news of America's mortification over the infamous breast incident spread to the Netherlands, resulting in the Dutch media having weeks of fun over the incident and resulting in the universal Dutch response of, "*We laughed our tits off over the overreaction of the Americans.*"

Being immersed into Dutch culture, one can easily observe the Dutch predilection for freedoms of expression. Many clubs and bars display pictures of their patrons having good times in an effort to encourage passer-bys to come inside. Many of these pictures include shots of half-naked people in provocative poses. Additionally, it's not uncommon for nakedness to appear on advertisements or covers of magazines in Holland. Nudity even runs rampant over the regular television stations, especially late at night. I've even heard some of the Dutch complaining that there's nothing to watch on television late at night other than sex shows. Viewers beware, channel surf at your own risk when in the Netherlands!

Dutch women will take any opportunity to express their freedom and individuality by baring their breasts, which they view as their inherent right. They consider being topless just as natural as men being topless - there is nothing sexual or licentious about it. They appear to bare their breasts with pride showing that as women they are entitled to the same rights and privileges as men. A Dutch friend of mine and his wife recently moved to Canada and during those rare beach moments his wife is always the only female on the beach with her breasts exposed. She does it defiantly in order to show her contempt for laws that infringe upon what she feels are the laws of nature and her intrinsic rights as a woman. Dutch KLM airline flight attendants are renowned for their nonchalant and open attitudes towards baring their breasts. I have met several American hotel concierges in my travels who have told me that they can't wait for KLM flight attendants to lodge at their hotels. The male concierges fight over who gets to bring the luggage to the Dutch girls' rooms because it's not uncommon for the Dutch women to open the doors completely topless or half-naked. Poolside behavior of the Dutch women is also agreeable to the male hotel staff members.

The absolute pinnacle of Dutch openness toward nudity lies within the confines of their numerous saunas. The Dutch find the dryness and comfort of saunas irresistible, undoubtedly due to the constantly damp weather. There are saunas scattered all around the Netherlands enabling the Dutch to relish in the dry refuge they so desirously seek. A typical Friday night for a Dutch couple is spending a couple of hours at the local sauna. While at the sauna, they can enjoy the numerous pleasantries that a Dutch sauna offers. Such pleasantries include a typical dry sauna; a Turkish steam bath; a compact swimming pool with frigid water and a strong current to swim against; hot and cold showers; foot massagers; masseuse services; and an ambiance that truly promotes relaxation and vitality. A typical sauna even has coffee and refreshments that the Dutch enjoy in comfortable lounge areas for further relaxation and to mingle with friends.

Many countries around the world have similar saunas and health spa facilities, but the one true distinction is that Dutch saunas are co-ed and nobody wears a stitch of clothing. Husbands, wives, boyfriends, girlfriends, young, old, singles all swagger around these saunas completely in the buff. Towels are provided and are used optionally for interim periods in between some of the sauna stations. The Dutch claim that wearing bathing suits or towels is restrictive and not nearly as refreshing or relaxing as being totally nude. They truly go for the whole mind-body experience. To the Dutch, relaxing, sweating, stretching and breathing therapeutically while completely naked in the saunas is as enjoyable and relaxing as just about anything, even with the mixed company. Towards the end of the working week, I often heard my Dutch colleagues stating their intense desires and anticipation of relaxing in a sauna.

Dutch saunas can certainly produce intense culture-shock for first time visitors. My first time in a Dutch sauna, in fact, left an indelible impression upon my mind, for that experience was unlike anything that had ever happened to me and even beyond my wild imagination. In short, the all-women aerobics class that I was gawking over during my Nautilus workout decided to join me, en masse, in the sauna room after their class ended. Being an unsuspected tourist at the time, needless to say my state of attentiveness, and even anxiety, immediately rose up as numerous long-legged, completely naked beauties settled in around me in the sauna room. Being the only man in this sauna, wearing nothing but a distressed look upon my face, in a foreign country surrounded by naked women speaking a foreign language, I knew then and there that the Dutch are truly a unique breed of people and that my stay in Holland was going to be anything but uneventful.

A distressed tourist visiting a Dutch sauna for the first time

WHEN YOU GOTTA GO...

In no other city in the world is it easier for men to find places to relieve themselves than in Amsterdam. Outdoor, and rather open, *pissoirs* are strategically dispersed throughout the city for men to relieve themselves at any given moment. These *pissoirs* aren't conspicuously placed or tucked away behind buildings, but are right out in the open and visible for all to see while happy patrons conduct their business. The permanent *pissoirs* are ideally placed throughout the city where there is usually a great influx of imbibing tourists, mainly in the Red Light District. On any given weekend night, a line of full-bladdered men can be seen waiting to use the odd-looking apparatuses. These green devices are situated alongside the canals, leaving no doubts as to where the draining is headed. It's a good thing that it rains often in Holland, for these structures can get rather foul and often times emit unpleasant odors. Even more remarkable, the Dutch built many of these structures in the most inappropriate places, such as adjacent to consecrated grounds comprising churches and somber memorials. Nothing like taking a picture of a sacred landmark with a green *pissoir* in the forefront or background!

The breathtaking Oude Kerk, with that lovely green pissoir in the forefront

Along with the permanent *pissoirs*, temporary ones are placed strategically around the city, usually during times when larger than normal crowds are expected, such as during festivals or football matches. These efficient devices can accommodate up to four willing participants at one time, although providing minimal privacy. But in the Dutch open society, this lack of privacy is no major concern and Dutch passer-bys have no desire to pry into the affairs of others, even if it's public urination on the corner of a busy intersection.

These vertical urine repositories are quite unique looking and rather humorous, especially when four Gentle Giants utilize one of them all at once. At any given time of day, one can witness

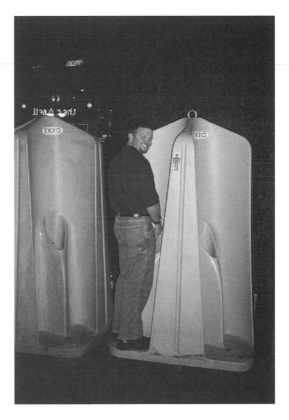

An obvious tourist enjoying his new found freedom

one-to-four men relieving themselves in one device while the industrious Dutch go along with their business, passing just inches away. The Dutch know exactly how many temporary *pissoirs* to place and the exact locations to place them. Before weekend activities or special events, trucks with flatbeds full of temporary *pissoirs* can be seen driving around town with the drivers stopping at strategic locations dropping them off. The Dutch are world experts of controlling water flows as proven with their successes at reclaiming land from the sea and regulating the country's water levels. Leave it to the Dutch to apply that knowledge to controlling the water flows of its occupants during times of congestion and revelry.

The Dutch like to poke fun back at the English and state that the only reason they place these *pissoirs* out in the streets is to keep the drunken English from using the inside facilities or relieving themselves on buildings or in the streets. That may be true, but Dutch men are commonly compared to dogs because much like dogs, they find it hard to pass up a good tree without peeing on it! Regardless of the reason for the numerous *pissoirs* dispersed throughout the cities of Holland, they certainly serve their purpose. It may be outrageous for visitors unaccustomed to such an open society where men can relieve themselves freely out in the open, but this peculiar custom is much more sanitary and orderly then the alternative of men ducking into alleys to conduct their affairs. Additionally, the restaurants and pubs are spared from the nuisances of men stopping in just to utilize the facilities, thus enabling the restrooms to remain clean for the legitimate customers. Leave it to the Dutch to solve a common problem experienced by all congested cities throughout the world with a simple, although outrageous to some, solution.

CONGRATULATIONS YOU'VE MADE IT ANOTHER YEAR!

I arrived to Holland just as my birthday was approaching. To most Americans once you reach a certain age birthdays are really no big deal. It's really just another day and business as usual. Usually you go out to dinner with your significant other and receive a present from him or her. You might receive a phone call from a relative you haven't spoken to in awhile and if you're lucky one of your friends will remember it's your birthday and will call you up to wish you a happy birthday. So when my birthday arrived while in Holland I figured it was no big deal and just another day, especially since I didn't know anyone just yet. I soon came to realize that the Dutch aren't so nonchalant when it comes to this special day.

I received a knock on my door on my birthday morning from a hotel staff member who was delivering a plant that a lady friend of mine had sent me for my birthday. I told the staff member, and as usual he was a 6 foot, 6 inch monstrosity of a man, that it was my birthday and he lit up like a Christmas tree. His enormous hands engulfed around mine as he excitedly exclaimed, "Congratulations!! Congratulations on your birthday! This is a special day. I wish you all the best. Once again, Congratulations!" Taken somewhat aback by the enthusiasm of this Gentle Giant, I thanked him and thought to myself, "They must really take birthdays seriously around here."

About thirty minutes later another knock on my door came and there were two more staff members with a bottle of wine, fresh cheese and fruit. This time they were Dutch girls, so my birthday was really starting to shape up! The hotel staff members were so kind for delivering such a thoughtful present to me on my birthday. Over and over they congratulated me on my birthday. I was absolutely incredulous with the excitement that my birthday generated and the fact that they kept congratulating me. I just didn't think that merely surviving another year at my age warranted such congratulatory remarks. Later that day I went down to the hotel bar for one of those tasty Dutch beers and the bartender congratulated me profusely on my birthday and even bought me a beer on the house. Even though I was in country for a short period of time, I was well aware of the infamous Dutch frugality. I came to the obvious conclusion that birthdays must really be special days in Holland if Dutch bartenders are willing to give drinks away on the house!

At work on the following Monday, word got out that it was my birthday over the weekend and the congratulations started up once again. E-mails were sent out to entire departments informing everyone of my major milestone in life. I originally didn't think that turning an insignificant number in my thirties as a major milestone. Once again I was embarrassed and couldn't believe what was transpiring. Another odd question I kept hearing was, "Where's your birthday cake?" Just about everyone asked me about my birthday cake. I figured since I was the new guy on the block, nobody really knew me well enough to buy me a cake, which I was totally comfortable with. With everyone continuing to ask me I felt like yelling, "Will somebody buy me a birthday cake so I don't have to deal with all of your questions anymore!"

A few weeks had passed and one day a Dutch colleague of mine showed up to work with two cakes. I initially thought that someone may have received a promotion or that someone may have just had a child. It turns out that it was *his* birthday and he was bringing in his *own* birthday cakes to share with everyone. Upon realizing this, I felt incredible sadness for my colleague because he had to bring in his own birthday cakes and had to throw his own little birthday celebration. Meanwhile, everybody showed up at his desk for pieces of birthday cake and delightedly congratulated him on his special day, to the complete satisfaction of the birthday reveler.

In Dutch culture, it's actually the norm for people with birthdays to buy or bake their own birthday cakes and to invite people to help them celebrate. My Dutch colleague, therefore, was just doing his part in Dutch society by throwing his own little birthday party. He was proud that it was his birthday and he wanted everyone to be a part of his special day and to celebrate it Dutch style. Whereas people in many cultures tend to hide the fact that it's their birthdays, especially in the latter years of life, the Dutch advertise theirs and want to celebrate it in the Dutch time-honored birthday tradition with those around them.

The Dutch take birthdays so seriously that they display birthday calendars in their bathrooms as constant reminders of upcoming special days to ensure that they don't forget loved ones' birthdays. Furthermore, it's even appropriate to congratulate relatives of a person whose birthday it is. For instance, the Dutch commonly pronounce statements such as, "Congratulations on your brother's birthday" or even "Congratulations on the birthday of your sister-in-law." For most cultures, this is definitely taking the birthday tradition a bit too far.

Dutchman throwing his own birthday party

Turning fifty in the Netherlands is celebrated as a major milestone and in a truly unique Dutch style. The usually restrained Dutch don't hold anything back when someone turns fifty and they celebrate this milestone with a rather unique tradition. When someone turns fifty years old, friends hang a picture or a stuffed life-sized figure of the Biblical characters Abraham or Sarah over the door of the lucky one to let everyone know that he or she has turned fifty. When a Dutchman or Dutchwoman hits the half-century mark, he or she is said to be "seeing Abraham'' or "seeing Sarah,'' which is a reference to the biblical couple who were too old to have children until an angel of the Lord intervened. In Holland, when someone asks you if you have seen Sarah or Abraham, they are merely asking your age.

Since the fifty year mark calls for celebrations and opportunities to make the newly turned fifty year old the butt of old-age jokes, the Dutch seize this rare opportunity and play rather outrageous, personalized jokes. Instead of a full-sized doll of Abraham or Sarah, newly turned fifty year olds may even find life-sized replicas of themselves hanging on their doors or on their sidewalks. Any physical distinction will be greatly exaggerated with these life-sized replicas. For instance, if a person has a big nose, the stuffed doll may have a cucumber protruding from its face, or if the person has a receding hairline, the life-sized replica may be completely bald. People will even post pictures from the childhood and teenage years of the newly turned fifty year olds on trees and telephone poles. This is one time where people are expected, and even encouraged, to be curious and to look at the pictures.

So the Gentle Giants do let their hair down once in awhile and have some great fun, even at the expense of their loved ones. In a shrinking world of disappearing cultures and traditions, it's refreshing to see the Dutch preserving those traditions that still provide meaning to their lives and respect for their culture.

No secret how old this resident is

Febo de *Lekkerste* and Raw Herring Stands

One of the most popular places around Holland for eating and mingling, especially late at night when the pubs and clubs let out, is a *Febo*. *Febo de lekkerste*, which means *Febo* the most delicious, is a food stand with pre-cooked (usually deep-fried) snacks stored in small glass containers. The doors of these containers can be opened by inserting small change into the slots, allowing access to the delicacies positioned within. Such delicacies include overly deep-fried croquettes, in the form of chicken, beef, pork, cheese, curry and other combinations; hamburgers and cheeseburgers; hotdogs; and chicken sandwiches. The croquettes are universally the favorite of the Dutch, which is truly amazing considering how deep-fried and unpleasant looking they are, both inside and out. But somehow the Dutch find these artery-clogging snacks delectable and devour them like they're going out of style. I must admit, these strange looking things sitting in their containers are somehow remarkably pleasing to the taste buds. My visiting friends and colleagues were almost always guilty of stopping at a *Febo* after a night at the pubs in order to indulge in these rather tasty snacks, usually ingesting more than just one. The mega-corporation, McDonalds, even realized the demand for such deep-fried treats and introduced the "McKroket" onto its menu in the Netherlands. The Dutch, meanwhile, find it more enjoyable to just drop a few coins into the slots at the *Febo* in order to savor these Dutch delicacies.

In addition to the pre-cooked, container snacks, the *Febo's* also serve ice-cream and soft drinks. A Dutch food stand wouldn't be complete without *Vlaamse frites* (French fries). The Dutch are passionate about their *frites* and are often seen walking the streets eating large containers of these potato treats. The Dutch favor putting mayonnaise on their *frites*, which many visitors find rather unique since most cultures throughout the word are accustomed to ketchup on their fries. But to the Dutch, *frites* and mayonnaise is as normal and enjoyable as could be. In the cinematic movie, *Pulp Fiction*, John Travolta tells Samuel Jackson about the disgusting Dutch habit of eating French Fries with mayonnaise. He emphatically stated that he had personally seen them do it and that they drown their fries with the stuff. The Dutch also enjoy curry sauce on their *frites*, a spice the Dutch have delighted in since the years of exploration and trade with far-reaching regions of the world.

In addition to the numerous *Febo's* in Holland, raw herring stands are strewn across the country and are just as popular as the deep-fried food stands. These raw herring stands are not bait shops for fishermen, but food stands that the Dutch swarm to in order to eat raw bait fish -- a delicacy that the Dutch, and perhaps only the Dutch, find truly delectable. These raw herring stands are situated alongside the murky waters of the Dutch canals, which leaves many visitors suspect as to where these fish actually came from. Some of the Dutch dip the herring in chopped onions prior to eating them. To eat the raw herring, the Dutch hold the fish by the tails, tip their heads back and slowly lower the entire fish

Deep-fried croquette anyone?

into their mouths. The mere sight of watching the Dutch devour these raw fish leaves many visitors queasy in their stomachs. The distinct aroma of dead fish doesn't help with that queasy feeling either. The Dutch also eat raw herring on white bread or cut it up into pieces and put on cocktail sticks. The Dutch can't seem to get enough of these little fish; the raw herring stands are always packed with eager customers. Even though most tourists try to abide by the adage, *when in Rome do as the Romans*, many visitors to Holland simply can't muster up the courage to take part of the Dutch tradition of eating raw herring at a street-side food stand along a murky canal.

An American colleague of mine and I were discussing the numerous Dutch peculiarities that we both observed while in Holland. When the topic of raw herring surfaced, my colleague turned green and became nauseous. After regaining his composure, he proceeded to tell me about his one, and only one, raw herring experience in Holland. On his first day of a business

A Dutchman ready to savor a true Dutch delicacy

trip to the Netherlands, my colleague and several Dutchmen went out to lunch. As they stumbled upon a raw herring stand along the *Rijn* river, the Dutchmen couldn't pass up the opportunity to savor their favorite little seafood delicacies. Being in Holland for the first time, my colleague was incredulous as all of the Dutchmen proceeded to hold these raw fish by the tails and slowly dropped them down their gullets. Being absolutely aghast over such a display, my colleague just wanted to continue walking and to be as far away as possible from this revolting raw fish stand. The Dutchmen, however, had other intentions.

One of the Dutchmen started describing how delicious the raw herring tasted and the integral role that these fish played in Dutch culture and throughout Dutch history. He then stated to my colleague, rather assertively, that it would be an insult to the Dutch if he did not try one of these seafood treats. As my colleague described, "I was surrounded by these really tall, intimidating Dutchmen, I couldn't say no." In their native tongue, the Dutchmen ordered up one of these tasty morsels and handed it over to the apprehensive American. As he held the fish by the tail, he just knew he couldn't stomach such a task, but didn't want to insult all of the Gentle Giants who were gathered around him. Perhaps observing the horrified look on his face, the Dutchmen agreed with the American to continue walking. Being quick on his feet, my colleague made sure he grabbed a few more napkins as they departed the stand.

The courageous American took a bite out of the raw herring, to the approval and applause of the Dutchmen. Being satisfied that the American fulfilled his obligation, the group proceeded to stroll along the river. Feeling queasy over that first bite, my colleague slowly dropped back behind the pack and stealthily disposed of the half-eaten raw fish that was still in his mouth into a napkin. There was no way he could actually *eat* the raw fish. Periodically, the Dutchmen would look back and my colleague would take another bite, usually with a thumbs-up sign falsely indicating that he was enjoying the Dutch treat. Once again the American would dispose of the fish remnants into a napkin at the first opportunity. This cycle continued until the entire herring was gone and all of his napkins were full of half-eaten raw fish. This American went above and beyond the call of duty, although surreptitiously, by honoring one of the local Dutch customs. Who says that Americans don't observe or respect other cultural traditions?

It is truly amazing how packed the *Febo's* and raw herring stands are on any given day. These food stands accommodate the busy and hard working lifestyles of the Dutch. It's very convenient for the Dutch to pull up to one of these food stands on their bicycles, pleasure in a quick croquette or raw herring, then move on to the business at hand.

DUTCH KISS

The Dutch have a very unique way of greeting one another. When the Dutch greet loved ones and close friends, they kiss each other three times on the cheeks, always starting with the right cheek. This custom is followed between men and women, women and women, and even between men and men (but less frequent). These kisses aren't gentle, and don't always land on the cheeks. The Dutch touch their cheeks together rather forcibly and usually end up kissing only the air. Even though the lips may not land entirely on the cheeks, the Dutch kiss is loud and has a distinct wet, puckering sound to it, which is shocking, and even disturbing, to members from "one kiss" cultures.

It's common for the Dutch to stop riding their bikes when they encounter friends or acquaintances in order to give each other the obligatory three kiss greeting, chat for a few moments, then to give each other the obligatory three kiss goodbye. Six kisses, consequently, can occur in the span of less than a minute with chance encounters between two people. When a Dutch person encounters a group of friends, the greeting and goodbye kisses can be rather strenuous. If a person encounters five friends on the street, for instance, that person ends up delivering thirty hello and goodbye kisses, that may span just a few minutes. With the way the Dutch slam their cheeks into one another and perform such exaggerated kisses, a person's cheeks and mouth may be quite sore after a day of running into old friends!

Americans are accustomed to the one kiss hello and goodbye, mainly reserved for men and women or women and women. Americans don't have to be concerned about learning the Dutch kiss prior to embarking upon a trip to the Netherlands, for the Dutch reserve such a custom for only those dear friends and acquaintances. Expatriates or long-term visitors partake in the Dutch kissing customs as they become closer with their Dutch neighbors and friends.

The American "one-kiss" ritual is rather dull in comparison to many European kissing customs. Blistex, the leading manufacturer of lip care products, discusses many European kissing customs on its website. Some European kissing customs are as follows:

France
For the French, kissing is a way of life and multiple kisses are normal. Paris adopted a four kiss greeting years ago and has stuck to it. The sequence is left cheek first - always. In Brittany they follow a three kiss routine and in most other parts of France they restrict themselves to a restrained two kiss greeting. The exception is the Côte d'Azur where a five or six kissing pattern is not unusual.

Italy
Kissing is restricted to very close friends or family in Italy. The number of kisses is optional and as there are no rules regarding which cheek to kiss first, there are frequent and sometimes painful clashes. Hugs and handshakes are good alternatives for friends.

Belgium
If you are about the same age as the person you are greeting, one kiss is the rule in Belgium. For someone at least ten years older than you are, then three kisses is seen as a mark of respect. This

could be hazardous - especially if you are not good at judging ages!

Spain, Austria and Scandinavia
Spain, Austria and Scandinavia are each content with the two kisses ritual. In Spain the rule is strictly right cheek first.

Germany
Germany tends to restrict kissing to family and very close friends. Handshakes predominate and all meetings begin and end with this formality.

U.K.
In the U.K. kissing is only just being extended outside of family and friends. Somewhat shy of physical contact, the British have tended to opt for a handshake or nod as the safest form of greeting. In today's less formal environment, "Hi!" or "How are you?" is a way of avoiding physical contact. But it must be remembered that when the British ask how you are they don't expect you to tell them.

As can be seen, there are many different flavors of kissing customs throughout the continent of Europe. One of the more interesting compliments I received while in Holland came from a nice Dutch lady whom I had to the privilege of taking out one particular evening. After months of observing hundreds, if not thousands, of Dutch kisses I finally had my opportunity to take part in this unique custom. Coming from a one-kiss culture, I must admit I was a little nervous embarking upon this endeavor. After I said good-bye to my lady friend in true Dutch form with the three kiss custom, she told me that I was a great kisser. I laughed the whole way home, but with a smile on my face.

Dutch Political Incorrectness

With the Dutch it's what you see is what you get. They are direct, blunt, brutally honest and, to some cultures, politically incorrect. The Dutch are not concerned with the presentation or delivery of the message, just the content of the message. They have no regard for embellishment or storytelling, for their industriousness won't permit it. The Dutch differ from other cultures where storytelling is a cherished part of their culture and the presentation of the content is just as important as the content itself. Ireland possesses such a culture where storytelling and long discussions on just about any topic are paramount to its inhabitants. The Irish take great pride in the skills of their spoken word and in their parlance. When an Irishman says, "Pull up a chair and let me tell you a story," one can expect an impassioned and rather lengthy narrative. The Dutch, meanwhile, would rather do without the extravagance and would rather get to the point at hand. After all, the Dutch strive to keep all things in life as modest and unpresumptuous as possible. Their penchant for timeliness and insistence on adhering to schedules, furthermore, won't allow them to sit through elaborate stories.

If you ask a Dutch person a question, such as "How do you like my haircut," you better be prepared for an honest answer, which may not be pleasant. I was initially taken aback several times when a Dutch person would tell me bluntly that they didn't like my tie or that I didn't conduct a meeting very well. On several occasions before delivering a presentation, my Dutch Manager would introduce me to the audience by stating, "This is one of those fast-talking New York types. You probably won't understand him, but do your best. I don't know why he talks so fast, but he does." Talk about breaking the ice! Not only was I nervous about my upcoming presentation, but now how to attempt to dispel the notion that I was just another one of those *fast talking New York types*. Thanks boss!

Working with the Dutch certainly requires thick skin at times. It is, however, comforting to know that they're not going to pull any punches and will tell you exactly what's on their minds. To some, such brutal honesty may take awhile to get used to. Even in the 17th century the Dutch were renowned for their direct and brutally honest manner, and once again the English had something derisive to say about such behavior. The English coined the term

Dutch Uncle as a tribute to the Dutch propensity for brutally honest opinions, even when they're not even asked for such opinions. The English refer to a person who speaks and admonishes frankly and sternly as a *Dutch Uncle*, for such a person acts like your uncle even though they're not. Other derisive terms towards the Dutch that the dry-witted English are credited with developing include *Dutch Courage* – false courage derived from alcohol, and *Dutch Concert* – a confusion of languages or sounds. I'm beginning to think that there's a love-hate relationship between the English and Dutch!

Political correctness, as carried out in countries like the U.S., hasn't made it to the Netherlands just yet. Some of the corporate behavior and actions I've personally witnessed in Holland would have been grounds for punishment and even dismissal in the U.S. For instance, at one company function, a senior-level manager presented an award to the sales person who showed the most intrepidness and audacity in achieving new business for the company. The award he presented was called the "Big Balls" award and he presented the recipient of this honor with two giant, inflatable balls. These two big balls, obviously, symbolized a male's nether-regions. As an outsider coming from a culture where political correctness runs rampant, I immediately looked over my shoulder to hopefully observe that nobody was offended. The room had a mixed gender audience and everyone found the award funny and not in the least bit offensive. I've also witnessed on several occasions senior-level managers delivering dirty jokes filled with numerous expletives to roomfuls of mixed gender audiences. Consistently, all found the jokes funny and not at all inappropriate.

What a far cry from America where political correctness runs supreme. Americans these days have to be so concerned with not offending other genders, races, religions, sexual preferences and anything else where people can actually get fired from their jobs and even sued by the offended. Recently, Senator Trent Lott was forced to step down as Senatorial Majority Leader because of questionable comments he made during Senator Strom Thurmond's 100th birthday party. Senator Lott was praising the elderly statesman by stating, "I want to say this about my state: When Strom Thurmond ran for president, we voted for him. We're proud of it. And if the rest of the country had followed our lead, we wouldn't have had all these problems over all these years, either." Senator Strom Thurmond ran for president in 1948 as the candidate of the breakaway Dixiecrat Party, which strongly favored racial segregation. Whether or not there were racial overtones in Lott's remarks, he was paying tribute to an American statesman who served in public office the majority of his life. Political opponents quickly lambasted Lott for being a racist because of these racially insensitive remarks, which had detrimental effects on Lott's life and political future.

CHRISTMAS TIME(S) AND *ZWARTE PIET*

The Dutch couldn't possibly be like everyone else and celebrate Christmas just once a year. It just wouldn't be *very Dutch* to do so. They actually celebrate Christmas twice -- December 5th and December 25th. The reason for celebrating twice is to separate the material celebrations, which take place on the 5th, from the spiritual celebrations, which occur on the 25th. The story of Santa Claus originated in the Netherlands. The Dutch kept the ancient legend of St. Nicholas alive. St. Nicholas dates back to the fourth century where he was a bishop of Myra in western Turkey and the patron saint of children. The Dutch originally spelled St. Nicholas as *Sint Nikolaas*, which eventually morphed into *Sinterklaas*. *Sinterklaas* eventually became anglicized resulting in its current form of Santa Claus. During the middle ages, Dutch children started placing their wooden shoes by the hearth in anticipation that they would be filled with treats by this mysterious man and his little helpers.

Sinterklaas has an interesting, but to some very politically incorrect, yearly ritual in Holland. *Sinterklaas* is tall, noble, wise, good-natured, authoritarian and white. His little helpers are not the cute little dwarf toy makers that most western civilizations are accustomed to. *Sinterklaas'* little helpers are rude, bad-tempered, undisciplined and black. These malevolent creatures are referred to as *Zwarte Pieten* (Black Peters) and the Dutch children are

179

terrified of them. Even more shocking, the *Zwarte Pieten* are actually white people wearing black make-up, kinky-haired wigs, earrings and pantaloons. The children fear that they will be taken from their homes by these strange looking black men who carry sacks around in order to capture bad children. When *Sinterklaas* and his little *Zwarte Pieten* come into town, children are terrified and can be seen crying and running away for safety.

Many of the Dutch like to placate those enraged over the racial insensitivity of the *Zwarte Pieten* by justifying the black faces come as a result of the *Zwarte Pieten* scurrying up and down chimneys delivering treats to the children. The blackness of their skin color, then, is a result of the soot from all of the chimneys. In actuality, however, the legend of *Sinterklaas* claims that Sinterklaas and his little helpers come from the Spanish capital, Madrid. The Netherlands was under Spanish colonial rule during a large segment of the middle ages, and this legend, invariably, derides such colonial rule with the use of *Zwarte Pieten*. Due to the early Moorish invasions of Spain and their subsequent occupation of the country, the *Zwarte Pieten* are allegedly of Moorish (African) descent. The outfit that he wears is supposed to resemble that of the ancient Moors. The legend of *Sinterklaas* and *Zwarte Pieten* has been alive and flourishing for centuries in Holland without hardly any repercussions to the insensitivities or to the stereotypes that go along with this time-honored legend.

Political correctness has made some inroads into the Netherlands, as the Dutch recently tried to be more racially sensitive by offering up multi-ethnic *Zwarte Pieten* when *Sint Nikolaas* made his entrance into Amsterdam. In true Dutch form, this gesture generated heated debate and even protests against the denigration of a Dutch time-honored tradition. As Dutch cities are becoming more and more ethnically mixed, people are starting to feel there might be more to this tradition than meets the eye.

THE AJAX CONTROVERSY

The legendary Ajax football team in the Netherlands is world renowned for its talent and reputation as a world class football club. It also has a rather curious reputation as a Jewish club, although hardly any of its members were ever Jews. Throughout the years, the Ajax football team jokingly exacerbated this Jewish reputation by calling themselves Jews, using Jewish words and eating only kosher meats. The Ajax fans even referred to themselves as Jews, even though nearly all of them were not. Additionally, the Ajax fans carried Israeli flags, mainly to irritate people, and referred to themselves as "Super Jews" and stated that "Jews are the champions."[6] The Ajax Star, a magazine for Ajax fans, even used the Star of David as its logo. Even more outrageous, opponents of the Ajax team, especially those from Feyenoord, provoked the Ajax team by chanting slogans such as "Hamas, Hamas, Jews to the Gas" and "Trains to Auschwitz leave in 5 minutes."[7] It was also common for opposing fans to make hissing noises in order to replicate the sounds of escaping gas. These chants and jeers happened so regularly that the police became ambivalent to them and paid little attention to the insensitivities. The Ajax reputation as being a Jewish club was so prevalent that many of the Dutch citizens thought that the blue and white flag with a star on it was an Ajax flag and not an Israeli one.

The origins of the Ajax Jewish reputation came about as a result of fans from the opposing teams entering into Amsterdam via trains and arriving at the Weesperpoort station. The streets outside of the Weesperpoort station had numerous Jewish street vendors and workers. These Jewish workers were the first people the opposing fans encountered upon entering into Amsterdam. Out of towners soon adopted phrases such as "we're going to the Jews" when referring to going to Ajax home games.[8] From the simple fact that Jewish workers congregated around the Weesperpoort station, the Ajax football team came to be known as a Jewish organization, and the Ajax players and fans took on this identity as their own.

In September, 1986, about a thousand of FC Den Haag fans yelled "We're hunting the Jews!" They also sang the German Nazi song "*Juden, wir kommen,*" which translates to "Jews, we're coming"[9] Police and authorities have been more cognizant of the ill-spirited rants of the opposing fans in recent years. In April, 2002, the Amsterdam police sent 670 supporters of the football club FC Utrecht back to Utrecht because they entered the stadium chanting "*Hamas, Hamas, alle Joden aan het gas,*" translating to "Hamas, Hamas, all Jews need to be gassed."[10]

WRAP UP

Dutch society is certainly an open society where individual liberties and freedoms are cherished and encouraged. The Dutch speak their minds freely and usually don't have to worry about any ramifications for doing so. The above examples, although insidiously offensive to some, are just ways in which the Dutch foster such an open society. The Dutch are tolerant and advance all forms of free speech and expression, even if it's derisive towards them. The Dutch, in turn, expect everyone else to show the same tolerance and concern for freedoms of expression.

As can be seen from this chapter, the land of the Gentle Giants is indeed a mysterious, bizarre, marvelous and unique place and the people inhabiting it are just the same. Many of their behaviors and customs date back centuries and have been leaving people throughout the world perplexed and flabbergasted ever since. The bedrock for almost all of their actions stem from their intensity towards tolerance and openness. They feel that there can be no compromising when it comes to a free and open society. To do so would be to disregard all of the struggles of their forebears in the creation of such a free and open society.

5.   DUTCH INDIVIDUALISM: FIRST AND FOREMOST

EGALITARIANISM

The American founding fathers were greatly influenced by the Dutch when staging their rebellion against Great Britain and crafting their form of government that would truly be of the people, by the people and for the people. The founding fathers were especially impressed with the liberties and rights bestowed upon all individuals throughout Dutch society. The Dutch had already endured the harsh tyrannical treatment of oppressive regimes centuries before; they were determined to let freedom reign and not to replace the overthrown, oppressive regimes with yet another form of oppression. This fervent desire for total freedom juxtaposed with the Dutch adherence to strict Calvinistic ethos, created social equality and a classlessness that have endured the test of time and is prevalent throughout the Netherlands today. Perhaps Thomas Jefferson had the Dutch in mind when contemplating the extent of individual freedom when he avowed, "all men are created equal" in the Declaration of Independence in 1776.

Egalitarianism is the modus operandi in the Netherlands where all people are considered morally equal and the rights of the individual come first and foremost. The Dutch are adamant about protecting the inherent freedoms of choice, speech, expression and anything else that the Dutch feel is a justifiable right for each and every individual. In capitalistic countries throughout the world a common aphorism, usually stated with cynicism, proclaims, "All men are created equal, but some more equal than others." This derisive adage is usually declared by the sanctimonious types who possess most of the wealth or by those ridden with animosity toward the wealthier classes. Unfortunately, some people are indeed more equal than others in many cultures throughout the world as evidenced by the numerous oligarchies and the alarmingly inequitable distribution of wealth. In Dutch society, however, nobody is more equal than others and nobody is the moral superior or inferior of others, no matter how much wealth a person possesses. All members of society play on a level playing field and the Dutch strive to maintain that equality.

Because moral equivalency is cherished in Dutch culture, asking for autographs of Dutch football stars or other illustrious figures is rare and derided. Even though someone may be an excellent sports player or famous singer, he or she is expected to maintain modesty and not to behave inexcusably as anyone's moral superior. In turn, the privacy and social space of these stars are respected. In the rare instances of famous figures being asked for autographs, it is common for these figures to turn the tables and ask the autograph seekers for *their* autographs, thus conveying the fact that nobody is above anybody else in Dutch society. This unassuming behavior can be starkly contrasted in star-struck cultures such as England and America. The paparazzi of England are dubiously renowned for their unrelenting pursuit of shocking stories or compromising photographs of England's most celebrated figures. The paparazzi feeds the English's insatiable appetite for good gossip by detailing the lives of revered individuals such as members of the House of Windsor, football stars like David Beckham and entertainers like the Spice Girls. In America, society's admiration and awe of individual stars is evident in the popularity of award shows such as the Grammy's and Emmy's. On just about any given night, throngs of salivating fans can be seen gathered outside the studios of David Letterman hoping to catch a glimpse of famous actors or to even pat them on their shoulders as they walk by. The price of stardom results in the loss of social space for celebrities in such star-struck cultures, although I'm sure most of them don't complain.

In the Netherlands, where that social space is revered, personal liberties are also greatly valued. The Dutch consider it their intrinsic right to do just about anything they please and to say whatever they want as long as it doesn't interfere with societal order or the personal liberties of others. The usually mild-mannered Dutch rage into conversational fury over any topic that deals with the infringement of personal liberties. On numerous occasions I voiced my concerns over how not just the Dutch police, but the police forces for many European nations, were expected to endure the violent actions of protestors against them, such as rock hurling and even pipe-bomb throwing! I claimed that police forces in such instances are justified in using force against the protestors for their blatant and hostile disregard of authority. My Dutch colleagues vehemently opposed my position and defended the individual rights of all people, even in such dubious circumstances.

Because the Dutch feel that all individuals deserve these liberties and rights, they are extremely tolerant of the actions of others. The Dutch are willing to overlook the personal, or even societal, infractions that other cultures deem highly offensive and even criminal. Marijuana, for example, can only be legally smoked in licensed coffeeshops throughout the country; however, Dutch authorities usually turn a blind eye when spotting an offender firing one up on a street corner. The Dutch feel that apprehending that individual would do more harm to society than by just letting the person smoke the marijuana out of harm's way. Dutch passer-bys won't even be offended or repulsed by such behavior for it is that person's right to do as he or she pleases. Parents would prefer their children learn the virtues of tolerance rather than malevolence toward one who has made an individual choice. This is especially true when the individual in question is less fortunate.

Dutch children are encouraged to be individualistic and independent. Pre-adolescent children can be seen frolicking around restaurants, airports and other public places with little parental supervision. Dutch parents feel that it is very important for their children to explore and learn the matters of life on their own. Such exploration by energetic little tykes can be quite a nuisance for members of other cultures where the virtues of discipline are of the utmost importance. German or Japanese elders, for example, wouldn't look too favorably on their offspring creating a ruckus in a restaurant or other public places. Dutch parents, however, place less emphasis on discipline and self-control; they expect other adults to respect their children's individuality and tolerate their learning processes, no matter how bothersome they may be.

Even as Dutch children enter the pubescent years they are encouraged to strengthen their individualism. Dutch teenagers constantly negotiate for more freedom and independence from their parents as they get older, with parents usually respecting such desires. Additionally, Dutch children are encouraged to question authority and to demand to be treated with respect for their own individuality, even though they are mere youngsters. I thoroughly enjoyed hearing stories from my Dutch colleagues about some of the arguments they would get into with their teachers. There is definitely reciprocal respect between teacher and student in the Dutch classroom. Rulers are used merely for measurement in the Dutch classroom, not for slapping knuckles as is still the case in many school systems throughout the world. Alarmingly to many people from other cultures, Dutch parents even encourage their children to openly discuss sex during their early teenage years. They feel that sex is a normal aspect of life and a pertinent stepping-stone in the maturation process. Of course, Dutch children are taught the essentials of safety and responsibility in dealing with such important issues.

Because of the importance of individualism in Dutch society, many young adults move out of the house to live on their own as soon as they turn eighteen years of age. Furthermore, many couples live together, even having children together, without getting married. These couples feel that mutual trust and respect for one another is more important than obtaining the official sanction of the state or church. In fact, the number of marriages has been declining in recent years and the number of illegitimate children being born has tripled since 1989. In 2003, one in three children born in the Netherlands were born out of wedlock.[1]

Individuality is even maintained by Dutch senior citizens. Dutch seniors rarely live with their children, even when becoming unable to support themselves physically. Numerous homes exist for the elderly where they are treated accordingly and their individuality respected. Dutch elders strive to maintain their independence and don't want to be a burden to their children and grandchildren. Most Dutch homes are nuclear families comprising just the father, mother and children.

The Dutch nuclear family model with all family members striving for individuality and independence is drastically different than many cultures throughout the world, especially the Latin cultures. In Italy, for instance, most homes comprise extended families, where grandparents and even brothers and sisters in-law live under one roof. The extended family, to include uncles, aunts and cousins, frequently get together to celebrate the numerous birthdays and holidays or just to enjoy home-cooked meals and homemade wine. The family is the most treasured aspect in such cultures. In Spain, as well as in Italy and Latin American countries, young adults are not expected to move out upon turning eighteen, but will stay in the household until marriage, which may occur late in their twenties or even thirties. A common stereotype is that young Italian men love their mothers' home cooking so much that they aren't willing to leave the household until a suitable replacement, in the form of a wife, is found.

Human rights and human dignity for everyone is top priority of the Dutch. Police brutality is virtually unheard of in the Netherlands. In fact, criminals are treated with just as much respect as law-abiding citizens, which can be difficult for other cultures to understand. Jailed criminals even have a room dedicated for sex, which the Dutch view as a healthy, inalienable right. Jailed criminals get more than an opportunity to just converse with their visitors through a one-inch thick glass via telephone! Drug addicts aren't demonized in the Netherlands; they're viewed as people with problems and the Dutch feel that society should do everything in their power to assist these people in trying to resolve these problems. Sweden also shows great sympathy for the downtrodden and people with problems. The Swedes strive for a minimum quality of life for everyone and minimizing differences between people. Like the Dutch, the Swedes have one of the world's highest tax rates and levies hefty taxes on the flourishing members of society in order to more equally distribute the wealth in their country.

Dutch laws also aim to protect the rights of the individual in the workplace. Employers can't wantonly fire or layoff workers in order to make the numbers look better, get rid of the "dead wood" or even because of poor performance. Employers are required by law to give workers ample notice of termination, usually around four months. Additionally, employers will endeavor to find work more suitable for those workers not performing to the expected standard in their current job responsibilities. Even before a worker is hired to a company, a three-month minimum trial period is allowed for both the employer and worker to feel each other out in order to determine if sufficient synergies exist between the two entities to allow for future employment. The Germans have similar employment policies. In Germany, fear of rampant unemployment still persists from the dreadful times leading up to World War II when unemployment reached unfathomable highs. The Germans take painstaking measure to place employees not performing to expectations in areas where they can do the least amount of harm as opposed to firing them.

The Italians are even more adamantly supportive of workers' rights than the Dutch and Germans. On April 16, 2002, millions of Italians workers throughout the country went on strike in protest of government plans to make it easier for employers to fire workers. The strike brought the entire country to a virtual standstill. Italian unions stated that 90% of the Italian workforce participated in the strike, which resulted in the stoppage of all public transport by road, rail, air and sea; deserted airports with air traffic controllers stopping work; hospitals providing emergency services only; schools, banks, post offices and government offices shutting down; no newspapers being published and no live television broadcasts. It is virtually impossible for Italian employers to legally terminate a worker. The government was merely trying to make it less difficult, even though it would still be extremely arduous, for Italian employers to terminate the services of their employees, if deemed necessary. Italian unions, however, argued that once the government begins to tamper with the existing labor legislation, workers' rights will continue to erode.

Non-union or non-governmental American employers, on the other hand, are not required to obey any special laws that strive to protect the individual from being wantonly terminated. American corporations, for the most part, follow the ethos of only one guiding paradigm – capitalism. Unions can provide some of the protection of individual rights that is afforded to the Dutch workforce. However, when a union is not present, many workers find themselves subject to the termination techniques utilized by American corporations. There is a myriad of reasons for employing these tactics, the primary one being an effort to stay competitive. The massive amount of layoffs after the burst of the Internet bubble is a testament to the principles of striving to remain competitive in a capitalistic society. Some corporations go as far to "get rid of the dead wood" on a regular basis in order to continuously raise the bar of excellence.

Jack Welch, American's CEO of the Century, is one who aggressively and continuously sought to terminate employees by implementing the *Vitality Curve* while at the helm of GE. The *Vitality Curve* required managers to rank workers in the 20th percentile, the A players; the 70th percentile, the B players; and the bottom 10th percentile, the C players. The A players were given incredible salary increases, huge sums of stock options, rewards and many other perks while the C players didn't fare so well; they were shown to the door! After several iterations of ranking people in accordance with the Vitality Curve, the C players just weren't that bad of performers! It didn't matter that these C players weren't necessarily poor performers; out the door they went. Below is a depiction of the *Vitality Curve*, beloved by some but dreaded by others.

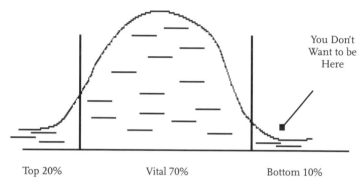

Top 20% Vital 70% Bottom 10%

The GE Vitality Curve

This Vitality Curve principle greatly contradicts the Dutch archetype of egalitarianism. Dutch members of society, and even Dutch workers, are considered to be morally equal and, thus, to be treated equally. Sure, Dutch workers are promoted for excellent performance and rewards are given out to the top achievers, but it's not even close to the extremes of some of the corporations throughout the world. Where there is great disparity between the income levels throughout the echelons of American corporations, the Dutch strive less for differentiation and more for parity in the income levels. In using a shotgun analogy to depict the differences in salaries between the two countries, the Americans have an incredibly wide shot group completely covering the target while the Dutch have a much tighter shot group, with little deviation from the median.

As can be seen, the disparity in salaries of workers in American corporations is much greater than those in Dutch corporations. This analogy doesn't even take into account tycoons such as Bill

Gates, Michael Dell or Warren Buffet; their salaries are so high that they're not even on the target! Even more alarming is that U.S. politicians are in the fray of the multi-millionaires. Forbes magazine publishes an issue outlining the country's richest politicians with their net worth. Michael Bloomberg, the mayor of New York City, incidentally, is the richest U.S. politician - worth $4.8 *billion*! Most people can't even fathom one individual, especially a public servant possessing such wealth. I can only imagine the incredulity that the Dutch must experience upon hearing of such a figure, especially were they to know the staggering numbers of people who live below the poverty line in New York City.

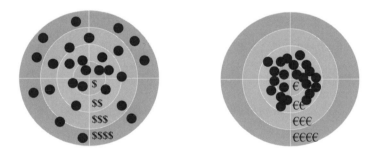

American Salary Shot Group   *Dutch Salary Shot Group*

The Dutch feel that no individual should possess such excessive wealth because no individual could possibly be worth all of those millions or, in the case of Mayor Bloomberg, billions. Due to their egalitarian ways, they strive for a more equitable distribution of the wealth as opposed to a system where a select few possess most of the wealth. It is ironic, therefore, that the Dutch Royal family is one of the wealthiest families in the world and benefits in capitalistic ways by owning parts of famous Dutch companies like Royal Dutch Shell, KLM Airlines, and some of the biggest banks in the Netherlands. To quote Mel Brooks in the popular cinematic film *History of the World Part I*, "It's good to be the king!"

Living in a Shoebox – Respecting Social Space

To an outsider, the Dutch may appear to be aloof, cold, distant and even standoffish. I remember my frustrations after living in the Netherlands for months and still not really understanding the Dutch people or even having any close Dutch friends. I regularly socialized with the British, Australian, and American expatriates, but rarely with the Dutch outside of normal business hours. The numerous expatriates would constantly offer to show me around the city, ask me to watch football, invite me to parties and take me to their favorite pubs. The Dutch never asked me to do any of these things; they were very cordial at work, but after hours, they went their way and I went mine. I soon began to realize why all of the expats sneered at me when I claimed that the Dutch were very helpful and would give me the shirts off of their backs when I first arrived in the Netherlands, which was truly my impression. They simply said, "Just wait a few more weeks, then come to us and say that." I just thought that other expats simply didn't have the social pizzazz or charisma to get along with the Dutch that I had. To me, the assimilation process was going to be a breeze. Or so I thought.

The Dutch were indeed very accommodating when I asked them questions or even asked for their assistance; they helped me out in the most genial manner. I soon became cognizant, however, that they rarely *offered* their assistance. They rarely went out of their way to ensure that I was adapting to their culture and even stood by idly at times when they saw that I was obviously struggling with something foreign to me. On more than one occasion while eating at a restaurant my jacket, unbeknownst to me, fell off of my chair and onto the floor. The Dutch waiters and waitresses went on with their normal duties and not only didn't pick my jacket up, but didn't even inform me that it was on the ground! I soon became frustrated with the Dutch and realized what the expats were referring to when they warned me about the Dutch hospitality.

As a firm believer that most things happen for a reason and similarly, that most people behave in certain ways for a reason, I was resolute in figuring out these odd Dutch behavior characteristics. It seemed to me that each individual member of Dutch society lived within his or her own domain and rarely ventured outside of that sphere. When walking the streets or hanging out in pubs, the Dutch rarely made eye contact with anyone outside of their immediate circle. Not even during social encounters with acquaintances or fairly familiar persons did the conversation go beyond the perfunctory. For these reasons, among others, the Dutch are perceived by outsiders to be reserved and unforthcoming.

A very different perception may be found in America, where people-watching is a favorite pastime. Americans like to walk the streets checking each other out, especially the attractive ones. At bars and in social environments it is common for American men and women to express themselves with slight smiles and brief moments of eye contact. The fairer-looking ones, furthermore, are constantly being examined, much to the chagrin of the average-looking ones. The sexual tension is so thick in most American bars that you can cut it with a knife. Such eye contact and blatant stares simply don't happen in the Netherlands. Many Americans find it frustrating that they can't strike up conversations with the opposite sex and that nobody "checks them out" like they do back home. My one friend, in particular, found it quite frustrating that none of the Dutch women would give him the time of day, not even an innocent glance. Coming from New York City with his *Sex and the City* lifestyle, he found it so unbelievable that he couldn't just put on his best duds, act chic and have Dutch women all over him. He tried all of the tricks of the trade but to no avail; even a fast talking New York city slicker could not overcome the Dutch impenetrable barriers!

My first encounter with the Dutch stoicism occurred on my plane ride over to Amsterdam on KLM, the Dutch airlines. The KLM flight attendants are known worldwide for their stunningly good looks, KLM blue uniforms and matching swimming pool eyes. So there I am, enamored with all of the 6 foot tall, long-legged Dutch beauties serving me Heinekens, thinking about the next phase of my life over in Europe. About halfway into the flight, one of these beautiful specimens trips over a careless passenger, spilling a tray of food all over herself, the floor and passengers all around her. I felt so bad for this previously sparkling young lady, for my initial thought was that she was going to cry, panic and fall to pieces. Well, without skipping a beat or showing any emotion she wiped off the passengers, cleaned up the floor then cleaned herself off. Not one frown, not one expletive, no signs of being flustered. My experience in similar situations with Americans and other nationalities has been quite different; reactions tend to be much more extreme and often include a variety of expletives that would make a drunken sailor blush! This Dutch flight attendant's face remained as austere as if nothing had happened.

So why is it that the Dutch maintain such stoicism and rarely venture outside of their own domains? Aren't the Dutch curious and even interested in other people, especially those of the opposite sex? Of course they are, but they possess an inordinate amount of respect for the social space of others. The Dutch regard social space as one's right to privacy. They feel people should be able to express their individuality without the scrutiny or prying eyes of others. This reverence for each other's social space is derived from the fact that they practically live on top of one another; the Netherlands has the highest average population density in the world with 459 inhabitants per square kilometer. Japan, a country historically known for its high population density, has only 334 inhabitants per square kilometer![2] With practically no physical space between one another, exacerbated by being the tallest people in the world, the Dutch need some sort of individual space in order to cope with living in a shoebox.

This deep desire for individual space manifests itself in a tremendous respect for social space. The Dutch don't drop by peoples' homes unexpectedly, don't make eye contact with strangers and don't go too far out of their way to assist people unknown to them. Offering such assistance may be perceived as an intrusion upon someone's social space and may even be construed as invasive. Being very individualistic, the Dutch assume that everyone else wants to be individualistic as well and left alone to make their own choices. In fact the literal translation of the Dutch word for hospitality is *gastvrijheid*, or guest-freedom. Once a Dutch person is *asked* for assistance, that person would happily and cordially give as much help as needed; *offering* such assistance, however, is usually taboo in Dutch culture, for it may infringe upon someone's social space. So when the Dutch waiters and waitresses passed by without picking up my jacket, they weren't being rude, but were just respecting my social space. Informing me that my jacket was on the floor may cause embarrassment to me, which certainly wouldn't be respecting my social space. Picking my jacket up for me, furthermore, may even give the impression that I'm not capable of handling my own affairs, which could be seen as a sign of weakness. With the Dutch incredibly high-regard for the individual, they would never want to embarrass anyone. The Dutch compensate for their lack of physical space in the Netherlands by respecting and adhering to the virtues of social space.

The Swedes also have a strong desire to respect social space and not interfere in personal matters. In Sweden, independence is linked directly to one's sense of self-sufficiency. It is imperative for Swedes to be in total control of any situation and to be capable of solving any problems or issues that are presented to them. Not being in control of such situations is a sign a weakness, and hence lacking independence. The Swedish term *duktig*, being capable, is deeply ingrained into their society and has serious emotional connotations. The Swedes are constantly being judged as to how *duktig* they are. A child who behaves at school and gets good grades is *duktig*. A person who is able to handle his or her affairs without the intervention or help of others is *duktig*. It's very important for a Swede not to be dependent upon or indebted to another person. Swedish couples, whether just dating or even married, in fact, often *Go Dutch* by splitting the bills equally. Doing so ensures that one is not indebted to the other. A person whose jacket falls onto the floor of a restaurant is not *duktig*. I'm sure my jacket would have remained on the floor in Sweden, as well, for the Swedes would not want to embarrass me by showing me that I'm not *duktig*. Like the Dutch, they would not want to intrude on my personal space and would rather afford me the opportunity to resolve the issues independently. Also like the Dutch, the Swedes are often perceived as aloof and distant, as a result of their innate respect for individuality.

It took me many months, many conversations with the Dutch, and many observations to truly understand and appreciate the Dutch esteem of social space. Unfortunately, many casual observers and short time visitors to the Netherlands don't have time to reach these deductions and view the Dutch as standoffish and cold. Additionally, many cultures, especially the Americans, have so much physical space that social space isn't even considered as being important. For instance, it's quite common for Americans to stop by each other's homes just to pay a visit. Americans, for the most part, will break bread with fairly unfamiliar people and even strangers. Upon meeting a new colleague at work or someone in a social environment, it's quite normal for Americans to inquire about each other's marital status, occupations, number of children, whether they rent or own their homes and just about anything else that satisfies each other's curiosities. Americans will also continuously offer their assistance to a new worker or new neighbor to show their hospitality and genuine concern. Such benevolent gestures are indeed appreciated and truly heartfelt, but in the Netherlands they can be construed as intrusive and disrespectful of one's social space.

The British and Australians are very similar to the Americans and diametrically dissimilar to the Dutch with regard to respecting social space. The Brits and Aussies are passionate about striking up conversations with strangers. They are very outgoing upon meeting strangers and love going to the Pub to have a pint or two to get to know each other better. When visiting the Netherlands, my British and Australian expatriate friends are more than willing to get together for some merriment and reminiscing. They go out of their way to see if any special events are happening during my visit and are willing to drop whatever they had planned should I give them short notice of my visit. My Dutch friends are willing to get together to catch up and to grab a few beers at the pub, but much more planning and structure is involved. They must have ample notice in order to clear it with their significant others; usually need to know where, when and for how long we'll be meeting; and once our visit is over, it's *dag* (good-bye) until the next time I'm in their homeland. Also, being late to such a reunion, even though it's on the most social of terms, is *verboden* for the Dutch. The Dutch maintain their formality even in such social situations.

On a recent visit to Amsterdam I met several of my close friends for some good cheer and merriment. Many of my Dutch brethren had to fight tooth and nail with their better halves to get a few hours away from their traditional Saturday night routines. As the night was concluding and since I was staying in the city for over a week, I felt it sensible not to say good-bye until my next visit, so I used social tact in saying, "Maybe we can meet for lunch sometime this week." Whether I meant that or not, in America we use such tact in order to avoid any uncomfortable situations of sad departures. A typical American response might go something like, "Yes that would be great. Give me a buzz and we'll meet up." The additional get-together may not happen, but the dialogue makes for comfortable departures. With the Dutch directness, concern over swaying too much out of their own domain and reverence for social space, the first response I received was, "No, no, no...we met already, this is enough. I'll see you next time around." The incredible jubilation I was feeling from a night of revelry and catching up with friends came to an abrupt halt as this statement brought me back to Dutch reality. My Dutch cohorts already deviated out of their routines and didn't want their social space interrupted anymore. Spending too much time together or getting too personal may lead to a disruption of their social space and personal sphere. Once our little get together was over, in a blink of an eye the Dutch went right back into their own little domains. Meanwhile my English mates couldn't wait for the next round of pints during my stay!

Even in restaurants, Dutch servers respect the social space of the patrons and only provide service when beckoned. Therefore, it is quite common to hear Americans lambaste the Dutch service at restaurants, as they are accustomed to a very different style. Americans customarily expect servers to be prompt, readily available and proactive. When Americans' drinks are near completion they expect to receive another one quickly or at least to be asked if they would like another one. Such service in the Netherlands is an intrusion upon one's social space. Dutch servers won't show up at the table unless requested, usually with a hand wave. Many Americans find the hand wave to be rude and too assertive, but such a practice is expected and normal in the Netherlands. Dutch servers have an uncanny ability to observe their patrons using nothing but their peripheral vision. Staring at the patrons or stopping by to see if everything is all right is an intrusion of the patrons' social space. A quick finger in the air is all that is needed for the Dutch server to be at your beckon call, ready to serve your needs.

Respecting Social Space, but not Physical Space!

The Dutch have a tremendous amount of respect for social space, but, ironically, have no regard whatsoever for physical space. Stand in line with the Dutch, whether at the movies, the lunch line or even getting onto a subway and you will invariably find crowding, reaching, bumping and pushing. One would think that living in a shoebox would yield reverence for the physical space as well as the social space, but the Dutch are so accustomed to cramped quarters that being physically close to one another in certain situations is just a normal way of living. While standing in lunch lines at work I've had trays hit me in the back and even armpits in my face as Dutch employees reached over my shoulder to grab something that they couldn't wait another three seconds for. Because everything in the Netherlands is small - except for the people themselves - and also very dense, the Dutch just accept the fact that they are going to be very close to one another. If they didn't accept this fate, they would be very uncomfortable in their houses, cars, restaurants, bathrooms, elevators and everyplace else where they'd be bumping into one another.

How do they fit?

If you're not used to being in uncomfortably tight situations, you better seriously hope that nobody gets on a typically slender Dutch elevator with you. Not too long ago I checked into a hotel in Amsterdam and entered one of these narrow elevators with quite a large duffel bag. I literally took up the entire space in the elevator - or so I thought. As the elevator door was about to close, a characteristically tall Dutchman comes along and without thinking twice proceeds to push his way into the elevator.

In America, this scenario would be out of the question but with the Dutch so used to being in cramped situations, they rarely give a second thought to entering such crowded places. Lo and behold the extremely slow elevator ride was quite uncomfortable as our two faces were mere inches from one another while our bodies were pushed up against each other's and against the walls of the elevator. Needless to say I was disinclined to take any deep breaths for any expansion of the chest would just make matters worse. This mortifying experience for an American like me was just part of a normal day in the life of the Dutchman.

Elevator ride – Dutch style

JUST DO YOUR OWN THING

The Dutch focus on their individual domains, while good-intentioned, can give the impression that they are an aloof and reticent people. This perception can be taken one step further in the work environment, where the Dutch focus on only their own tasks and responsibilities can be construed as laziness. I was initially flabbergasted in the Dutch workplace upon encountering their penchant to do simply what is expected of them and nothing else. This is not to say that the Dutch are not hard workers or good at what they do, but they are extremely focused at their tasks at hand and seldom venture beyond their focal areas.

As an American I'm used to getting most of my questions answered via e-mail. Most questions in the daily business grind are fairly straightforward and only require a simple response. I find that e-mail is a very effective means of conducting this sort of business. In getting into the swing of things in my new job I relied heavily on the e-mail system and sent out a barrage of e-mails to various workers throughout the organization, most of whom I haven't met yet, in order to get off to a good start. With practically zero responses I assumed the e-mail system was down or not functioning properly. I again sent out the same barrage of e-mails to the same group of workers and received the same dismal response. I soon realized that sending e-mail messages to Dutch workers outside of my immediate work area was like sending one into a black hole of nothingness! Turning to the reliable telephone to get in touch with these people produced similar results. Hardly any of my voicemail messages were returned.

In turning to my expatriate colleagues for assistance, they enlightened me by telling me that the only way to get information out of people not in your immediate vicinity is to physically go to their desks and stand over them until I received what I was looking for. As an American, this appeared to be an incredible violation of one's social space, let alone physical space. Tracking people down is usually the last resort in obtaining information.

In the Netherlands, if the information being requested is outside of Dutch workers' responsibilities, you better get ready to tighten up those shoelaces and do some walking! For the next several months, I found myself scaling stairs, traveling to remote facilities and even getting to work early in order to be the first person in peoples' queues to obtain the requisite information in order to do my job effectively. The quickest way for the Dutch to get me out of their social and physical space was simply to give me the information I was looking for. I employed the tactic of many European waiters and waitresses of standing over the person until I received what I was looking for; whereas they received payment for the bill, I received the business information that I was seeking.

This extremely focused behavior transcends the Dutch corporate world into other areas of society. On one particular visit back to Amsterdam I stopped by one of my favorite pubs for a cold one and to converse with one of my Dutch bartender friends. After some casual talk he told me about a particular incident that happened the previous night at the pub. He informed me that there were about twenty Irish tourists having a grand time and just getting warmed up for a night of jollity. The beers were flowing, the Jenever shots were being devoured and the Euros were flying out of their pockets like doves out of a cage. Overall, it started out as an outstanding business night for the pub, with even greater cash flow to be expected for the rest of the evening. My Dutch friend's shift ended at 9 pm and he was then to be relieved by one of his colleagues. 9 pm was soon approaching and no replacement was to be found, which caused great disconcert for my friend. At exactly 9 pm, when his shift was officially over, he stopped serving drinks, made everyone finish their beers and asked all of them to leave, much to the frustration of the Irish revelers. He proceeded to close shop and then went home for the evening. Since working past 9 pm was outside of his work responsibilities, he was willing to perturb a throng of customers, to endure resentful complaints and to forfeit substantial revenue for the pub. Being in total bewilderment upon hearing this story, I had to ask why he didn't just stay a little longer or call his manager. In a typically nonchalant Dutch way he said, "It's not my responsibility." I can't imagine how an American bar owner would react to such a statement from an employee and to the lost profits!

After living and working in the Netherlands for a couple of months it became clear to me that the Dutch strive to perform to expectations, nothing less and nothing more. In fact, only 11% of Dutch men and less than 5% of the women work more than 40 hours a week, the lowest percentage in the developed world. In comparison to other countries, the U.S. is at 80% and 60% and the Czech Republic at 90% and 80%.[3] This is a great disparity indeed in the work mentality of these three nations. You can set your clock to 5 pm every day as the hordes of Dutch workers can be seen departing their employment facilities. I must reiterate that the Dutch do indeed meet the expectations made of them and thoroughly fulfill all of their responsibilities. They perform what is expected of them in the utmost professional and conscientious manner. Anything that falls outside of the realms of their responsibilities, however, is a different story. Residing within their own domains and focusing on their own areas of responsibility are not attributable to laziness or lack of caring, but out of deeply ingrained cultural indoctrinations. The Dutch cherish individual freedom, quality of life and order. Venturing too far outside of their domains can only serve to disrupt these cherished values.

As an American growing up in a capitalistic and competitive environment, it disturbed me greatly observing how the Dutch seemed to strive for mediocrity. Never have I seen such physical potential among a group of peoples. The expression "raising the bar" is used quite often to motivate people to strive for that elusive bar, to tap their full potential in order to achieve excellence. For the Dutch, raising the bar really doesn't serve as a motivator in many aspects of life, even in competitive sports. In Dutch culture, striving for the extreme and doing something outside of the norm is actually looked down upon. A common phrase in the Netherlands is *act normal, that's weird enough*. Striving for financial advancement, chasing the almighty Euro, or spending money excessively is taboo in the Netherlands. This mindset is well represented with their very socialistic government.

Dutch psychoanalyst and novelist Anna Enquist has studied extensively the causes for this Dutch pattern of underachievement. She postulates that the underlying causes for such non-aggressive and non-competitive behavior stems from the Dutch early roots of Calvinism. She cites that the Calvinistic culture makes it deeply shameful to be the best. Furthermore, she stipulates that if you're better than average in Dutch culture you're singled out and criticized. Calvinism teaches that if anything good happens to you it's from god and you must be very humble. But if anything bad happens it's your fault because you've committed some sin or you're not good enough.[4] It's quite common for Dutch students to turn in tests while only completing portions of them once they're confident that they've achieved the minimum standards. Many Dutch students won't exert any more energy in completing the remaining portions, but will be satisfied with meeting the minimum standards. Additionally many Dutch workers will actually decelerate their work efforts in order to finish their tasks on the expected due date rather than finishing up early. The Dutch certainly live within their own domains and do little to break out of that domain in order to avoid bringing too much unwanted attention to themselves.

The Scandinavian countries (Sweden, Denmark, Finland, Norway and Iceland) possess similar views to the Dutch when dealing with individualistic extremism or pompous behavior. As with the Dutch, Scandinavians cherish the liberties and privacy of all individuals, as long as they don't abuse this individualism by possessing a moral high-ground to those around them. Scandinavians greatly abhor self-promotion, boasting and expressions of vanity. In fact, ten commandments have been written in a popular book espousing the virtues of moderation and humility. In *A Refugee Crosses His Tracks*, by Aksel Sandemose, these commandments serve as guiding principles for Scandinavians and calls for socially enforced humility and self-restraint. These Laws of Jante, referred to as *Jantelagen* in Swedish or *Janteloven* in Danish, are as follows:

1. Thou shalt not presume that thou art someone
2. Thou shalt not presume that thou art as good as we
3. Thou shalt not presume that thou art any wiser than we
4. Thou shalt never indulge in the conceit of imaging that thou art better than we
5. Thou shalt not presume that thou art more knowledgeable than we
6. Thou shalt not presume that thou art more important than we
7. Thou shalt not presume that thou art going to amount to anything
8. Thou are not entitled to laugh at us
9. Thou shalt never imagine that anyone cares about thee
10. Thou shalt not suppose that thou can teach us anything

I used to joke with one of my tall, well-built Dutch friends that he should quit his job and join the National Football League in America. His response, typical for a Dutchman, was, "Why would I want to hit somebody and possibly hurt them? Why would I risk the chance of getting hurt myself?" What a far cry from a typical American boy growing up eating his Cheerios salivating at the thought of blind-siding a Quarterback and ripping his head off! My Dutch friend recently had a son, so of course I sent him an American football for his first birthday. Since it's not round and white, however, I'm sure it was tossed into the trash can.

The legendary American coach of the Green Bay Packers, Vince Lombardi, was so fanatical about winning that he stated, "Winning isn't everything, it's the only thing." Mr. Lombardi's audacious statement is reflected in many competitive cultures throughout the world, especially when it comes to competitive sports, and especially world football. In Colombia, for instance, one of the football players, Andres Escobar, was actually brutally murdered by his fellow countrymen upon returning to his homeland after he inadvertently kicked the ball into his own goal in the 1994 World Cup tournament, knocking Colombia out of the tournament. Research at Leicester University, England, has shown that between June 1996 and October 1999 there were three football related murders in England, 5 in Italy and 39 in Argentina, due mainly to fans' passion for their teams and to winning.[5]

The Dutch also have a passion for football and their national team; however, the Dutch penchant for performing to expectations and not being *the tall tree that catches the breeze* even transcends into this extremely competitive realm. To the Dutch it's how you play the game that's important and not whether you win or lose. One of the Netherlands' most admired and best-loved coaches, Foppe de Haan, stated, "Winning is not the most important thing. The most important thing is to play a good game." Other Dutch coaches, fans, players and reporters echo those sentiments about the importance of playing a good game rather than winning at any cost.

The Dutch are extremely contemptible of what they see as the unprofessional football tactics, like "defensive play" as practiced by neighboring countries, such as Italy, Spain and Belgium. Furthermore, they loathe the tactic of kicking the ball into the stands and taking the easy way out instead of trying to continue play. English fans applaud their players for such maneuvers while the Dutch will actually boo this casual style of play. Because Dutch players are not expected to perform or behave in any way that may make them too conspicuous or appear to be striving for the limelight, just as in Dutch society, the players focus at performing to the best of their abilities in the most professional manner.

The Netherlands has only won one major football tournament, the 1986 European tournament, although experts of at the game feel that they possess the talent to have won many more. This lackluster winning percentage is clearly indicative of the Dutch approach to performing to expectations and living within one's own domain. The Dutch coach Leo Beenhakker summarizes the Dutch mindset by stating:

> *"At a world cup or a European Championship, ninety percent of the teams are there to win. But there's always one country who only wants to show how good they are. And that's Holland. It's our drama. With all our talent, our technical and tactical skills, our offensive football, we have only once won a major tournament and that was by accident. We love the game, but we lack something. We are like a boxer who boxes very well but doesn't have a knockout punch. We don't have the mentality to take him by the throat, but sometimes you have to ...(squishes throat) strangle? Yeah. We have no killer touch. That's been the problem during the whole history of our football."[6]*

For the Dutch it's much better to come in third place while playing a good, professional game than by coming in first place playing sloppily or haughtily.

While the Dutch are applauded for having one of the highest qualities of life and one of the highest life expectancies in the world, undoubtedly attributed to their restrained and undemonstrative lifestyles, critics of the Dutch point out that such impassivity and indifference is harmful in an ever-shrinking, communal world. The Dutch are still criticized for their blasé and careless attitude during the time leading up to the Nazi invasion of WWII. The Dutch didn't take the necessary precautions in preparing for such an attack, even though the Nazi war machine was amassing troops and machinery all along the Dutch border. Critics state that the Dutch just continued on with their normal lifestyles with blind obedience to their daily rituals. The Dutch initial resistance to the invasion lasted only five day, leading to their humiliating defeat and agonizing five-year occupation. Even during the occupation, it is said that the Dutch turned a blind eye toward the horrific atrocities being committed. In fact, more Jews were deported from the Netherlands than from any other Western

European city.[7] Even more distressing is that only one in seven Dutch Jews survived the war, and in the city of Amsterdam, only one in sixteen.[8] These figures are truly staggering and disturbing, but it must also be pointed out that there were many heroic men and women in the Dutch Resistance that went well above and beyond the call of duty.

More recently, an event occurred in Bosnia where the massacre of over 7,000 unarmed men and boys were brutally killed as Dutch peacekeepers stood by. In 1995, Bosnian Serb forces overran the enclave of Srebrenica, which was under United Nations protection and at the time under the protection of Dutch peacekeepers. Over 200 Dutch peacekeepers were responsible for patrolling the area when the massacre took place. It has been reported that the Dutch government and troops didn't exercise proper judgment and didn't take the necessary steps to avert the massacre. This incident so severely shocked the Netherlands that the entire cabinet of Prime Minister Wim Kok resigned.

These two historical events are surely black eyes for the Dutch and much guilt is felt over them. All countries have ominous episodes at one time or another. What is important is how a country deals with its past to ensure that evil history doesn't repeat itself. Today the Netherlands is one of the biggest contributors to philanthropic causes throughout the world. The Dutch constantly struggle with some of their past and continuously search for ways to make the world a better place. In walking along the beautiful canals and 17th century townhouses several of my Dutch friends commented how shameful it is that these picturesque buildings were built with the riches obtained from their forebears by plundering and exploiting all parts of the world. Upon encountering persons representing charitable organizations such as the Salvation Army, the Dutch, who are notoriously known for their frugality, are quick to reach into their pockets to make donations. It's quite common for one of these charity collectors to walk into restaurants and bars seeking money from patrons. As I felt it was an incredible intrusion upon my privacy for a person to shake a tin can in front of my face while trying to enjoy a meal, the Dutch went out of their way to make their generous donations. In America such solicitation is detested and management usually throws these solicitors out before they disturb any of their patrons. The Dutch passion for a better world and, perhaps, their guilt over their questionable past cause the Dutch to be amenable to having even their sacred social space violated in certain situations.

It is evident that the Dutch are committed to the virtues of individuality and personal space. These concepts may be difficult for outsiders to embrace but an effort should be made to understand. In so doing, visitors will feel more comfortable in Dutch society and can more fully appreciate and enjoy the experience and unique charm of the Netherlands.

Behind all of the activity, especially in big cities like Amsterdam, are the tenets of order, decency and consistency that produce a somewhat yielding chaos or acquiescent pandemonium. Much like busy little bees, the Dutch go about their business, which appears at times to be sheer madness, in their unique, methodical ways and in the end produce their own intricate, tightly woven beehive in the form of an orderly, conforming societal structure.

One might think that with the heavy emphasis placed on individuality and the obdurate protection of the rights of each and every individual that the Netherlands would comprise a population of nonconformists, anarchists and rabble-rousers. It's true that the Netherlands has seen its share of radicals, most notably the *Provos* of the 1960s - protestors similar to those demonstrating throughout the world during that tumultuous era. However, overall members of Dutch society are law-abiding, conforming and particularly orderly. Even though the individual members of Dutch society have carte blanche to do just about whatever they please, the Netherlands remains, remarkably, one of the most orderly and conforming countries in the world.

This issue of societal conformity versus individuality has been raised in a philosophical debate amongst officers of the U.S. military who pose the question of "What's more important, the overall mission or the lives of the individual soldiers?" This sensitive issue has even resulted in the Reserve Officer Training Corps (ROTC) program adopting the motto, "Mission first, people always." Though the motto doesn't directly answer the question, it communicates the utmost importance of both the mission and the soldiers. In Dutch society, a similar motto can be postulated, "Societal conformity first, individualism always." Although individualism is revered intensely, each and every individual is expected to abide by the laws of society and to adhere to the prescribed societal norms. Much like fraternal twins, individualism and societal conformity are distinctly different but in Dutch culture they are remarkably intertwined.

Examples of the important role of orderliness in Dutch life may be found in the home where dinner is steadfastly served at 6:00 in the evening and coffee at 7:00. These daily rituals are not to be interrupted for just about anything, for they are cherished traditions in Dutch culture. In fact, one of my Dutch colleagues who accepted a position for a firm which required shift work and off-hours support, negotiated contractually to be free of any obligation from the hours of 6:00 to 7:00 in the evening for that was when he had dinner with his family. He was willing to sacrifice a career advancement in order to preserve this time-honored tradition of his family. This request was granted without question by the management of the firm. To do otherwise would show disdain for deeply ingrained Dutch cultural characteristics.

Dutch homes themselves are legendary for their cleanliness and orderliness. The Dutch possess a peculiar custom of leaving the curtains wide-open with the lights shining brightly so that everyone can see the inside...although no one is expected to look. Looking would be a major intrusion of their dearly beloved social space. Dutch families keep their curtains open to show that they have nothing to hide and that their homes are clean and orderly in accordance to the unwritten rules of Dutch society. Closed curtains lead to suspicion; passer-bys may assume that residents are hiding something behind these closed curtains and are not living up to the societal expectations bestowed upon them. Such a custom, although peculiar to some, strengthens and enforces Dutch societal order and conformity.

On numerous occasions I would depart the bustling city life of Amsterdam to appreciate the serenity and peacefulness of the Dutch countryside and to enjoy the comforts of the numerous small towns. In wandering around these small towns I noticed an uncanny likeness in the appearance and arrangement of all of the houses. With their curtains wide open, I was able to peer through their unusually large windows, as clandestinely as I could of course, and see the entirety of their homes and as far as their backyards. The insides of all of the homes were meticulously clean, fairly simplistic in their furniture arrangements and never cluttered. The outsides of the homes also portrayed a neatness and orderliness that is testament to the fastidiousness of its inhabitants. The Dutch garden, no matter how small, is one of the most cherished attributes of Dutch culture. These gardens can be found in both the front and backyards of Dutch houses, and more often than not, the Dutch can be found scrupulously cultivating these gardens. Finding a weed in a Dutch garden is analogous to finding that proverbial needle in a haystack. Beyond the manicured gardens, the porches, walkways and even sidewalks are laboriously swept and scrubbed to ensure spotlessness and to ensure conformity with their persnickety neighbors. One can say that this behavior is predicated upon the notion of keeping up with the Joneses, or in this case the von Joneses. Not doing their part in conforming to neighborhood standards would surely result in the sneers and discontent of their fastidious neighbors.

The Dutch insatiable desire for cleanliness and order has been observed and written about for centuries. Even the early Dutch settlers to New York City, or *Nieuw Amsterdam*, were infamous for their immaculate homes and painstaking measures to keep them that way. Washington Irving, author of the world-renowned novels of *Legend of Sleepy Hollow* and *Rip van Winkle*, wrote about the industrious Dutch and their pristine homes in his first novel *A Knickerbocker's History of New York* under the pseudonym of Diedrich Knickerbocker:

> *"In those good days of simplicity and sunshine, a passion for cleanliness was the leading principle in domestic economy, and the universal test of an able housewife — a character which formed the utmost ambition of our unenlightened grandmothers. The front door was never opened except on marriages, funerals, new years' days the festival of St. Nicholas, or some such great occasion. It was ornamented with a gorgeous brass knocker, curiously wrought, sometimes in the device of a dog, and sometimes of a lion's head, and was daily burnished*

with such religious zeal, that it was oft-times worn out by the very precautions taken for its preservation. The whole house was constantly in a state of inundation, under the discipline of mops and brooms and scrubbing brushes; and the good housewives of those days were a kind of amphibious animal, delighting exceedingly to be dabbling in water.

The great parlour was the sanctum sanctorum, where the passion for cleaning was indulged without control. In this sacred apartment no one was permitted to enter, excepting the mistress and her confidential maid, who visited it once a week, for the purpose of giving it a thorough cleaning, and putting things to rights — always taking the precaution of leaving their shoes at the door, and entering devoutly on their stocking-feet. After scrubbing the floor, sprinkling it with fine white sand, which was curiously stroked into angles, and curves, and rhomboids, with a broom — after washing the windows, rubbing and polishing the furniture, and putting a new bunch of evergreens in the fire-place — the window shutters were again closed to keep out the flies, and the room carefully locked up until the revolution of time brought round the weekly cleaning day."[1]

Washington Irving would be pleased to know that the Dutch haven't lost their proclivity for cleanliness and order even in today's frenzied world. As a rather interesting aside, the term Knickerbocker, which is widely used today, especially in the New York region, is a direct result of Washington Irving's first book where he used the pseudonym Diedrich Knickerbocker. Irving conceived the name Knickerbocker when he was twenty six years old in 1809. The word *Knickerbocker* has come to signify any descendant of the original Dutch settlers to the *Nieuw Nederlands*, modern day New York, New Jersey, parts of Delaware and Connecticut. The word *knickerbockers* (lower-case k), or *knickers*, is used to identify those loose fitting breeches tucked in below the knee that were an integral part of the clothing of those early Dutch settlers. The basketball team, the N.Y. Knicks (capital K), derives its name from this legendary author and pays homage to the early Dutch settlers of the New York metropolitan region. Very few New Yorkers, even sports enthusiasts, know the true meaning or origins of the name of their beloved team, the Knicks. At least one common attribute still exists between today's basketball players on the Knicks and the early Dutch settlers from which their name is derived – their extreme height!

The layout and structure of the countryside is testament to the Dutch penchant for order and detail; straight ditches, unswerving canals and symmetric, rectangular fields abound the Dutch landscape. The Dutch suburbs are even neatly structured and arranged with modest homes and proportioned yards. The electrical and telephone cables are even neatly buried underground to avoid disorderly appearances found in so many parts of the world. You won't see the unsightly mess as shown below anywhere in the Netherlands!

Manmade Spider web in beautiful Hoboken, New Jersey

The Dutch are passionate planners and they intensely prepare for just about everything. Intense planning even stretches to the realm of determining where street signs should be placed in cities and towns. The calculated placement of these street signs ensures that orderliness is maintained for there will be fewer lost pedestrians or motorists disrupting the instinctive, orderly flow of society. The Dutch have some of the most peculiar street signs that I've ever seen. The street sign depicted below is placed strategically in the Red Light District, providing passer-bys, and in many cases drunken revelers, with valuable information.

No need to understand the language with this sign

The buildings across the Netherlands are orderly and consistent in size and architecture. There are hardly any skyscrapers or elaborately designed building. As the Dutch abhor pretentious people who stick out in society, they detest high peaks and prefer to keep everything level, like their landscape. As the Dutch adage goes, "*When your head is above the level of the grass it will be cut off.*" The Dutch prefer everything level and unassuming, just like their terrain. Anything to the contrary simply serves to disrupt the order and conformity they so acutely desire.

Must be on Time!

Every time I return to Amsterdam I am immediately amazed with what appears to be the amount of organized mayhem, or controlled anarchy as my lady friend at the cocktail party so precisely described. In departing Centraal Train Station, usually jet-lagged and bleary-eyed, I am immediately awoken with the intensity of the activity transpiring throughout the city. There is an abundance of focused pedestrians, resolute cyclists, speeding cars and busses, rambling streetcars (trams), canal boats disappearing and emerging underneath the plethora of bridges and obvious tourists struggling for survival, darting in and out of all of this bedlam.

For the newly arrived tourist to Amsterdam, this is indeed pandemonium, but to the Dutch it's just their natural societal flow. As long as everyone stays focused on his or her own mode of transport and doesn't interrupt other modes, the orderly flow of traffic is maintained. Nothing infuriates the Dutch more than absent-minded pedestrians drifting into sections of the numerous bike paths causing cyclists to slow down or even coming to an abrupt halt; such transgressions interrupt the natural societal flow causing much maligned disorder. Speeding Dutch cyclists convincingly warn unsuspecting pedestrians who have wandered onto the bike paths by vigorously ringing their bike bells, usually causing sudden panic in the pedestrians. This sudden panic, invariably, causes them to immediately scurry back to their own walkways and that alarming bell leaves indelible impressions upon them causing them to be cognizant of where they are walking at all times.

With all of this activity, you can set your watch to the arrivals and departures of the trams and trains. Even with all of the pedestrians, cyclists and motorists engulfing the streets, the infamous Dutch trams and buses miraculously make their tight timelines. Anything but on-time arrivals and departures is simply not acceptable to the Dutch. In those rare instances when they may be running a little behind schedule, the resourceful, yet impatient, Dutch anxiously check their watches with looks of perturbment. Drivers of these trams and busses are unyielding in their pursuit for on-time arrivals and departures. It is highly advisable to stay out of the paths of these resolute drivers for they don't offer much leeway for careless pedestrians. Throughout the city people are constantly running frantically out of the way of oncoming trams and busses. In fact, one time when I carelessly wandered approximately one foot into a bus lane I was actually hit by a bus knocking me back onto the sidewalk! It was a good thing that I had my laptop computer bag on the side facing the bus to absorb most of the blow. Instead of being apologetic, the bus driver shot me a derisive scowl as if to say, "That'll teach you for being in my bus lane." Getting hit by one of the thunderous, intimidating tram machines would not have resulted in such an innocuous ending.

Dutch services such as refuse collection and street cleaning also adhere to strict time guidelines. The intense and deliberate planning that the Dutch put into everything enables these services to be consistently on time and thorough. Additionally, stores open up at the prescribed times and prescribed dates, not a minute before and not a minute later. Even if Dutch merchants are prepared to open shop early, they will still wait to open up at the exact opening hour, even if there are customers waiting. Being on time is indeed a Dutch characteristic. When something is supposed to occur at 1:00 pm, 1:02 is not acceptable. Being on time applies to services, meetings, social and business functions, family affairs and just about everything else where a start time is applicable. All societal members must adhere to this Dutch tradition of timeliness in order for their time-honored system to work. Not doing so ruins the whole system causing a dire chain of events; if one person or train is late for an appointment or station stop, then the schedules of all parties are detrimentally affected for the rest of the day.

In Spain and many of the Latin American countries, such strict adherence to time schedules is simply not honored and is even detested. These Latin cultures have a much more relaxed attitude towards meeting their time commitments. In the Spanish cultures, there is much leeway in attending to appointments. In many circumstances, especially social ones, it's not uncommon for people to show up at 11:45 for an 11:00 appointment and not consider themselves late. In most social situations, an hour leeway is an acceptable time period to show up for an engagement. Additionally, schedules don't rule supreme in these cultures. Missing a scheduled appointment, with proper justification, is not necessarily a bad thing and doesn't bring their daily lives to a screeching halt.

The Dutch live and breathe according to their schedules. They are constantly abreast of the time of day or night. Clocks can be found almost anywhere in the Netherlands and the Dutch frequently check their wristwatches to constantly remind themselves of the exact time. Most of the Dutch, even children, carry planning calendars with them and use them frequently. Once an appointment is set in a person's planner, that person's time is allocated for that appointment and nothing else. Appointments are strictly planned from hour to hour. Always being on time is fundamental in order for everyone to make all of their appointments at the prescribed times. The Dutch always know where they are going to be or what they are going to be doing at any given time. For this reason, unexpected visits and even chance encounters are severely loathed. Someone not familiar with Dutch culture who shows up unexpectedly, even during non-working hours, may be mortified with the Dutch frigid welcome, terse conversation and obvious desire for the unannounced visit to conclude so they can get on with their planned activities.

Arriving late, showing up without prior notice and taking more time than what was allocated only serves to disrupt the Dutch penchant for orderly lifestyles. *Tipping over the applecart* is not advisable in Dutch culture. In other cultures a popular maxim is *the squeaky wheel gets a greasing*, meaning that the person who persistently makes the most noise and who constantly stands out in the crowd will be rewarded because of the lasting impression, no matter how obnoxious it may be. The Dutch, meanwhile, won't provide any grease for those squeaky wheels.

A somewhat trivial observation that I made, but one which really shows the genuineness of the Dutch approbation for timeliness and exactness, is that the clocks in all of the pubs and restaurants are set to the exact time. This may seem rather inconsequential, but in the U.S., just about all of the pubs have their clocks set fifteen minutes or more ahead of time. The justification for setting the clocks ahead of time is to mislead the patrons into thinking it's later than it really is so they leave earlier than the closing time allowing the staff to close up on time. Additionally, bartenders have more leverage in dealing with the drunks who are trying to get one more for the road. Although done with good intentions, the Dutch would abhor such deception and demand that the clocks be set to the exact times.

DUTCH CONFORMITY

Everybody is expected to be a decent citizen in Dutch culture and to act decently in conformance to Dutch norms. This means that people are expected to be cordial; keep their houses, windows and sidewalks clean; be presentable; and to adhere to the norms of society. This mindset can be found in all of the service establishments throughout the country, such as restaurants, pubs, hotels, and other businesses. On a recent trip to Amsterdam a friend commented to me, "The service industry is still alive in Holland." By the tone of his voice I can tell there was some resentment towards the service industries back in his homeland and in other countries he had visited.

The service in all of these establishments is remarkably similar; everyone is professionally dressed, very polite but not overly courteous, and certain minimum standards can be expected of the establishments such as cleanliness and freshness. In fact, a bartender will never pour a beer in the same glass without properly cleaning the glass first or using a new one. A rather unique Dutch custom that bartenders perform is scraping the excess foam from the tops of the glasses before serving a beer. I've never seen this in any other country, except in the *Nederlandia* portion of Belgium where adherence to Dutch customs is prevalent. Most bartenders don't know why they perform such a custom. I've asked numerous bartenders and the usual response I get is, "Everybody else does it." As can be deduced from such comments, conformity is valued in Dutch culture and people rarely sway from established conformance. The reason that they perform this unique custom is to ensure that everybody is served the same amount of beer, nothing less and nothing more. The Dutch expect to be served exactly what they pay for. By scraping off the excess foam, a Dutch customer can be assured he is getting the appropriate amount of beer and not an excess amount of foam. An appropriate amount of foam in Dutch society is the width of two fingers. Amazingly, just about each and every beer I was served in Holland had exactly two fingers width of foam! The Dutch expect to be on a level playing field with everyone else; if one person gets preferential treatment, then others are being taking advantage of. *The squeaky wheels don't get a greasing.*

Due to this desire for a level playing field and consistency across the board, Dutch bartenders won't offer *buy backs* for patrons. Nothing is *on the house* in the Netherlands. Adopting such a custom would merely disrupt the Dutch natural societal flow and introduce greatly maligned disparity. The Dutch expect to pay for all of their drinks and if they have to pay for their drinks, so should everybody else. Otherwise, some members of society will be taken advantage of and, thus, the level field becomes askew. Since the Dutch expect decent service, cleanliness and consistency, tipping is not customary. They feel that since such service is expected and demanded as per Dutch culture, tipping is unnecessary. The usual custom is to just round up to the nearest Euro.

The Dutch cultural characteristic of conformity and attitude towards tipping varies greatly from that of the U.S. In the U.S., tipping is a core component to the services industry and better service usually dictates higher tipping. Furthermore, Americans expect to have a round or two of drinks bought for them if they've been imbibing for a while. If such rounds aren't bought for them, the tips are usually lessened or even eliminated. Americans will frequent establishments where they know they will be taken care of with *on the house* drinks and avoid places where they won't. The customary tip in America for good, decent service is fifteen to twenty percent. For exceptional service the tips will exceed twenty percent and for poorer service they will drop below ten percent and may even reach zero.

With such an incentives-based model in place, services vary greatly from establishment to establishment. Servers who give extraordinary service and work in a popular establishment can do extremely well for themselves financially. Coveted Friday and Saturday nights are reserved for those who have paid their dues and have earned the right to work these lucrative evenings. In some of the trendy hotspots in the big cities, for instance, it's not uncommon for servers and bartenders to rake in salaries of six figures a year, most of which is under the table. The Dutch don't believe in the notion of getting something for nothing or having such a disparity in the quality of service. To them conformity is the only way of ensuring that nobody benefits and nobody gets taken advantage of, thus keeping their cultural playing field level.

Although it may seem rather trite to analogize Dutch conformity with that of their tavern rituals and beer consumption, Dutch beer and comfortable, cozy taverns are as integral to Dutch society as just about anything else. In fact, today there are approximately

1,200 taverns in Amsterdam alone, most noted for their fine quality beer and to a lesser degree, Jenever, or Dutch gin. Beer drinking and gathering at the local tavern has always been an integral part of Dutch culture. In fact, In Haarlem during the 1570s there were already 50 operating breweries and 50 years later that number had doubled. In Amsterdam alone, in 1590, there were 180 breweries![2] (Although not nearly as many breweries populate the Netherlands today, the Dutch still preserve that time-honored tradition of unwinding and conversing with locals over a few cold beers after an honest day's work). Today Heineken, Amsterdam's biggest brewery, is world-renowned and is in the top three of the world's best selling beers along with Budweiser and Guinness.

As Dutch as it gets!

I was asked recently by a colleague embarking upon a journey to Amsterdam, "Can you recommend any good bars or restaurants?" I started thinking about my response and was about to rattle off a few of my favorite places then hesitated and simply informed him that they're all very good. I told him just about any place you go will be extremely clean; have decent, professional service; and won't vary too much from the next place. I've tried them all, from 5-star restaurants to local Mom and Pop shops and the consistency in service and quality is remarkable. Being that the Dutch abhor extravagance and excess, even the higher-end restaurants display an unassuming nature and the service is consistent with all other eateries throughout the country. Regardless of where one goes, the coffee will always be freshly made and refills will never be served with the same cup and saucer. Additionally, as part of a Dutch custom, all cups of coffee will be served with a single cookie or biscuit to enjoy with the freshly made coffee. Hardly any restaurants or cafes, deviate from such Dutch customs and etiquette, no matter how high or low scale the establishment.

Rules are Rules

With the numerous liberal social policies and the live-and-let-live attitudes of the Dutch, foreigners usually view the Netherlands as a country with very few rules and regulations. Quite the contrary, the Netherlands is laden with an inordinate amount of strict laws for just about all aspects of society. Expatriates who come to live and work in the Netherlands expecting free reign are surprised, and even frustrated, with the tight control that exists in order to preserve the highly sought after societal order and conformity. Expatriates often complain about the numerous bureaucracies and red tape they encounter when trying to settle into their new lifestyles. Obtaining certain societal privileges that were rather easily acquired in their homelands turn out to be quite hassles for expatriates in the Netherlands. Prolonged waiting periods, extensive paperwork and strict codes exist for privileges such as residence permits, work permits and driver's licenses. Innocuous activities such as placing a fence or planting a tree in a yard require approval from the local authorities and even rigid licenses. Building designers and contractors find it very difficult obtaining approval and securing the required licenses in order to construct new edifices. Local boards scrutinize every last detail in order to ensure conformance to societal specifications and that the designs are aesthetically pleasing, but not overly pleasing, as the Dutch strive for moderation in all aspects of life.

Because of the strict rules and detailed planning that is pervasive in all aspects of Dutch society, entrepreneurship is often times stifled. In addition to the required licenses needed for just about everything, entrepreneurs must even exhibit certain qualifications to prove that they are worthy of such ambitions. Furthermore, Dutch authorities actually control the amount of competition that exists within a certain radius within city or town limits. Too many competing entities operating in proximity to one another cause over-competition which only serves to disrupt the harmony and order of Dutch society. This mentality is starkly in contrast with that of the other countries where if a McDonalds is located on a busy street corner, chances are great that a Burger King is across the street, a Wendy's cattycorner and other competing fast food chains nearby. In fact, business models of many corporations call for allowing the number one business in their market to make the first move and then to follow in their footsteps executing the exact maneuver in the exact location. Since the Dutch exhibit both socialistic and capitalistic tendencies, societal order and harmony must not be sacrificed with rampant commercial competition.

Once a decision is made or once a rule or regulation is put into effect, the Dutch will follow it steadfastly and without question. This unwavering support and strict adherence to policy often times leads to inflexibility and even irrationality. A common phrase often heard in the Netherlands is *dat kan niet*, or that's impossible, which is testament to their unwillingness to bend the rules or to deviate even slightly from established procedures. Expatriates and even Dutch nationals are often times frustrated in dealing with the numerous bureaucracies in applying for certain permits or seeking to obtain certain licenses. Much to the chagrin of these expats and Dutch nationals, the answer they hear quite often to many of their requests is simply *dat kan niet*.

A personal encounter of mine in dealing with the staff of a reputable hotel chain in Amsterdam illustrates this Dutch unyielding commitment to rules and regulations. I was residing in a corporate suite of a rather notable hotel for six months, consistently paying my bills on time, spending lavishly at the hotel restaurant and bar, and being an overall solid and reliable customer to the hotel. Prior to embarking back to the States, I decided to take advantage of the inexpensive flights on KLM and take one last weekend trip to another country in Europe. I traveled to Austria on that weekend to reflect on my incredible European experience and to purchase trinkets for my family and friends back home. It was a perfect ending to an amazing chapter of my life.

That perfect ending came to an abrupt halt upon my return to the hotel in Amsterdam. My magnetic key didn't work in the door, so I went down to the front desk to receive a new one or to have it reprogrammed. I informed the young lady behind the counter of the situation and she replied, in the usual stoic Dutch manner, "Sir, we had to move all of your belongings to another room in another building because you were scheduled to depart yesterday." Thinking she was obviously confused or mistook me for someone else I told her that I've been at the hotel for six months and that my departure date was in two days. Again as unemotionally as possible she stated, "Sir, you are clearly scheduled in the computer to depart yesterday so we had to remove all of your belongings and put them in another room in another building." Realizing now that there was no confusion or case of mistaken identity, I thought of the pain of settling into a new room as the hour of midnight was upon us. My mild demur turned to that of total incredulity; I couldn't believe that such rigidity could be possible. Furthermore, I deliberated on all of my belongings, and especially my high-value items that I even kept hidden, and began to dread the possibilities of anything missing.

After several minutes of discussing the issue at hand with the young lady I then asked to speak with the manager. Again I received the similar responses that it's company policy to remove the belongings once the computer shows that a customer's time has expired. I accentuated the fact that I'd been a corporate resident at the hotel for six months, always paying my monthly bills on time and even spending generously in the restaurant and lounge. It didn't matter; my time was up so out the door I went.

The manager told me that they tried calling me to inquire about the status of my departure date. I did receive a call from the hotel on my mobile phone when I was in Austria, but didn't answer for I didn't want to be bothered on my last weekend retreat in Europe. I assumed that if there was a matter of importance that the caller would leave me a message. No message was left. It's clear that the hotel's policy is to call the customer prior to rummaging through their personal belongings, but the regulations don't state to leave a message or to call more than once. A simple voice message would have alleviated this entire mess. However, I'm sure the Dutch hotel staff member referenced the policy and saw that it called for making one phone call, nothing less and nothing more. A simple voice mail message would have been going way above and beyond the call of duty, and to a Dutch person that means venturing outside of his or her beloved own domain.

Shortly thereafter I had the dubious privilege of dealing with the heavy bureaucracy of the Amsterdam Police, for there were indeed high-value items missing from my belongings. I tried in vain for several months to track down my missing items with numerous queries to the hotel staff, concierges and cleaning people, but eventually capitulated. The conversations with the cleaning people, who had the onerous chore of moving my belongings, were quite futile for they didn't speak English, or even Dutch for that matter; they were recent immigrants from African countries who were brought in to the country to fulfill the numerous job vacancies. At this point I would have been satisfied with an offer of a complimentary weekend hotel stay for my troubles. Such a small gesture is not only appreciated in the U.S., but expected. I did receive a rather lengthy letter from the hotel management which exhaustively detailed the rules and regulations of their missing items policy. Although the hotel management expressed their deepest apologies for my losses and inconvenience, they didn't offer any kind of hospitable gesture to try to make amends for this unfortunate event. I guess if you can't get a beer on the house in the Netherlands after a night of imbibing, since that would give one an unfair advantage over others, a free hotel room is out of the question.

TRIBAL COLLECTIVISM

As distant and independent each member of Dutch society appears to be, an underlying fundamental common bond perpetuates that unifies these societal members. This unification of the Dutch can be viewed as a sort of tribal collectivism; each individual member of society yearns for commonality, homogeneity and familiarity. In considering the origins of the Germanic tribe that settled this inhospitable, marshy wasteland of Northern Europe, and the endeavors of its current inhabitants just to stay dry, it's no wonder that such tribal collectivism exists. Legendary coach Mike Krzyzewski of the Duke University basketball program states, "People want to be on a team. They want to be part of something bigger than themselves. They want to be in a situation where they feel that they are doing something for the greater good."[3] Knowing that their homelands can be engulfed in a torrent of sea water upon any given wicked storm, the Dutch are cognizant of their perpetual vulnerability. This tenuous situation leaves the Dutch longing for communalism and to be part of something bigger than themselves.

This tribal collectivism can be observed in many facets of Dutch culture. When I first arrived in the Netherlands and made my initial observations I concluded that the Dutch were people who liked to *jump on the latest bandwagons.* Whether it was fashion, music or other forms of entertainment, when the Dutch embraced something, they embraced it fervently. I was amazed in observing the usually mild-mannered, reserved Dutch go absolutely ballistic when the trendy, flavor of the week song came over the airwaves. The busy little bees would stop everything they were doing, turn up the volume and lose themselves in song and dance for the duration of the song. Even a quiet, cozy pub would erupt with enthusiasm upon hearing the song that was all the rage. Rather remarkably, one can guarantee that all activities ceased in every establishment throughout the country at the time when that trendy song came on the radio or when the video came on the television. As soon as the song ended, it was back to business as usual; the volume was turned down and the industrious Dutch continued with their duties. With the Dutch wholeheartedly embracing the latest musical hit, that song could be heard throughout the day more times than imaginable, eliciting the same frenzied response each time. Once a new flavor of the week came along, however, it was out with the old and in with the new without skipping a beat. Just as the Dutch support decisions once they are made with unwavering support, they collectively firmly embrace the latest trends with tribal passion.

Homogeneity is evident in the Dutch manners of fashion. Once again, once the latest fashion trend has been established, nobody would be seen without sporting that trend. In walking around a city such as Amsterdam, it would appear that the Dutch are all wearing the same clothes. With the conservative nature of the Dutch and the unremitting mist, these fashions aren't going to start any major trends in sub-tropical climates around the world. The Dutch prefer dark colors, notably black, and overall neatness in the way they dress. When I was living in the Netherlands, the latest trend was to cuff the pant legs approximately three or four inches. It was mind-boggling at first witnessing everybody, and I mean everybody, walking around with extremely wide pant cuffs. Fashion designers have been known to use Amsterdam as a test bed for trialing out their latest designs since they know that if a certain style takes off, it will take off like wildfire.

Tribal collectivism in its rawest form can be found in the Netherlands on *Koninginnedag*, or Queen's day. *Koninginnedag* is the celebration for the Queen's official birthday and is celebrated on April 30th of every year. April 30th is actually *not* the official birthday of the reigning queen, Queen Beatrix. This date is the birthday of Queen's Beatrix's mother, Queen Juliana. On the day of Queen Beatrix's investiture, she desired to keep the official holiday on April 30th out of reverence for her mother. The first official Queen's Day celebration occurred August 31, 1891 after the death of King William III and when Wilhelmina received her appointment to queen. The reason for this celebration was to promote national unity and to mark the end of the summer. National unity is clearly evident on this day as throngs of Dutch revel in the streets clad in Dutch orange from head to toe waving the national flag high above their heads. The Dutch cannot specifically state why they celebrate this day with such zeal and revelry; most state that it's just the thing to do on Queen's day. The Dutch absolutely adore the queen and never a bad word is said about her. If negative comments are made in reference to the queen, the Dutch will zealously come to her aid defending her with the justification that she is not present to defend herself. Ironically, very few Dutch can state why they adore the queen so much or why having a monarch is a good thing. Supporting and venerating the queen with unyielding fervor is just another example of Dutch collective tribalism.

Football is the national passion in the Netherlands. The usually mild-mannered Dutch are fanatical for their beloved national team. On game day the Dutch can be found waving their colors enthusiastically with orange wigs and cramming into the trains to get to the stadium. The modern day Dutch deplore the stereotype that they still wear wooden shoes, but on game day I've actually observed giant Dutchmen walking around in those very same wooden shoes. Such a sight is certainly worth the price of a ticket!

After a major victory, the Dutch celebrate with cheers and singing in the city centers. Rembrandtplein, Leidseplein and the Dam Square are mobbed with raucous beer drinking revelers. Even non-football enthusiasts are out in the streets celebrating. When I inquired into why even the non-sports fans partied in the streets after a victory, the usual response I received was, "It's just what you have to do...If you're Dutch you simply have to do certain things." Football plays a major role in keeping Dutch tribal collectivism strong. In fact, the biggest party ever seen in the Netherlands after Liberation day in 1945 was when the Dutch national team beat their archrivals, the Germans, in 1998.

SMOKING

Tobacco has always played an essential role in Dutch culture. As with many other Europeans, the Dutch are passionate about their tobacco. Although the number of smokers has dissipated in recent years, large segments of their population still carry on the age-old tradition of cigarette and pipe smoking. It comes as no surprise that the oldest cafes in the Netherlands are referred to as *Bruin* (brown) cafes due to the tarnishing of the ceilings and walls from so much tobacco smoke over the years. In the mid 18th century, French traveler Grosley counted three hundred smokers in a single modest inn at Rotterdam and complained that the Dutch were so indifferent to the poisoning of confined spaces that the fumes from traveling barges drove foxes from their lairs as they passed. [4] Upon entering a café or pub in the Netherlands, one can expect to immediately be besieged by a hazy cloud of tobacco smoke in cramped quarters.

The vast amount of smokers in the Netherlands is directly attributable to the tribal collectivism mentality that pervades throughout the country. Teenagers fondly remember their dads smoking pipes in the evenings when they were growing up. Many smoke simply because they don't want to stick out in the crowd by being a rare non-smoker, since *the one whose head is above the crowd will get it chopped off*. The Dutch, being seafaring people living in an international hub of commerce and tourism, have even left an indelible mark upon other lands and visitors with their incessant smoking. A common observation at home and abroad was that "a Hollander without a pipe is a national impossibility, akin to a town without a house, a stage without actors, a spring without flowers. If a Hollander should be bereft of his pipe of tobacco he could not blissfully enter heaven". [5]

Recent earth shattering legislation called for the cessation of all smoking in public places starting in the year 2004. What an incredible transition considering the Dutch penchant for smoking and going out. "Holland," wrote Claude Saumaise, "is a country where the demon gold is seated on a throne of cheese, and crowned with tobacco".[6]   Holland may just have to find another crown if this legislation remains unchallenged. The reason for such legislation is for the protection of the multitude of employees working in the exceedingly smoky bars and restaurants throughout the country. Once again the Dutch are showing their innate respect for the rights of the individual. In this particular case, however, the rights of the few may be stampeding on the rights of the many. It will be interesting to see if the masses rise up in solidarity in an attempt to evoke such legislation. But with the Dutch, once a decision is made there's usually no turning back.

Gezelligheid – Dutch Coziness

Another reason the Dutch maintain such societal order and conformity is in their endless pursuit of *gezelligheid*. *Gezelligheid* is a Dutch term that isn't easily translated into English. *Gezelligheid* is very similar to coziness, contentment, or a sort of mild happiness resulting from being in a comfortable, stress free atmosphere. A Dutchman smoking and drinking with close friends in a small, cozy pub is an example of *gezelligheid*. A woman working in her small garden on a sunny day is another form of *gezelligheid*. In fact, the universal desire for almost all Dutch men and women above everything else is to have gardens in their front and backyards. Being stuck in a traffic jam or being hurried in a frenzied restaurant is certainly not *gezelligheid*. The Dutch strive for this state of mild happiness in just about everything they do. For this reason, it's not uncommon for visitors to find the Dutch rather nonchalant and laid back.

The Dutch *gezelligheid* is very similar to the German *Gemuetlichkeit*, which can be heard in the famous beer drinking and toasting song:

> *Ein prosit* (a toast)
> *Ein prosit*
> *Gemuetlichkeit.*
> *Ein prosit*

Ein prosit
Gemuetlichkeit
Ein, zwei, drei, G' suffa! (1, 2, 3 chug!)

As with the Dutch *gezelligheid*, the German *Gemuetlichkeit* isn't easily translatable. It's a mixture of comfort, friendliness, good-nature, and pleasantness. This special feeling can be evoked while sitting in an open fire with friends in a beer garden or simply in the arms of a loving companion.

The American dream of having a comfortable home, a white picket fence, 1.5 kids and a dog is probably the American equivalent of *gezelligheid*. *Gezelligheid* is a sort of snugness that pervades throughout the Dutch culture. Their desire to avoid risk is much greater than in other cultures; the Dutch have a strong preference for stability and continuity. In fact, the beloved Queen herself honors those subjects who have attained the coveted 40-year mark for employment with the same company, thus rewarding their stability and continuity. A common expression in Holland is, *"Don't skate over one night's ice."* The significance of such an idiom is that one should not take the risk that the ice is completely frozen before skating on it but should wait another day to absolutely ensure that the ice is completely frozen.

Another common aphorism in the Netherlands states, *"More than enough constitutes a feast."* The Dutch strive to attain the perfect level of comfort, nothing less and nothing more. The acclaimed Dutch painter, Jan Steen, captures the essence of *gezelligheid* in his painting *Grace Before Meat*. This work of art depicts a simple family gracing their meal with an inscription based on Proverbs 30:7-8 pinned to the wall which reads:

Three things I wish and nothing more:
Above all else to love my Lord and God
No overflow of riches' wealth
But to desire what the wisest prayed for:
An honorable life in this vale.

OVERLEG

The Netherlands draws a multitude of foreigners from all corners of the globe to fill the numerous professional vacancies. With only 16.2 million inhabitants and a Gross National Product (GNP) ranking in the top twenty in the world, there just aren't enough Dutch nationals to occupy the necessary jobs for the Netherlands to remain as one of the most productive economic engines in the world. Most of the desired skill sets are in the field of Information Technology (IT). The Netherlands has numerous technology-oriented, as well as telecommunications companies, and serves as a major hub on the worldwide Internet backbone. With the Netherlands' inimitable permissiveness towards sex, drugs and individual freedom, and the IT industry being dominated mostly by young, male professionals, the Dutch have little to no problems filling these occupational vacancies!

These outside workers, invariably, are initially befuddled and disturbed at the way the Dutch conduct their business. For a small country with such a strong economy and international presence, most visiting workers expect the Dutch to conduct their business affairs with strikingly fast precision and efficiency. These outsiders, however, are initially incredulous with what they perceive as inefficient, ineffective and burdensome working procedures. Their expectations of a fine-tuned economic machine turn out to be the reality, or at least what appears to be the reality, of a rusty, outdated economic clunker. As always with the Dutch, initial impressions and expectations don't always turn out to be the most accurate ones.

This initial perception of inefficiency stems from the fact that the Dutch hold extremely long meetings with a shockingly large amount of participants where decisions are usually not even made. The leaders of these protracted meetings act more as facilitators than authoritarian figures and encourage the flow of communication rather than directing the meetings towards finality with decisions as the ultimate result. All of the participants, furthermore, are expected to speak their minds, no matter how significant or insignificant a role they play in the overall decision-making process. When one meeting participant has the floor, all others listen attentively with calm demurs, never interrupting and allowing that person any amount of time to get his or her point across.

Non-Dutch meeting participants, conversely, are usually the ones fidgeting in their chairs, constantly checking their watches during these long, deliberate processes. They can usually be found periodically loosening their ties, tapping their fingernails, rolling their eyes and even letting out conspicuous sighs when the nonsensical or even absurd ideas are brought to the table. The Dutch, however, treat every person and every idea with reverence and sincerity. Since all participants speak their minds at these meetings, and the Dutch love speaking their minds, the only decision at the end of a meeting is usually the decision to hold another meeting to further discuss the topic at hand! Such a decision can be the last straw on a camel's back for an outsider. After all, having another meeting to deliberate over the same topic is just another hour or so of wasted time, so an outsider usually believes. The Dutch, meanwhile, leave the meeting with cordiality and feel that the session was productive and time well spent.

Such a deliberate and time-consuming decision making process can indeed be shocking for certain cultures, but for the Dutch it

Frustrated visitor experiencing the Dutch deliberation process

is just the way that business gets done. There are fundamental reasons, in fact, that the Dutch take the necessary time and allow for all, even the ones on the lower rung of the ladder, to have a voice in the decision making process. This long-term planning is done consciously and is conducted with a matter of pride. These extensive meetings, deliberations and consultations are referred to as *overlegs* in Dutch. *Overlegs* are derived from the Dutch innate respect for the rights of the individual and their seriousness on just about all issues. Additionally, the Dutch feel that *overlegs* foster team building and produce desired results that satisfy all parties. The overall decision or outcome of an *overleg* may not be the most optimal one, but one that usually results with a compromise where all interested parties achieved, at least minimally, their sought after outcomes. Perhaps the most significant attribute of an *overleg* is the unwavering support that the Dutch give to the decision once it is finally made. Once that decision is made, there is no turning back. The Dutch will be in 100% compliance and will support that decision without question. All of the questions have already been asked and all of the issues have already been raised during the *overleg* process; there is no need for further deliberation. What they may have lost with consensus building and compromise, they gained with unyielding support and incredible momentum going forward.

The Dutch approach of consensus building and compromise is radically different than approaches taken by other cultures throughout the world. In America, for instance, such long-term planning and consensus building is negatively viewed as inefficient and disadvantageous; after all, time is money and money is everything in Corporate America. Decisions need to be made fast and they need to be the most optimal ones that yield immediate, positive results. For this reason, the highest-ranking managers, the most dynamic leaders, or even the most convincing personalities make most decisions in American businesses. Since America is more hierarchical-oriented than many cultures, the more senior a person in an organization, the more clout and respect that person commands. For this reason, the words of these senior-level people are viewed as gospel and many are reluctant to refute such consecrated words.

Because efficiency is desired and hierarchy respected in the U.S., most workers will just go along with the flow and support the decisions made by the higher-ups rather than adding their input, even though it may be of significant value. For these reasons, many decisions are made in haste and not everyone supports them. Although the decision was made quickly and efficiently, many times the issue at hand will have to be revisited and modified due to lack of support or identified flaws in the hastily made decision. Effectiveness, in many instances, has been sacrificed for expediency.

In America, these expedient decisions are usually modified as time goes along, eventually yielding desirous results, as evidenced by America's economic might. Americans tend to be more flexible in business, preferring to react quickly to any market fluctuations that may affect their bottom-line. Whereas the Dutch plan extensively up front then execute the plan with unwavering fury, the Americans plan less up front and then modify and optimize the plan going forward. Below is a graphical depiction of the differing approaches taken by the Dutch and Americans in executing decisions and producing desirable results.

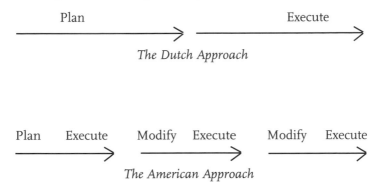

The Swedes take a similar approach to the Dutch in the planning and decision-making process. They feel that quick decisions are usually the act of poor judgment and eventually yield undesirable results. The Swedes spend the necessary time up front planning for an event because they feel that such proactive measures will ensure efficiency with the implementation of the decision, as intricate planning will result in fewer changes being needed. Studies show that the Swedes allocate approximately 50% of time for planning while Americans allocate only 15% of time for planning and 85% for execution. As with the Dutch, Swedes favor achieving consensus among the various members of the group in formulating plans and making decisions rather than through individual competition.

The Germans also spend a great amount of time planning and scrutinizing issues at hand before making decisions and executing on them. In fact, the Germans are renowned for their intricate planning and analysis of even the most minuscule of elements. The Germans strive to understand the *why's* first, then will conduct long, theoretical discussions planning for virtually every *what-if* possibility. They are very methodical in their approaches, processes and procedures, thus ensuring that no stone has been left unturned.

A recent Beck's beer commercial even satirizes the German methodical and precise behavior. An unemotional German comedian is on stage and breaks the ice with the terribly clichéd opener of "I just flew in from Berlin and boy my arms are tired." This undemonstrative comedian then attempts to dispel the notion that Germans are exceedingly methodical and systematic, but his intentions backfire by prefacing his first joke with, "Joke number one...." The Executives at Beck's must think they can sell more beer by crafting a parody of the German penchant for order and precision. Doesn't necessarily make me want to go out and buy a six-pack of Beck's!

Such precision and methodical processes augment the world renowned German scientific and engineering prowess. Germans have been world leaders in the acutely technical fields of science and engineering for many centuries. The German proclivity for order, exactness and intricacy undoubtedly assisted in attaining such levels of prominence in these fields. The German language, furthermore, even contributes to their affinity for the technical sciences. The German language calls for an extraordinary amount of memorization for even the most basic of grammatical principles, which indoctrinates German children into the world of exactness and strict attention to detail at early ages. For instance, all German nouns are specified as either masculine, feminine or neutral. Such categorization is not unlike many other languages, but the Germans use absolutely no rhyme or reason in designating these distinctions. For example, a desk is masculine, while a box is feminine and an automobile is neutral. The German word for the English definite article *the* is either *der (masculine)*, *die (feminine)* or *das (neutral)* and their use is dependent on the gender of the noun.

For instance,

> The desk translates to *der Schreibtisch*
> The box translates to *die Schachtel*
> The automobile translates to *das Auto*

Furthermore, the indefinite article "a" is translated into German by using *ein* (for masculine or neutral) or *eine* (for feminine).

> A desk translates to *ein Schreibtisch*
> A box translates to *eine Schachtel*
> An automobile translates to *ein Auto*

To further complicate matters, the adjective describing the noun changes notation based upon whether a definite article "the" or an indefinite article "a" is used. For instance, the adjective *klein* (small) changes in the following examples:

> A small desk translates to *ein kleiner Schreibtisch*
> A small box translates to *eine kleine Schachtel*
> A small automobile translates to *ein kleines Auto*

> The small desk translates to *der kleine Schreibtisch*
> The small box translates to *die kleine Schachtel*
> The small automobile translates to *das kleine Auto*

These examples are just the tip of the iceberg when dealing with the complexities of grammar in the German language and the necessity for intense memorization. When other grammatical principles such as the accusative case (example: 'I have a car') and prepositions are introduced, even further obstacles arise. For instance, when dealing with prepositional phases such as "to the store," "with a man," or "from the country," the definite articles *der*, *die* and *das* become *dem*, *der* and *dem*, while the indefinite articles *ein*, *eine*, *ein* become *einem*, *einer* and *einem*. As can be seen from these simple grammatical examples, the German language is quite complex and requires a high degree of precision and meticulousness, along with unyielding memorization, in order to speak it correctly. Other languages, such as Spanish, use gender in categorizing its nouns. The Spanish language, however, uses only two genders, masculine and feminine. Alleviating the burdens of strict memorization, all feminine nouns end in an "a" and the preceding definite article is "la." The definite article for masculine nouns is "el." For example:

The house translates to *la casa*
The exit translates to *la salida*
The train translates to *el tren*
The station translates to *el estacion*

Meanwhile, in using the indefinite article, the above examples become:

A house translates to *una casa*
An exit translates to *una salida*
A train translates to *un tren*
A station translates to *un estacion*

As can be seen, the Spanish language is much less complex and requires significantly less memorization than German. Perhaps this is an underlying reason why the Spanish are more known for their relaxed lifestyles and fine cuisine rather than their scientific and engineering prowess. The Dutch language is very similar to the German language, but doesn't require nearly as much memorization, although requires bizarre guttural sounds found in no other language!

Struggling for Survival against the Sea

It is hard to imagine that the Dutch are able to maintain such discipline and perseverance in their decision-making process in today's fast-paced, globalized marketplace. After all, business success, quite often, is bestowed upon those who strike fast and beat their competitors to the punch. This attitude is indicative of the slogan of one of the most renowned multinational corporations, UPS. UPS claims to be *"Moving at the Speed of Business."* Additionally, Nike's *"Just Do It"* slogan conveys action and decisiveness. So how is it that the Dutch continue to strive for consensus and compromise in almost everything they do without a fear of falling behind? This atypical behavior with its heavy emphasis on planning before acting is actually ingrained into the Dutch due to centuries of struggling for survival against the constant threat of being engulfed by the sea.

As discussed in previous chapters, the Dutch are in a perpetual struggle with the sea with more than sixty percent of the current population living below sea level. The province of Flevoland, in fact, just recently emerged from the commanding sea that had submerged this new landmass since the beginning of time. So as their forebears have done for centuries before them, the modern day Dutch are still living in constant danger of the potential catastrophic consequences of a rising sea. In fact, with the current trend of increasing temperatures, the threat may become even greater as the icecaps begin to melt causing the water levels to rise. Thus, even in today's society, proper planning, pooling of resources and commitment by all is a necessity to ensure the Dutch domination over the threatening sea. As recently as 1953, great floods engulfed the Netherlands resulting in horrifying deaths and dreadful destruction. The great flood disaster of 1953 caused more than 1,800 deaths. On January 31, 1953 there was a fateful combination of gale force winds, a deep depression and a spring tide. A tremendous volume of water was driven southwards into the North Sea between England and the Netherlands. The result was a huge surge tide which raised the sea level by an incredible ten feet. The catastrophic results of these floods are indelibly sketched into the minds of Dutch survivors and younger generations are keenly aware of these events and understand that such a tragedy may happen again at any given time.

In the 13th and 14th centuries, when the Dutch began reclaiming land from the sea in earnest, they didn't have the luxury of modern day technology or even a committee whose sole purpose was the regulation of the water levels, as they do today. The responsibility of planning for such an ambitious endeavor was that of everyone, not just a select few. Each individual was thought to bring some sort of value to the planning process. After all, a dam is only as strong as its weakest link, so no matter how insignificant someone may appear in the big scheme of things, that person's input may be just the required bit of information to strengthen that weakest link. A popular saying in the Netherlands is, *"God made the world but the Dutch made Holland."* Such an axiom demonstrates the Dutch pride, and perhaps a little arrogance, in their proficiency in reclaiming land from the sea.

It's no wonder that Hans Brinker, the fictitious little boy who stuck his thumb in a leaking dike to save the town from a torrent of sea water, is still talked about with such zeal. The moral of the story is that big deeds can come from little people. Furthermore, Admiral Piet Hein, a Dutch Naval hero for conquering a fleet of Spanish ships more than double his fleet's size, is still revered today for similar reasons. Songs are even sung about his miraculous victory at football games. Below is an excerpt of the song, *De Zilvervloot*, The Silver Fleet.

DE ZILVERVLOOT

Heb je van de zilveren vloot wel gehoord
(Have you heard about the Silver Fleet)
De zilveren vloot van Spanje?
(the Silver Fleet from Spain?)
Die had er veel Spaansche matten aan boord.
(It had all kinds of Spanish stuff on board)
En appeltjes van Oranje!
(and little apples colored Orange!)

Piet Hein, Piet Hein, Piet Hein, zijn naam is klein,
(Piet Hein, Piet Hein your name is small)
Zijn daden bennen groot, Zijn daden bennen groot:

(Your deeds are great, your deeds are great)
Die heeft gewonnen de zilveren vloot,
(You have captured the Silver Fleet)
Die heeft gewonnen, gewonnen de zilvervloot.
(You have captured, captured the Silver Fleet)

The moral of this song is to not underestimate the Netherlands just because they are a small country. Even though they are small, the Dutch can still accomplish magnificent feats, just as Piet Hein had done in centuries past. Given such fables and stories, it is quite apparent that the Dutch hold each individual member of society in the highest regard. This high regard for the individual is reflected in the many liberal social laws throughout the Netherlands. A dike built for the purposes of reclaiming land to ensure survival was never taken lightly and long, deliberate planning processes were necessary to ensure that the most practical decision was made to ensure everyone's total commitment, and thus, long-term survival.

The centuries of struggling against the sea and the resolute solidarity amongst the Dutch inhabitants has carried over into today's society. This solidarity is so palpable that the English fashioned a term describing the Dutch paradigm of consensus building and compromise as the *Poldermodel*. A *polder*, a Dutch term, is a piece of land completely surrounded by a dike. The purpose of the dike is to protect the land within against raging high waters. Flevoland is an example of a *polder*, and is also the largest one in the Netherlands. In order to protect this *polder* and the people living on it, tight cooperation between the inhabitants is of the utmost importance. The smallest mistake can lead to dire consequences. For these reasons, the inhabitants of the *polder* formed a tight bond where everyone adhered to established norms and supported all decisions once they were finally made after long deliberation processes. Should the inhabitants of the *polder* not do so, their already tenuous situation may become exacerbated, causing not only danger to themselves but also danger to the entire *polder* community. Even though Dutch men and women in business, politics and other areas in the Netherlands where decisions need to be made aren't usually debating life or death situations like those living on the *polder* in centuries past, they still adhere to the time-honored tradition of *overleg*. This tradition has proven itself time-and-time again to be brilliantly effectual as evidenced by the additional land masses acquired from the sea and the exceedingly high standard of living that the Dutch so readily enjoy today.

The Dutch struggle against the sea wasn't only in the form of *polders* and rising waters, but also came in the form of long, global sea voyages of the early Dutch merchants. These early Dutch merchants, especially in the 17th century during the Dutch Golden Age, were prolific traders and explorers who established trade routes along all sectors of the globe. In order to ensure survival on these grueling voyages, the Dutch merchants relied on tight cooperation with one another and consensus building. Additionally, in order to garner all of the riches that the world had to offer, individual ships liaised with one another instead of competed, for the strength of the masses was certainly greater than that of each individual ship. The Dutch merchants even pooled all of their resources and cargo goods together and spread them equally amongst all of the ships ensuring that most of the acquired riches made it back to their homeland in the unfortunate event that an individual ship plunged into the depths of the sea. For such a small country as the Netherlands with its limited resources, the Dutch would not have been able to have traded, explored and even colonized the various areas throughout the eastern and western hemispheres were it not for their intense collaboration, calculating planning and unyielding unity towards the common goal. The early Dutch merchants were indeed masters of international trade. Even today the Dutch are still experts at international trade, with this element accounting for fifty to sixty percent of their Gross Domestic Product (GDP).

DEALING WITH *OVERLEG* AS AN OUTSIDER

After centuries of accomplishing colossal feats with scarce resources and limited people, the Dutch aren't likely to abandon this tried and true method of consensus building and compromise any time soon. As a non-Dutch person living and working in the Netherlands, it is prudent to learn more about the uncanny Dutch and to accept their intriguing methods of conducting business. My initial actions while working in the Netherlands certainly weren't conducted in the spirit of *overleg*, but more like that of a, according to the Dutch, "typical American cowboy shooting from the hip." This stereotype of Americans is greatly intensified in the Netherlands with the current President of the U.S. being from Texas. The fact that President George W. Bush even wears a Cowboy hat and boots whets the Dutch appetite even further to taunt the Americans whenever they get a chance. Being on the receiving end of all kinds of stereotypes involving wooden shoes, tulips and windmills, the Dutch love to give it back once in awhile!

Alas, I gave the Dutch more fodder to feed their image of Americans by being the impatient fella in those long, drawn-out meetings checking his watch and letting out those conspicuous sighs. I initially couldn't believe the inefficiency of these meetings and the patience that everyone showed while even the lowest man or woman on the totem pole was allowed to ramble on and on about absolutely nothing of significance to the matter at hand. I often asked myself, "How do these Dutch get any work done with all of these ridiculous 'gossip sessions' taking place?"

My impatience with these *overlegs* reached a point where I devised a scheme to liberate myself from these tortuous meetings. Since I was usually the only English speaker present in a roomful of Dutch nationals, I "sacrificed" by offering to espouse my issues and concerns at the beginning of the meeting so that I could depart immediately thereafter allowing the Dutch nationals to resume in their native tongue. Even though the Dutch are multi-lingual and fluent in English, some of the meeting participants appreciated my hospitable gesture. After all, speaking a foreign language in their own country, no matter how fluent the Dutch are in English, adds an extra strain to the brain and an inconvenience they would rather do without if they had a choice. Many of my Dutch friends and colleagues couldn't wait to get home after an entire day of speaking English just so they could go back to their native tongue to avoid the cerebral strains involved in speaking a foreign language. I found my scheme of ducking out of the meetings quite satisfying initially, but by doing so I left the impression that I didn't take the matters at hand seriously enough and that I didn't respect each of the individual opinions. (For the record, I did take the matters at hand seriously, although I did think some of the individual opinions were preposterous and that some of the individuals were galling!) Regardless of my opinions, I lost credibility with the Dutch. Instead of being viewed as a serious player in the *overleg* process, I was viewed as just another "typical American cowboy shooting from the hip."

After spending more time in the Netherlands, it became quite obvious to me that the Dutch were indeed a peculiar bunch and did things in their own, unique way. Determined to learn more about the Dutch and to be accepted into their society, I reevaluated my aggressive, American approach and began to live and work like a Dutchman. While performing my duties as a consultant for a Dutch company, I formulated a strategy of bringing their products to market faster and more efficiently. Learning from all of my previous blunders in interacting with the Dutch, I was determined not to make a single faux pas in presenting my idea to the Dutch and to bring my strategy to fruition by following the *overleg* process.

In seeking counsel with my Dutch project sponsor, he advised me to coordinate a plethora of meetings with numerous groups throughout the organization. I was setting up meetings with not only people I had never heard of, but departments that I didn't even know existed! The project sponsor emphasized that the plan would never fly unless I had total consensus amongst all of the individuals within the numerous departments throughout the company. My idea wasn't that radical or earth shattering that I felt I had to get approval from just about the entire organization. Adopting the "when in Rome do as the Romans" philosophy, I was determined to do as the Dutch in order to gain Dutch acceptance of my proposal.

In the U.S., an idea such as the one I devised would be presented to a manager, who may in turn run it by his or her manager and select colleagues and then if everyone was in agreement, the decision would be made to go forward with the idea. The management would then inform the organization of the new policy and it would be implemented. In the Netherlands, however, even the smallest proposed changes are debated until a consensus has been reached. After countless weeks of meetings and deliberations, and after modifying my original idea to the point where I received the much sought after Dutch nod of approval, I was able to get a consensus. Getting this consensus, initially, wasn't very rewarding since I felt that the efforts far outweighed the results, and I had to modify my original strategy to the point where I felt it wasn't nearly as effective. But what was rewarding was the commitment and speed in which this plan was implemented once it was approved. There was no hesitation, no resistance to change and everybody in the organization worked toward the common goal of bringing their products to market faster by adhering to the new policy.

In dealing with the Dutch on all matters that require some sort of decision, outsiders can expect to go through what may appear to them as an inordinate amount of time deliberating the topic at hand. A decision that may take a couple of days in their cultures may take weeks, even months in the Netherlands. Gaining acceptance and reaching a compromise on all decisions is the Dutch model of doing business. Outsiders must accept this cautious behavior or they will immediately get frustrated and discouraged. Obtaining signatures on final deliverable documents, for instance, from a Dutch manager is like squeezing water from a stone! A Dutch manager will not put their John Hancock, or since we're dealing with the Dutch, their William of Orange, on a document unless all of their people have thoroughly read through it and have made all of their modifications and recommendations. As one can imagine, this process is extremely time-consuming, especially for a foreign consultant trying to achieve immediate results. Outsiders need to be cognizant that once a compromise has been attained, it's full steam ahead shortly thereafter. This steadfast commitment by the

Dutch once a decision has been made is truly a motivating factor for outsiders to accept the *overleg* process.

DETESTATION OF HIERARCHY

With the Dutch extraordinary high-regard for the rights of the individual, it is not at all surprising that they absolutely detest a rigid hierarchical structure. The Dutch truly feel that all individuals, no matter what their position in an organization or society, are morally equal and all put their pants on one leg at a time. No one person is better than anybody else; the Dutch live in a classless society. The Dutch have achieved greatness throughout the centuries not by the means of Herculean leaders, but by the unity of the individuals. For these reasons, the Dutch despise being told what to do by authoritative figures without elaborate deliberation first. To do otherwise would be to abandon the principles set forth by the Dutch throughout their existence. Dutch police don't even bark out orders to offenders of the law; they usually just calmly discuss the altercation, allowing offenders the rights to verbally defend themselves.

In Dutch business and society, very few direct orders are given; leaders more or less discuss the issues at hand first and then ask their employees to perform a particular task. If Dutch employees are treated with dignity by their bosses and are encouraged to discuss the matters at hand, they will willingly perform any task being requested. If, on the other hand, a Dutch employee is given a direct order, that employee will think of every excuse under the sun not to follow that order, even if it would take just a couple of minutes of their time to obey it! John Calvin taught that every individual should read the bible and decide the meaning for him or herself. The Dutch still adhere to this Calvinistic viewpoint and definitely march to the beat of their own drum.

When I first started working in the Netherlands, I was absolutely incredulous observing the Dutch obstinacy when it came to following directives of people in higher positions. Being an American with a military background, I tend to follow reasonable requests of the people higher up in the pecking order, as do most Americans. I happened to have a Dutch colleague consulting alongside me at a Dutch company. This company was growing incredibly fast and was particularly strapped for resources, especially human resources. The main Project Leader of the organization would brief my Dutch colleague and me in the mornings on all pertinent issues and ask us to perform certain tasks. The Project Leader was so busy at that point of the project that he didn't have the time to go into detail on all of the issues and the reasons why he was asking us to do certain things. He would usually just speak his piece and scurry off to his next meeting. Since my Dutch colleague felt that he wasn't privy to all of the information and that he wasn't given the opportunity to discuss the issues at hand, he was adamant about not performing those tasks asked of him. He felt it was his individual right to know why he was being asked to do something and his right to deliberate on that request. Because we were working as a team and I felt it necessary to put our best foot forward early on in the project, I wanted to accomplish all of the tasks given to us as efficiently and effectively as possible. Needless to say, my partner and I had numerous, heated debates. My Dutch colleague would rather spend forty-five minutes complaining about following a directive from the boss than performing the task that would take him less than five minutes to accomplish!

The Dutch don't bestow respect upon individuals in higher positions simply because of their titles or levels of authority; such respect has to be earned. Such indifference towards authority creates unpleasant and frustrating situations for leaders in all elements of Dutch society, including sports, especially if said leaders are of non-Dutch origin. In England and America, head coaches of sports teams are usually immediately given respect by their players for they are in charge, call the shots and hopefully will lead their teams to positions of eminence. In the Netherlands, however, such respect has to develop over time. In 1978, Ernst Happel, an exceptional Austrian football player in the 1970s, was appointed head coach of the Dutch national team prior to the World Cup. Being from Austria and from a culture that has profound respect for authority, Ernst Happel was immediately chagrined when observing the contempt that the Dutch players had for him. He realized that the only way he was going to earn the respect of his players was to prove himself worthy of being the head coach of the highly-esteemed Dutch national team. He rectified the situation by not saying a word, but by demonstrating his incredible football talents to the entire team. He lined up a string of balls on the eighteen yard line and proceeded to kick each one with striking precision against the crossbar of the goal![1] Respect was earned and his players began listening to him immediately thereafter.

It is no surprise that the Dutch attitude toward authority is reflected not only in the realm of sports, but in the workplace, as well. There are very few plush, corner offices in a typical Dutch organization accommodating high-level executives. Most of the managers are out on the floor rubbing elbows with the rest of the workers. Very few privileges or perks are bestowed upon managers and they are treated with the same respect as all other workers in an organization. One Dutch idiosyncrasy that used to give me mild heart attacks was how Dutch employees would make senior-level people wait their turn in queues when all they needed was a quick answer to one of their questions. Such a senior manager would have to wait if the employee was talking to someone else or even talking on the phone. It was astonishing how these Dutch workers wouldn't even acknowledge their executive's presence! When, and only when, that employee was done completing the affairs at hand would the senior-level manager even be acknowledged. In cultures where hierarchy and authority are respected, most people would hang up the phone or put the person on hold, excuse themselves from their current conversation and address the executive. In most cases, the senior-level manager has a simple question that can be answered in a couple of seconds. For the Dutch, however, there is no differentiation between the ranks; everybody is treated with the same respect and dignity. First come, first serve.

Because the Dutch greatly value equality, empower their employees, and resist authority, a typical organizational structure is very flat and decentralized. Most organizations in Sweden also possess a flat, decentralized structure with few levels of management. In countries such as the U.S., Germany, Austria and Japan, where hierarchy and authority are acknowledged and respected, organizations tend to have more layers. People in prominent positions are treated with more reverence and are venerated for having the wisdom, skill and intellect needed to obtain that position. These leaders, in turn, are expected to display strong leadership and to drive an organization or department towards success. Workers, for the most part, will follow the directives of the higher echelons within an organization without question. There may be some rumblings about certain decisions, but since these cultures are very hierarchical oriented, the desires of the bosses are usually accommodated. A Dutch worker would have a very difficult time working in such hierarchical environments where the directives of the senior-level managers are followed usually without question or deliberation.

German corporations are particularly well known for their rigid hierarchies and vertical organizational structures. German corporations have strict chains of command and clearly defined levels of responsibility. Even though the Germans are moving more in the direction of consensus building, they still follow a very autocratic style of leadership. German leaders are expected to give direct orders to their subordinates and to place high demands on them. The workers, in turn, are expected to follow these orders and directives without hesitation. Very few compliments are given to workers, especially for just doing what is expected of them. In fact, there's a popular German saying that expresses this viewpoint -- *Nicht geschimpft ist Lob genug* (if you weren't criticized that's praise enough).[2] Individuals from other cultures working in German organizations can find such rigidity overwhelming and even intimidating. In fact, numerous cultural clashes occurred after the merger of the two monolithic juggernauts Daimler-Benz and Chrysler. Even though Americans, for the most part, are inclined to adhere to hierarchical principles, the German model proved to be too rigid and structured for many Americans. Numerous business and psychological studies were conducted which focused on the numerous growing pains encountered with this colossal merger.

The Austrian method of doing business is quite similar to the German method. One particular week I took a few personal days and flew down to Vienna to catch an opera and to enjoy the exquisite Viennese culture. On the flight back I found myself sitting next to a disheveled, stressed out Dutchman – quite a rarity for a Dutchman to be in such disarray! As this giant of a man was hunched in his seat with his tie loosened, sleeves rolled up, hair unkempt and a look on his face as if he had seen a ghost, I asked him if everything was all right. I could only imagine that he had some sort of unfortunate encounter prior to boarding the plane. It turned out that the unfortunate encounter he had was with the hierarchical structure of Austrian business! An Austrian firm recently purchased his Dutch company and he was down in Vienna for a couple of days attending to business. It would be an understatement to say that this Dutchman experienced severe culture shock. He proceeded to tell me how the Austrians barked out order after order and that nobody questioned any of them. He went on to say that even during lunches and dinners the Austrians were all business and didn't stand for any kind of jocularity. He said that he felt like he did months of work in the few days that he was down there. The rigidity and hierarchy was too much for this Dutchman; he told me that he was immediately going to look for employment in a Dutch firm upon his return to his homeland.

The business model of the Dutch is clearly less rigid than that of their German and Austrian brethren. In the same manner that the Dutch business structure promotes equality, so does their approach to leadership. There are no flamboyant, hard-charging, charismatic, dictatorial-type leaders running Dutch organizations. Such ostentation is looked down upon; modesty is the norm and the expected behavior of even the highest-ranking officials. Leadership behavior is certainly a characteristic differentiator between the Netherlands and the U.S. In the Netherlands, leaders don't make the exorbitant salaries and receive the astonishing perks common to corporate leaders in the U.S. Furthermore, Dutch leaders rarely bask in the limelight but behave in the same conservative manner as the rest of the Dutch population. The Dutch people would have it no other way.

In the U.S., strong, charismatic leaders are idolized. The American people will rely on one person to turn situations around for the better and will willingly give that person the deserved credit. Stock prices skyrocketing or plummeting at the announcement of a hiring or resignation of a senior-level executive is indicative of the trust bestowed upon leadership in America. The stock price of Sunbeam Corporation, incredibly, rose nearly fifty percent in just one day on the announcement of the hiring of "Chainsaw" Al Dunlap. Leaders in America are expected to act with strikingly fast precision and to obtain desirable results immediately. Long-term planning is simply not an option many times because quarterly earnings are too imperative to ignore.

Jack Welch, the retired CEO of General Electric (GE) has been dubbed the "CEO of the Century" for the leadership that he demonstrated while at the helm. Jack Welch's principles on leadership reflect the general consensus of what Americans expect out of their leaders. Jack Welch's principles on leadership and the attributes he looks for when hiring managers are as follows:

GE Leadership Ingredients - E^4

Energy	Enormous personal energy -- strong bias for action
Energizer	Ability to motivate and energize others.....Infectious enthusiasm to max organization potential

Edge	Competitive spirit...Instinctive drive for speed/impact....strong convictions and courageous advocacy
Execution	Deliver Results

Looks like Mr. Welch overlooked the part about consensus building and compromise! I'm confident that the Dutch would not deem Jack Welch to be the CEO of the century with his hardnosed tactics. In fact, I don't believe Mr. Welch would have lasted very long in a Dutch company for the Dutch would not stand for his authoritative and Machiavellian methods. Consensus building and compromise are too tightly woven into the Dutch culture and psyche for them to abandon these principles for just about anything or anybody.

POLITICS AND POLITICAL DEBATE

Even the Dutch form of government is indicative of the culture of consensus building and compromise. The Dutch Lower House of Parliament is elected by proportional representation. The Dutch government comprises a group of coalitions. If a coalition wins 10% of the vote in an election, that coalition will represent 10% of the government. If another coalition wins 43% of the vote, they will represent 43% of the government. The largest coalitions in the Netherlands are the Labor Party, the Christian Democrats and the Liberals. This form of government is suitable for the Dutch for at any given time it represents nearly all political affiliations in some shape or form. Everybody benefits, whether greatly or minimally, in that most of the Dutch population is represented by some percentage of political influence.

In contrast, in the U.S. if the Republicans win the majority of the Electoral College, no matter how slim the vote, the Republicans will then control the Executive branch of the government for the next 4 years. In fact, in the election of 2001, George W. Bush didn't even win the popular vote (i.e. more people throughout the country voted for Al Gore) but because he won the majority of the Electoral College, the Republicans obtained power in the Executive branch for the ensuing 4 years. The democrats will have absolutely no representation in the Executive branch of the government for those years.

Dutch politicians are generally moderate in their views and coalition building is a top priority for them. Being consistent with the rest of the Netherlands, most politicians aren't flamboyant or extreme in their mannerisms. The politicians know that the Dutch people vote on issues and views that are consistent with theirs and not for the individual politician. In true Dutch form, political debates are known to go on for hours and into the latter parts of the evening and early parts of the morning. The Dutch political system can be described as a slow moving system of consultation, discussion, checks and balances with no drama, sudden shifts or changes in direction.

Even though Dutch politicians are public figures, little is known about their personal lives. Their incomes, marital affairs, family affairs and even extra-curricular love affairs are kept out of the spotlight. The Dutch people respect their individuality and don't find it necessary to know of such personal things. Wow, is this drastically different than in the U.S.! To this day Monica Lewinsky is still a household name. Americans want to know everything there is to know about their politicians. Americans drill down to the level of detail of knowing that Ronald Reagan loved jellybeans; that George Bush Sr. hates broccoli; that Bill Clinton didn't inhale, wears boxer shorts and has a thing for female interns; and that George Bush Jr. had a wild drinking streak during his college years and that his daughters are following in those same, wild college footsteps.

8.   Dutch Tolerance

Introduction

The Netherlands has the honorable, but sometimes dubious, distinction of being the most tolerant country in the world. Many people, furthermore, consider the Netherlands to be the most progressive nation in the world with its liberal, and often controversial, social policies. The Dutch are quick to defend their "live and let live" attitudes and can usually do so with supporting facts and figures that lend credence to their liberal social policies. The Dutch feel that despite the easy availability of drugs, sex and a merciful death, fewer people in the Netherlands die of overdoses, contract sexually transmitted diseases or kill themselves to end suffering. Individual freedom, they argue, does not have to mean chaos. The Dutch feel that their liberal policies towards such matters as prostitution, drugs, euthanasia, same-sex marriages and abortion are simply common sense, pragmatic solutions to everyday, but serious, social issues that are universal throughout the world. The Dutch look at harm reduction as a way of dealing with such social problems as opposed to total elimination, the preferred method of most cultures throughout the world. The elimination of such social concerns is simply not an option for the Dutch; these social phenomena, along with numerous others, have always been present in civilizations throughout the history of mankind and always will be. The Dutch, therefore, strive to reduce the harm done to individuals engaged in such activities by not punishing or ostracizing them, but by tolerating and regulating such activities to ensure the least harm is done to those individuals, as well as to society.

Dutch children are introduced into this world of tolerance at very early ages and the indoctrination process continues throughout the rest of their school years. The Dutch are proud of their history of tolerance throughout the centuries and educate their inhabitants on this righteous virtue. This tolerance carries over into today's society where the Dutch have been at the forefront of tolerating and even legalizing many activities deemed taboo in other cultures. Incidentally, many of the countries that lambasted the Dutch for their social policies, such as Great Britain, France and the U.S., are now following suit and implementing their own policies of tolerance based on the Dutch model.

The Dutch will quickly point out the flawed policies of the U.S. where the percentage of citizens in prison (approaching 2 million) is the highest in the developed world. Even with U.S. politicians advocating stringent prohibitions of increasing numbers of *immoral* behaviors to win elections, as the Dutch like to point out, rates of youth drug use and abortions soar. The Dutch analogize these disturbing trends with that of *mopping the floor while the faucet is still running.* No matter how much water is being mopped up, there is more and more on the way to replace what was already mopped up. You can mop all that you want, but it will be to no avail. Not tolerating and even condemning certain behaviors will not end those behaviors, but more than likely only exacerbate them. The Dutch feel that the social problems in the U.S., as well as in other industrialized countries, will not be solved and will continue to deteriorate as long as draconian social policies and intolerance exist.

There are many myths and stereotypes about the Dutch because of their tolerance toward issues that are taboo in other cultures. Popular film and media, for instance, exacerbate such fabrications about Dutch cities and culture. In the popular cinematic film *Pulp Fiction*, John Travolta and Samuel Jackson glorify and embellish the drug use policies of Amsterdam in the opening scene of the movie. Samuel Jackson is incredulous upon hearing about the relaxed drug laws in Amsterdam and states emphatically that he must visit this decadent place. In walking around the Red Light District in Amsterdam, a tourist may find it to be the quintessential *Sin City* with all of the scantily clad prostitutes in the windows, the numerous sex shops selling the most outrageous of merchandise, the sex theaters that promote live sex shows, the smells of burning cannabis emanating from the numerous hash houses, and other sights and sounds that simply can't be found in other cultures (unless behind closed doors). The Dutch insist, however, that their country is no more decadent than others, just less hypocritical. People smoke marijuana throughout the world, prostitution exists in all cities and even small towns, gays fall in love, and sick people seek an end to their suffering no matter what, they argue, and hence these behaviors might as well be out in the open where it can be discussed and regulated.

In this chapter we will explore the world of Dutch tolerance and attempt to debunk the numerous falsehoods and myths that exist about the Dutch and many of the risqué activities that transpire within their borders. Specifically, the contentious issues of prostitution, same-sex marriages, drugs, and euthanasia will be explored.

DUTCH HISTORY OF TOLERANCE

Throughout the centuries, The Netherlands was always the Mecca of tolerance. With Amsterdam being Europe's main port city throughout history and with the Dutch being such prolific international merchants, Amsterdam had its share of cultures, religions and nationalities passing through its gates on a continual basis. Dutch tolerance and willingness to accept new, and often alarming cultural differences stem from being such a small nation, dependent on trade with numerous foreign nations. In order for the Dutch to continue to thrive as merchants and as a nation, they couldn't discriminate as to with whom to conduct business with. Early Dutch merchants couldn't be concerned with religious or social ideologies of its many trading partners;

such ideologies had to be tolerated in order for these merchants to build and maintain its economic prowess throughout the world. Dutch tolerance also goes back to the times of Prince of Orange who defeated the Spanish in 1576. The Spanish Inquisition was demoralizing and left horrific memories for the Dutch. The Prince wanted to undo years of intolerance and abuse by the Spanish. The Dutch populace, consequently, was encouraged to live their lives according to their own conscience and not be forced into something against their will. This tolerance has survived the ages and continues to be a vital element in Dutch culture.

The Netherlands has long had a reputation as a humanitarian haven. Since the 16th century, refugees and immigrants have been attracted to its shores because of its tolerance and the individual freedoms it offered its inhabitants. In the 1600s, the Netherlands attracted many Jews, Huguenots, Protestants and others yearning for religious freedom from areas such as France, Germany and England. While wars over religion were fought in many regions of Europe and while religious minorities were persecuted according to slogans such as *un roi, un loi, un foi* (a king, a law, a belief) or *huius regio eius religio* (in whose territory you live, his religion you have), the Dutch practiced religious tolerance. In Holland, everybody was permitted to practice his or her faith no matter if it conformed to the state religion or not. The majority of Amsterdam's citizens of the 17th century originated from Antwerp, which was taken and sacked by the Spanish in the latter part of the previous century. Amsterdam's diamond cutting trade, coincidentally, was established by these refugees from Antwerp.

Many notable figures living in Holland during the 17th century were able to explore and even question the most sacred of things, such as religion, while others doing the same in different parts of Europe were being persecuted. Many had sought refuge in the Dutch Republic at one point or another in their lives to either escape persecution in their homelands or to take advantage of the tolerance and freedom that the Netherlands afforded them. One prominent person was the Jewish philosopher Baruch Spinoza, who took full advantage of the freedoms afforded to him in Holland by questioning firmly established religious notions. In his philosophical works, Spinoza denied the immortality of the soul; strongly rejected the notion of a providential God -- the God of Abraham, Isaac and Jacob; and claimed that the Law was neither literally given by God nor any longer binding on Jews. Even though the Dutch tolerated such questionable religious philosophical views, ironically the Sephardic community of Amsterdam excommunicated Spinoza for his blasphemous ways!

Another notable figure, Rene Descartes, also sought refuge in the Dutch Republic. Descartes was a French mathematician, philosopher, and physiologist who first explored the mind/body relationship. He gave much thought to choosing a country suited to his nature and chose Holland because of the limitless freedom it provided him. While Descartes was enjoying the liberties of Holland free to delve into any subject matter, his ingenious counterpart Galileo fell victim to the Inquisition in Italy for his controversial belief that the earth rotated around the sun. He was, subsequently, condemned to house arrest by religious authorities. Interestingly, in October, 1992, 350 years after Galileo's death, Pope John Paul II gave an address on behalf of the Catholic Church in which he admitted that errors had been made by the theological advisors in the case of Galileo. He declared the Galileo case closed, but he did not admit that the Church was wrong to convict Galileo on a charge of heresy! So much for forgiveness.

The French writer and satirist, Voltaire, the undisputed leader of the Age of Enlightenment who was a staunch crusader against tyranny and bigotry, also sought refuge in Holland. Outside of Holland his essays did not gain the approval of authorities, especially when he attacked the government and the Catholic Church, which caused him numerous imprisonments and exiles. Voltaire defended freedom of thoughts and religious tolerance, and thus found the Dutch Republic to be the perfect place to live and work during his numerous times of exile from France.

Montesquieu, the famous writer and philosopher during the 18th century, was banned in his native land of France for criticizing the lifestyles and liberties of the wealthy French, as well as the church. Montesquieu's book *On the Spirit of Laws*, published in 1748, outlines his ideas on how government would best work and is accredited with being the groundwork for the American Constitution. Montesquieu argued that the best government would be one in which power was balanced among three groups of officials. Montesquieu called the idea of dividing government power into three branches the "separation of powers." He thought it most important to create separate branches of government with equal but different powers. That way, the government would avoid placing too much power with one individual or group of individuals. According to Montesquieu, each branch of government could limit the power of the other two branches; therefore, no branch of the government could threaten the freedom of the people. His ideas about separation of powers became the basis for the United States Constitution. Fortunately for the United States, Montesquieu found safe refuge in Holland enabling him the freedom to philosophize on the principles of sound government.

An interesting historical event often overlooked is that America's original Pilgrims, the English Puritans, even traveled to the Netherlands seeking religious freedom before embarking to Massachusetts. They journeyed to the Netherlands on the Mayflower and settled in Rotterdam for several years practicing their religious beliefs and maintaining the religious lifestyles they were so desperately seeking. Perhaps the Netherlands was *too* tolerant for the English Puritans with its welcoming ways of other religions and cultures, causing the Puritans to seek more seclusion on the other side of the Atlantic Ocean! Several centuries later during World Wars I and II, thousands upon thousands of political refugees fled to the Netherlands. Even the famous Beatle, John Lennon, found the Netherlands to be the ideal place to stage a world protest. In 1969, John Lennon and Yoko Ono went to bed for a week in front of the entire world in the Amsterdam Hilton in a bid for world peace. Most recently, the Netherlands has been a haven for asylum seekers throughout the world. During the mid-1990s, asylum seekers numbered over 40,000 per year, up from 3,500 – 14,000 in the latter half of the 1980s.[1]

Even today visitors to the Netherlands are pleasantly surprised with the Dutch tolerance of foreigners and even foreign languages. With most of the Dutch being fluent in other languages such as English, French and German, visitors find it easy and enjoyable conversing with the locals. The Dutch do not begrudge visitors for speaking their native tongues or for not even attempting to speak Dutch. Such tolerance is not found in many parts of the world, especially in the neighboring countries to the Netherlands. In France, for instance, many French won't even acknowledge tourists if they're not attempting to speak French. Most French are fairly fluent in the English language, but won't speak it to Americans or other English speakers if these visitors are not attempting to speak their beloved French. In my earlier years while on my first backpacking trip through Europe, my friends and I visited a café right outside of the Paris train station hoping to enjoy a few cups of good French coffee. Being so close to the train station, the café must have been inundated with foreigners speaking a multitude of languages. With English being the universal language one might think a French merchant in such an area would be amenable to conducting business in English, after all money is money no matter what language. My friends and I soon came to realize that the French language is indeed more important than money for many French merchants. Upon ordering six cups of coffee in English, the French waitress simply yelled something at us in French. Holding up six fingers and saying "café" infuriated the waitress even further. Needless to say we didn't receive our six cups of coffee at that café. Our money was not good there because we did not attempt to speak their language! Off to the next café we went. Many visitors to France relay similar stories on how the French locals treat them with contempt merely for not speaking the cherished French language.

Even French speakers in Belgium and Canada are adamant about speaking only French and demanding to be spoken to only in French. Upon finishing a business meeting in Brussels, which is a French speaking city in Belgium, I boarded a cab and told the driver in English, "Please take me to the train station." The driver wailed at the top of his lungs something in French and flailed his arms about in the air. I was somewhat taken aback and simply reiterated my request in a more cordial manner. My second request, although cordial, was also in English, frustrating the driver even further, for his moans and flailings were even more exaggerated. I realized that I was dealing with one of these notorious French language zealots and figured, since I had to catch a train, I'd appease him by attempting his language. I then stated in horrific French, *"La station de tren s'il vous plaît."* Satisfied, he immediately began driving to the station! The French Canadians, meanwhile, are so passionate about their language that the French speaking provinces have been trying to secede from the nation for decades. The most recent vote on secession was quite close but the overall majority dictated that the nation remain intact, even though areas such as Montreal and Quebec defiantly speak French while all other provinces speak English.

Many Germans aren't much more welcoming to foreign tongues than the French, especially in the less cosmopolitan regions. In restaurants and bars, the Germans, for the most part, will serve tourists speaking foreign tongues but aren't shy about shooting nasty glances indicating their dissatisfaction with the tourists' lack of effort in speaking German. Visitors are often looked upon with suspicion and the German speakers tread cautiously in dealing with these strangers. I have found a foolproof way of breaking the ice and getting a German to let his or her guard down -- buy a German a drink by stating *"Ein Bier für meinen freund bitte"* (a beer for my friend please). Beer is an integral part of the German culture and they revel in the quality of their beer and their comfortable *Biergartens* or Pubs. I've never had an encounter where a German refused my hospitable gesture or had an unpleasant experience afterwards. Germans will

Prost a stranger and become forthcoming with him or her upon receiving such a cordial gesture. They figure that the stranger made an attempt to assimilate into the culture and that such a gesture indicates appreciativeness for the host country.

I've never experienced an unpleasant situation in dealing with the Dutch in English. In fact, they prefer that visitors speak English in order not to waste their precious time by struggling with their rather difficult language. Even if you do attempt to speak Dutch to them they'll more than likely answer you back in English. I witnessed a Dutch woman and an Italian man attempting to conduct business in a bike rental shop prior to embarking on a leisurely bike ride through the countryside. The man could only speak Italian and the Dutch lady, although fluent in at least four languages, couldn't speak Italian. The Dutch lady was actually apologetic to the man and to the people in line because she couldn't speak Italian, and therefore, held up the progress of the line. She felt awful that the business transaction wasn't as smooth as all of her other transactions. Instead of being intolerant of the man, she persisted and did her best to ensure that the transaction went through, even though there was a line of people ready to rent bikes in English, Dutch, German or French languages in which she could easily understand.

A major drawback, however, to the Dutch tolerance of foreign languages is that it allows visitors to be mentally lazy while in the Netherlands because they can maintain speaking their own languages and still get along in a foreign country. Many expatriates and long term visitors to the Netherlands can hardly speak any Dutch, even after living and working there for many years. In France and Germany, visitors are expected to at least attempt to learn the language immediately. Speaking and understanding a foreign language can be one of life's most rewarding endeavors. Even the tolerant Dutch do become indignant, however, when expatriates haven't learned the Dutch language after living and working there for many months or even years. The Dutch have to speak English whenever dealing with these expatriates. After many months of accommodating these expats, they feel that it's only practical, and even respectful, that the expats learn and speak the language of the country in which they live and earn a living. These resentments are exacerbated when first and second generations of immigrant families can't even speak the Dutch language. After all, even Dutch tolerance has its limits.

SEX AND PROSTITUTION

Leave it to the Dutch to legalize, regulate and tax sex. The Dutch exhibit to the world their methods of solving everyday social problems with practical, common sense solutions. There isn't a city in the world that doesn't have the oldest profession in its midst. Prostitution, according to the Dutch, has always been prevalent where there is enough cash flow and always will be. The simple economic concept of supply and demand dictates the inevitability of prostitution, and Mother Nature keeps that primal demand for it quite strong! Realizing this simple concept, the Dutch cultivate Red Light Districts in many of their cities with legalized prostitution that is regulated, relatively safe and the least harmful to society and its citizens. The Dutch believe that the alternative to such Red Light Districts is illegal prostitution that is unsafe, rampant, and a persistent problem for society as a whole, the workers and the customers.

The Red Light District in Amsterdam comprises only a small portion of the overall city and if visitors choose to abstain from entering this area, they can easily do so. The Red Light District in Amsterdam is actually a beautiful, historic part of the city that has incredible architecture, numerous shops, restaurants and some of the best cafes in the city. At the heart of the Red Light District is the oldest and most beautiful church in Amsterdam, the *Oude Kerk*, built in the 14th century. Only Dutch tolerance could sanction countless streets of prostitution surrounding the most historic church in the city! The Prostitution Information Center (PIC) is in proximity to the *Oude Kerk* and offers literature, souvenirs and information on all aspects of prostitution and the Red Light District. As the old adage goes, "location is everything!"

The juxtaposition of the PIC with the 14ᵗʰ Century Oude Kerk – now that's tolerance!

Even more alarming than the Prostitution Information Center conducting business across the street from such hallowed grounds is the child day care center located in the heart of the Red Light District. This day care center invites children from all over to learn the ABCs and the virtues of Dutch tolerance. Tourists are incredulous after meandering through the streets of the Red Light District taking in all of the truly unique sights and sounds and then stumbling upon pictures of Mickey Mouse and other Disney characters. How better for children to learn about the virtues of Dutch tolerance while on their way to the day care center than by passing countless prostitutes in windows and possibly their neighbors seeking extra-curricular activities? It's more important to the Dutch that their children learn tolerance and respect for individuals than to shy away from social issues and even to cast aspersions on those participating in objectionable activities. By being exposed at early ages to the questionable elements of society, Dutch children learn to accept individual choices and to tolerate societal phenomena much more easily than children, and even adults, in other cultures.

This ideological mindset of Dutch parents is vastly different than that of most parents in the U.S. and other countries. The thought of sending young children to school in a neighborhood where prostitution is widespread is utterly abhorrent and contemptible in these other cultures. A parent would be ostracized from a community for even entertaining the notion of having children coexist with prostitutes and sex shops. In fact, the famous Mayor Rudy Giuliani of New York City went on a rampage to close or clean up all sex-related businesses such as topless dancing establishments, video stores and sex novelty shops within a certain radius of school districts and neighborhoods. Consequently, the once legendary 42nd street went from Sleaze Land to Disney Land due to his untiring efforts. It used to be a rite of passage for teenage boys to walk 42nd street on their way to Yankee or Met games to purchase fake IDs and to survey the unusual sites. Now it's more like walking through a strip mall in the heart of Disney with its numerous fast food chains, children stores, Starbucks, Gaps and video arcade parlors. Mr. Giuliani did indeed do a fantastic job of cleaning up the city in certain areas, but prostitutes and the sex industry are still thriving, just in different parts of the city. His actions resulted in a mere displacement, not elimination, of such social phenomena. All one has to do is walk a few blocks to the Port Authority Bus terminal and 8th Avenue or to one of the boroughs outside of Manhattan to witness the displaced illicit street transactions. As the Dutch would say, he *"mopped the floor with the faucet still running."*

So how did these Red Light Districts come into being? With the Dutch being seafaring people and maintaining trading posts in all corners of the world, the long sea journeys didn't provide much companionship for the men onboard the ships. When these seafarers returned to port in their homeland they were looking for something a little more than a good night's sleep. The Red Light District in Amsterdam is only a few blocks from port and the sailors would be able to take care of business right away.

In addition to wanting a warm body upon returning from a long journey, the sailors wanted to imbibe in local gin mills, hence all of the *oude bruin* (old brown) cafes that still exist today in the Red Light District. In Dutch, the area is referred to as *de Wallen*, which refers to the medieval walls that acted as the city's defenses in centuries past. The approximately twenty streets of the Red Light District are lined with red lights, red curtains and even bridges decorated with red lights spanning the numerous canals. All of this redness is a result of an old folklore which asserts that working women in centuries past carried red candles through the streets of Amsterdam showing their availability. Once the candle was blown out, shop was closed for the time-being.

The infamous Lady in the window

Prostitution didn't actually become fully legalized in the Netherlands until October 1, 2000. Only after this date were prostitutes able to elude the stigma of working in an illegal profession. The Red Light District, however, has been operating for centuries openly to the public and to Dutch authorities. The Dutch relied on its form of *gedogen*, or regulated tolerance, to ensure that the Red Light District was not harmful to society or its active participants. Prostitution was going to exist regardless, so Dutch authorities tolerated the practice and strived to make it as safe as possible. In October, 2000, the Dutch went one step further in regulating this thriving industry by making it fully legal and, therefore, making it safer, enabling reasonable pay and providing full health coverage to the workers much in line with the Dutch liberal social welfare system. As with any legalized profession, taxes are now being levied and collected much more efficiently, much to the chagrin of many of the prostitutes. When prostitution was merely tolerated, it was easier for the working girls to collect their wages under the table, or in this case under the mattress. It is unknown precisely how much the Dutch government collects from the estimated one to two billion euro industry, but financial experts have calculated that if all sex workers and brothel owners paid tax, the government would rake in almost 450 million euros annually![2]

With the legalization and even stricter regulation of the sex industry, Dutch officials are striving for improved working conditions, reduced crime and increased tax revenue. Additionally, the Dutch are working diligently to ensure that forced and child prostitution don't exist and that the minimum age for all workers is 18. Such heinous crimes exist in cities throughout the world and the Dutch are taking proactive measures to ensure that they don't happen within their borders. In addition to the safety provided by the Dutch government, the prostitutes actually have their own hooker's union, or *Stichting de Rode Draad*, to ensure further safety and to guarantee their inherent rights. This hooker's union is a tightly knit organization where all members look after one another. In the event of a violent or undesirable incident, a worker simply presses a button and, since most of these window brothels are connected to others via passageways, help can arrive immediately. Additionally, when a foolhardy tourist snaps a picture of one of the ladies in a window, a plethora of prostitutes converge on that unsuspecting individual like vultures on a carcass! It's quite amusing observing jovial Asian men, well renowned for their proclivity for snapping pictures at just about anything, being accosted and browbeaten by a horde of scantily clad prostitutes. A picture of the look on one of their faces is worth a thousand words! Even in the land of tolerance some things are still anathematized. Many women working in the Red Light District come from other parts of the world where they work as prostitutes in order to earn enough money in a short period of time to go back to their homelands to start careers or to buy land. They don't need the specter looming over them that incriminating pictures are floating around of them working the Red Light District of Amsterdam.

In addition to prostitution in the Red Light Districts throughout the Netherlands, other sex related activities are tolerated. For instance, outside Amsterdam is a drive-through brothel where clients can pull up in their cars and make a selection from among the many working ladies (or even men). Paying customers then park in a stall with corrugated metal dividers, negotiate the deal, and then toss whatever it is they need to toss in specially provided waste bins once the deal has been consummated. Such regulated procedures provide clients with the convenience of taking care of their business without leaving the confines of their front seats. Some may find it incorrigible that the Dutch tolerate such activities, but then again the Dutch know that such activities will transpire anyway, so regulating such activities, no matter how vile they may seem, reduces the harm towards individuals and to society. Although not as prevalent as years past, hookers can be found loitering around the entrances of tunnels to New York City ready to jump in a potential client's car to make the journey through the tunnel a little more pleasurable for the driver. These street workers, invariably, get out on the other side ready for a repeat performance, this time in reverse. Obviously, such behavior is extremely dangerous for all involved parties. The

Dutch feel that regulating such activities is a much more viable option than just letting it occur recklessly and dangerously.

The Red Light District in Amsterdam is replete with all things relating to sex. In one of the famous theaters, the Casa Rosso (or its smaller equivalent across the street) such sex related activities take place such as strip teases; sexual performances with various paraphernalia, to include candles, beads, whips, dog collars and other risqué devices; humorous skits with audience participation, much to the embarrassment of many men once full of bravado; and many other scintillating activities. This theater is not hard to find for it is the one with the famous fountain across the street of a giant penis with rotating testicles! The Dutch don't have any statues of great statesmen or war heroes, for that would honor individual greatness, which rewards people who *stick their heads above the crowd,* but they proudly exhibit the infamous penis with rotating testicles statue. There are more pictures taken of that infamous statue than the most cultural sites throughout Europe!

Only in Holland!

Perhaps the most offensive or pleasurable activities, depending on one's take in the matter, are the live sexual performances between consenting adults on stage. Performers actually get on stage, whether it man/woman or woman/woman, and perform sexual activities with one another in front of a captivated audience. Such a concept is truly mortifying to many. But since the Dutch tolerate and regulate all activities in the Red Light District, these shows are conducted with as much decorum and decency as possible, as unbelievable as it may sound. The venues for these live performances are quality theaters; they are not sleazy, back alley dives. In fact, waiter service is even available at the Casa Rosso so that audience members can order and receive drinks without leaving the comforts of their plush theater seats. Analyzing and critiquing art certainly requires subjectivity. These live sex performers are considered true artists by scores of people. All of the movements on stage are actually choreographed and the performers maneuver into various positions with grace and precision. It's quite obvious that much planning and practice, true to Dutch form, goes into these performances.

There are numerous establishments throughout the Red Light District that center on the theme of sex. In fact, Amsterdam hosts a Sex Museum that depicts the history of sex and many of the social repercussions experienced due to sexual relations throughout time. Interestingly, men and women from all walks of life and of all ages patronize these sex-related enterprises. These commercial establishments aren't just reserved for drunken Englishman, as some may presuppose. The infamous *Bananenbar*, perhaps the most risqué of venues, operates in the Red Light District where ladies of all shapes and sizes perform tricks on top of the bar with various phallic (and at often times airborne) devices, the capstone being their legendary banana trick. Ok, this particular establishment may be reserved for drunken Englishmen and other rowdy types!

Numerous peepshow establishments, as well as sex merchandise stores, are found dispersed throughout the Red Light District. The number of sex related establishments, however, is small compared to the number of *normal* businesses that operate throughout the Red Light District. Common, everyday businesses such as delicatessens, restaurants, ice-cream parlors and bakeries function just as normally as in the rest of the world with hardworking employees striving to make a living and aiming to please their customers. Since tolerance is ingrained into the minds of these merchants, they simply view the prostitutes and sex related entities as neighboring merchants striving for the same goals as themselves.

In commuting to and from work everyday, I had to walk through the heart of the Red Light District in order to enter and exit the *Nieuwmarkt* train station. In doing so I was able to observe the social dynamics of the various businesses and the efforts required to maintain their success. A prostitute in a window brothel (which is indeed an entrepreneurial business in itself), a sex merchandise store and even a live sex theater all had to ensure that their businesses were clean, were run efficiently, were advertised properly and treated their customers with respect and dignity in order to maintain profitability. By legalizing and regulating such activities, the economic principles of supply and demand ensure high levels of quality, dictate market value prices and prevent a proliferation of such businesses since the inefficient ones simply wouldn't be able to compete in this market driven industry.

Even though many nations condemn the Dutch liberal policies on sex and prostitution, these same countries are actually clandestinely collaborating with the multi-billion dollar sex industry, reaping the incredible profits while exploiting young women throughout the world. In the United States alone, the sex industry is estimated to be an astounding $10 billion, which is more than the combined revenues of the National Football League (NFL), National Basketball Association (NBA) and Major League Baseball (MLB) combined! Furthermore, the sex industry in the U.S. makes more money than the movie industry with the summation of all movie tickets sold annually! The government is collecting enormous taxes on corporate behemoths greatly benefiting from the sex industry, like General Motors (owns hotel chains), AOL Time Warner (media), Comcast (cable) and the numerous hotel chains such as the Hilton. Forty percent of all hotel rooms in the U.S. support pornographic channeling, which draws incredible sums of monies to these corporate giants. These corporations, however, do not publicize or even report the profits that they reap from actively participating in this highly lucrative industry. Diane Sawyer produced a documentary on the profitable sex industry on the television show *Nightline* in January, 2003 and she exposed the defiance that these corporations exhibited upon confrontation with their involvement in this unregulated, very unsafe industry.

While these megalomaniacal corporations are reaping enormous profits from the thriving sex industry, young girls are being mercilessly exploited and abused. Even though corporate executives are profiting tremendously off of this exploitation, they do nothing to ensure the safety and basic human rights of the countless workers in this industry. Girls as young as eighteen years old are being paid nominal fees to perform in pornographic movies where they have no benefits whatsoever. *Nightline* reported that these young women make up to only $1500 per movie, and that's only if they're willing to perform with multiple partners at once. The lump sum payment decreases significantly the older a woman gets and the less risqué they are willing to be. There are no unions to support and defend the rights of these young women and no Occupational Safety and Health Act (OSHA) requirements to ensure safe working conditions. Even though employees of these powerful corporations enjoy medical, dental, vision, life insurance, profit sharing, stock options, pensions, and numerous other benefits, the workers in the sex industry, from whom they are profiting generously, aren't even acknowledged.

The government collects huge sums of monies from these corporations in the form of taxes but does nothing to ensure the safety of these young women. The government supports a plethora of organizations that defend the rights of anything from animals, to nature, to blasphemous arts, but does nothing to protect the rights of young adults working in this $10 billion a year industry. It can be argued that endangered species such as the Pennsylvania Cave Amphipod, Florida Fairy Shrimp and American Burying Beetle are being taken care of better than U.S. citizens working in the sex industry. While I was in the Army stationed in Fort Bragg, home of the prestigious 82nd Airborne Division, the endangered Red Cockaded Woodpecker demanded more respect than any 3-Star General on post! Military maneuvers were interrupted, curtailed and even terminated because of this precious little creature. The nation's fighting elite, the first Division deployed to war, was being severely hampered in preparing for its crucial mission because the environmentalists deemed this diminutive woodpecker more essential than a well-prepared, combat ready force. Needless to say, most members of the 82nd Airborne Division salivate at the thought of that little creature sizzling in their frying pans or stuffed and mounted over their fireplaces! The fines levied for harming even the slightest feather on one of these beloved birds would deter even a Special Forces Airborne Ranger Infantryman. It seems that the rights of the young workers in the sex industry should be more in line with those of the numerous endangered species. Even the former U.S. Surgeon General, Dr. C. Everett Koop, calls for the House and Senate to address the need to regulate this industry to ensure basic safety and that OSHA requirements are being met for these workers. These workers may participate in a questionable business, but ethics and morals aside, they certainly have just as many rights as any Red Cockaded Woodpecker or Florida Fairy Shrimp!

The Dutch absolutely abhor what they see as the hypocrisy of other nations when dealing with such touchy subjects as sex and prostitution. While other nations are sweeping these inevitable social quandaries under the rug, the Dutch are taking these problems head on and solving them in pragmatic ways ensuring that safety and decency are upheld for all. In the U.S. a newly turned 18 year old girl can perform, on camera, unsafe sexual acts with multiple partners for practically nothing for distribution to the world but has to wait three more years to legally drink a beer!

The Dutch scoff at such hypocrisy. One state in the U.S., however, is taking measures similar to the Dutch in ensuring the safety of workers in the sex industry. Some brothels in Nevada are now legal, such as the infamous Chicken Ranch, and impose strict regulations to ensure safety for workers and customers. In such brothels, working ladies aren't exposed to the highly probable misfortunes that illegal working ladies of the streets encounter such as robbery, abduction, rape and even murder. For the same reasons that the Dutch tolerated, but regulated, for many years and then legalized prostitution, the U.S. and other countries may slowly be following their lead and adopting the philosophy that prostitution is inevitable and the only way to make it safe is to regulate and control it.

GAY NETHERLANDS

True to form, the Dutch tolerate homosexuality perhaps more than any other place in the world. Many reports suggest that the incidents of homophobia and hate crimes in the Netherlands are among the lowest. Gay men and women travel to the Netherlands from all corners of the globe to enjoy the Dutch unparalleled tolerance and to avoid the stigma of being gay in their homelands. As one homosexual declared:

> *"Living in Holland, we can easily forget that in other countries you can be fired, beat-up, imprisoned, murdered with impunity, evicted from your home, banned from teaching and other professions, subject to ridicule, excommunicated, ostracized, barred from holding public office, prevented from visiting your children and denied the financial and social benefits of marriage - just because you're gay."[3]*

Gay men and women are fully integrated into Dutch society and can be as open as they please with their sexual preferences. Gay people do not feel compelled to congregate in the same neighborhoods and aren't laden with pressures to belong solely to all-gay institution or clubs.

Amsterdam hosts the world's largest Gay Pride parade once a year. On the first Saturday in August, gay men and women put on a spectacular show that leaves little to the imagination. This water-borne extravaganza attracts more than 100,000 spectators and displays remarkably decorated floats carrying passengers dancing passionately to blaring music. The canals throughout Amsterdam are strewn with such sights and sounds and people of all ages laugh and cheer along the canal banks as the merriment floats by. Once the parade finishes, parade participants can be found carousing the streets and imbibing in pubs wearing outrageous costumes or as little as a smile. The city is certainly full of energy, electricity and incredulity on this yearly occasion.

As an American growing up in conservative suburbia, to say that the Gay Pride parade was quite an eye-opener is an understatement. I had no idea that such an event took place and was expecting to go about my normal Saturday routine on the day of this big event. Upon departing my apartment, situated along the Amstel River, I was immediately taken aback with the throngs of people out in the streets and the numerous floats sailing down the river with frolicking, practically naked men and women. Reluctant to ask anyone what was going on to avoid being marked as an outsider, I cautiously strolled along the streets and observed people of all ages, and even parents with their small children, camped out along the banks of the rivers and canals truly enjoying these bizarre sights and sounds. With the Dutch being tolerant of all lifestyles and behaviors, they set out to enjoy a day of uniqueness and expressions of individuality as seen nowhere else in the world. Once I was over the initial shock of seeing men dressed in nothing but spiked leather pouches for their private parts and women with nothing but creative, colorful concoctions for theirs, I was able to go about my business for the day. I must admit, however, that I conducted my affairs with some trepidation for the spiked, leather pouches worn by some of these naked men made me a bit uneasy!

In 2001, the Dutch were the first to allow marriage rights to gay couples equivalent to those enjoyed by heterosexuals. This law is the most liberal gay marriage law in the world. Dutch homosexuals have full marriage rights and benefits, which include adoption, divorce, pensions and inheritance. The only difference is that gay couples may not adopt children from abroad, out of deference to the sensitivities of other nations. Parliament approved such a measure with relative ease since the majority of the population supported the rights of gay couples. Countries throughout the world are decades, if not centuries behind the Netherlands in passing such liberal gay marriage laws. Belgium is one country that followed the lead of the Dutch and enacted similar same-sex marriage laws in 2003. Sweden, Luxembourg, Spain and Switzerland are all proposing similar legislation and are targeting allowing same-sex marriages in 2005.

Tremendous controversy recently emerged in the U.S. over the New York Times' desire to post gay marriage announcements. With the New York Times being one of the most liberal newspapers in the U.S., they made the decision to include gay marriage announcements along with the traditional marriage announcements. Many subscriptions were canceled due to this breakthrough decision. This is a big step for gay rights in the U.S., but many gays feel there are still many hurdles and obstacles that need to be overcome in order to attain the rights and privileges afforded to gays in the Netherlands.

Homosexuality is not hidden and is simply a normal component of Dutch society. Amsterdam even commemorates its gays with its *Homomonument*, located near the *Westerkerk*, the famous church that Anne Frank peered at through cracks in her window blinds. This monument comprises three pink granite triangles, which extends into the *Keizersgracht* (Emperor's Canal). The triangles represent the pink patches that had to be worn by gay concentration camp inmates during the Nazi era. Many homosexuals wear the gay rainbow flags on their lapels, even to work. While working for a Dutch company, my department hired a new gentleman and on his first day, much to my surprise, he came in wearing a rainbow flag on the lapel of his suit. He wanted people to have the first impression of him as a proud gay man. Water cooler conversations in other cultures about a man wearing a rainbow flag on his first day would have been unremitting, but to the Dutch it was no big deal.

The Dutch military freely allows gays, which is a far cry from the "don't ask, don't tell" policy of the U.S.'s Clinton administration. Numerous rainbow flags garnish neighborhoods throughout the country and gay couples candidly hold hands while sauntering through the streets. Such hand holding in public is taboo throughout most parts of the world. There are areas in the U.S., however, where gay couples are free to be open with their sexuality. Such areas are extremely liberating for visiting couples who normally have to repress their sexuality in their hometowns. In Greenwich Village, New York and San Francisco, California, for instance, visitors come from all over the U.S. just so they can be free with their sexuality and hold hands with their partners openly and without prejudice while walking the streets.

Gay emancipation in the Netherlands has not worsened the AIDS crisis. The number of AIDS cases per 1,000 people in Holland is 0.28, slightly above Germany at 0.20, but below France at 0.75 and well below the United States at 2.33.[4] The Dutch realize that homosexuality exists and will exist regardless of what stringent measures a society or even a government may impose on this form of sexuality. As with all individuals with differing lifestyles, idiosyncrasies, religious inclinations, political views and any other individual preferences, homosexuals are tolerated and accepted into Dutch society and entitled to reap the many social benefits available to all members of the community. The Dutch form of tolerance means no discrimination whatsoever.

DRUGS

There are numerous misconceptions about the drug laws and the use of drugs in the Netherlands. Many people throughout the world view Amsterdam as a drug-crazed, decadent city where all of its inhabitants are addicts and high on drugs. This couldn't be farther from the truth. Laws do exist in the Netherlands that allow for the purchase of small quantities of soft drugs, or cannabis, which includes marijuana and hashish, only in designated and regulated business establishments. As always, the Dutch debated at length on first the toleration, and then the legalization, of such drugs. The *overleg* process was in full force and they formed a clear consensus of what they thought was the most pragmatic and safest way to deal with the common societal occurrences of cannabis use. The drug policies of the Netherlands depict soft drugs as virtually harmless and hard drugs, such as cocaine, heroin, LSD, amphetamines, crack and ecstasy as extremely dangerous. The Dutch drug laws concerning hard drugs are very tough, and active measures are taken to prohibit such use. The Dutch view the responsible use of soft drugs, however, as victimless and harmless to society and do not criminalize or feign moral outrage over such recreational drug use.

In typical Dutch form, the use of cannabis was tolerated for over twenty years before being legalized. This toleration, or *gedogen*, called for authorities to look the other way when common sense dictated. As long as businesses were conducting their affairs ethically and within the prescribed societal norms and people weren't abusing these tolerant drug policies, authorities would refrain from probing into their affairs. The Dutch tolerated the sale and use of soft drugs because it separated the soft drug users from the extremely dangerous hard drug arena. Tolerating soft drugs makes it less likely that someone desiring cannabis would end up purchasing a more dangerous drug, and keeps a whole market away from the illegal drug trade.

Even though the Dutch adamantly oppose and resist the use of hard drugs, they view hard drug users as people with serious problems and seek to help them rather than to persecute them. The Dutch take exhaustive measures to help these people with problems to clean up and to become fully functional members of society. The Dutch socialistic government is responsible for the general health of its citizens and, therefore, its drug policies depict soft drugs as virtually harmless and hard drugs as extremely dangerous. Even with the Dutch strong stance against hard drugs, the Netherlands is the biggest producer and distributor of the harmful drug ecstasy. This chemical concoction has made it onto the shores all over the world and has caused numerous societal and health problems, especially with the teenager and young adult segments. The Dutch need to initiate their *overleg* process and strive for their usual consensus on how best to deal with this disturbing hard drug problem occurring within their borders.

The sale, purchase and use of cannabis became fully legal in the Netherlands in 2000. Businesses participating in the soft drug industry are regulated by the government on a local level and are required to obtain licenses and to pay taxes. As with prostitution, the Dutch government legalized cannabis as a way to even further regulate and to ensure the safety of all who are willing to participate in this activity. Businesses are allowed to sell a maximum of only five grams of cannabis to an individual customer. They used to be allowed to sell up to thirty grams, but the Germans and French, strong opponents to the Dutch liberal drug policy, insisted that the Dutch tighten its controls over their sinister drug policies. What the neighboring Germans and French fail to realize is that most of the drugs entering the Netherlands come via routes through Germany and France! These drug establishments are permitted to stock no more than five hundred grams of cannabis at any given time. There are no laws that allow for the production and distribution of large quantities of marijuana and hashish, but somehow these lucrative establishments always find a way to stockpile their maximum of five hundred grams on any given day. The production and distribution is one element of this industry where the Dutch still exercise *gedogen*, or looking the other way when common sense dictates. These businesses are permitted to operate as long as they pay their taxes and don't disclose where they received their drugs.

Another common misconception is that since soft drugs are readily available the Dutch probably use and abuse them on a regular basis. Many Dutch citizens may have experimented with soft drugs in their lives, but by far the majority of them don't use them regularly. By far, the most active participants in smoking cannabis are the tourists. Since the Dutch grow up with easy access to soft drugs, these drugs are treated like any other commodity. When people want it, they simply get it. It's not considered a big deal or "cool" to be able to smoke marijuana or hashish in the Netherlands.

I associate this nonchalance towards smoking cannabis to children of Italian immigrant parents growing up in the U.S. These children drank wine with their dinners nearly every night; it's part of their culture. These children, consequently, were least likely to binge drink on the weekends or to have strong desires to drink excessively upon entering their teenage years. Drinking responsibly was always tolerated in their households so weekend binge drinking was not eagerly sought out. As soon as people are told that they can't do something is when their desires to do it become ardent.

The United States was practically turned upside down when Prohibition was introduced in the roaring 1920's. Bootlegging and illegal profiteering took place during these tumultuous times with an increase in organized crime and violence. Many similarities exist between Prohibition and the existing U.S. drug policies. Even though cannabis is illegal, there are no purported decreases in its usage and drug dealers are profiting tremendously. The Dutch further argue and prove that their toleration and legalization of cannabis doesn't create a more violent society; the murder rate in the Netherlands is 1.8 per hundred thousand, less than one-fourth the U.S. rate and among the lowest in the European Union.[5] With 16.2 million people, the Netherlands has fewer homicides each year than many individual U.S. cities!

DUTCH COFFEESHOPS

The legal entities participating in the business of selling marijuana and hashish are all referred to with one common name; that name, surprisingly, is "Coffeeshop." Every single place of business which sells pot, and there are over four hundred of them in Amsterdam alone, is referred to as a Coffeeshop. A Coffeeshop is a unique Dutch institution that has operated with quasi-legal status in the Netherlands for over twenty years. Not only can one get a tasty cup of Dutch coffee, but can also purchase and smoke marijuana or hashish right on the premises. Some Coffeeshops offer a full array of beer and liquor, some offer tasty treats and some are true Coffeeshops that serve only coffee and fruit drinks, and, of course, cannabis! If you enter a *Koffiehuis*, a regular Café or even a Coffee House, you won't be able to purchase or smoke cannabis; the business must explicitly state "Coffeeshop" on the front façade. One can easily identify a Coffeeshop by the sweet smell of burning cannabis and pictures of marijuana leaves, Jamaican reggae singer Bob Marley or other drug related references on the storefront windows.

More than just coffee in here!

Since there are numerous, competing Coffeeshops in cities such as Amsterdam, each Coffeeshop strives for a particular ambiance or theme to appeal to certain segments of the population. Such themes include rock n' roll, jazz, Caribbean, sports and just about anything else that appeals to one's imagination while under the influence of drugs. Some may offer comfortable couches, television sets, pool tables, foosball tables and even Internet access. It's quite common to observe tourists e-mailing their friends at home boasting that they're currently smoking a joint in a public place. Since all of these Coffeeshops compete with one another, all of them have menus depicting the choices of marijuana and hashish with their corresponding prices. Regular cannabis users can passionately tell you the best types of cannabis to get along with reasonable prices that you should pay. A typical Coffeeshop menu, prices in Euros, is shown below.

Grass	25,00	12,00	20,00	115,00 (Group Price)
Super Skunk	4,3 gram	2,0 gram		22 gram
Orange Bud	4,3 gram	2.0 gram		22 gram
White Widow	4,1 gram	1,8 gram		21 gram
Northern Light	4,1 gram	1,8 gram		21 gram
High Hydro	4,1 gram	1,8 gram		21 gram
Purple Haze	5,0 gram	2,2 gram		30 gram
Jamaica		2,5 gram	5,0 gram	40 gram
Sensimilla		2,5 gram	5,0 gram	40 gram
Thai		2,5 gram	5,0 gram	40 gram

Hash	25,00	12,00	20,00	115,00 (Group Price)
Old Amsterdam	3,3 gram	1,5 gram		20 gram
Temple Hash	3,3 gram	1.5 gram		20 gram
Super Kachmir	3,3 gram	1,5 gram		20 gram
Charras	3,3 gram	1,5 gram		20 gram
Buddha's Fingers	2,3 gram	1,0 gram		12 gram
Sky High (Dutch)	1,0 gram			5 gram
Super Afghan		2,5 gram	5,0 gram	30 gram
Black Bombay		2,5 gram	5,0 gram	30 gram
Zero Zero		2,5 gram	5,0 gram	35 gram

Choices, choices, choices!

Some Cannabis smokers may just be interested in getting good deals, rather than the quality of the pot. Cognizant of such frugal pot smokers, Coffeeshop owners realize the importance of good old-fashioned advertising.

Only in the Netherlands....What a bargain!

As can be seen there is a clear distinction between marijuana and hashish. Marijuana is simply the leaves from marijuana plants while hashish is the resin from the hands of the workers picking the leaves of these plants. This resin is then compacted to form a solid mass. Smokers of hash burn sections of this mass structure and mix small pieces of it with tobacco to roll a joint. Hash smokers must truly delight in the effects of such a drug considering its rather unsanitary origins of being resin from field workers' hands.

Worldwide Cultural Drug Trends
Due in a large part to the successful and virtually harmless drug policies of the Netherlands, marijuana decriminalization

is becoming the worldwide drug policy of choice as numerous nations are revising their drug laws to be more in line with that of the Dutch model. The majority of the countries in the European Union have removed the criminal element for possessing and using cannabis. Not only are countries decriminalizing the possession and use of soft drugs, but are actively pursuing the decriminalization of the cultivation and sale of such drugs.

In Switzerland, for instance, government officials recently endorsed draft legislation that recommends police stop enforcing laws prohibiting the cultivation and sale of small amounts of marijuana. This move comes on the heels of a nationwide poll indicating that more than one-quarter of the population has used the drug, and more than fifty percent favor liberalizing marijuana laws. These measures would even tolerate the creation of private establishments, similar to the Dutch Coffeeshops, where business proprietors could sell soft drugs to its patrons.

Several Industrialized countries throughout the world have been tolerating businesses similar to the Dutch Coffeeshops for the last few years. The *HC Marijuana Users Teahouse of Canada*, recently opened without incident in Vancouver, British Columbia. The Teahouse allows patients licensed by Health Canada to consume pot openly, but does not sell or distribute cannabis on the premises. The Canadian government legalized the use and possession of medical marijuana for qualified patients at the turn of the century.

In England, the *Dutch Experience* café is fully operational and allows recreational users to openly consume cannabis on the premises. This fully legal business establishment draws approximately five hundred patrons per day and attracts only minor attention from the police. Additional cafes of this nature may soon be opening in other cities in England. The success of the *Dutch Experience* café is indicative of the growing support for cannabis law reform in England, as well as other nations. Colin Davis, the pioneer who opened the café, is fondly remembered for handing the Queen of England a bouquet of flowers mixed with cannabis buds! Wonder what went on behind closed doors at Buckingham Palace that night.

Many European nations have been practicing their own forms of *gedogen* when dealing with individual marijuana use for many years. They've realized that such recreational use, especially among the younger segments of society, are going to exist no matter what types of laws are implemented. I've been traveling to Germany quite often for business and pleasure over the past fifteen years and invariably, have witnessed marijuana use right out in the open on numerous occasions. Many Germans will roll marijuana or hashish joints right in a pub and smoke it out in the open. These activities are usually preceded by a quick glance over the shoulder to ensure that no authorities are in the immediate vicinity. Pub owners and customers simply tolerate such behavior as long as those participating in it are in control and aren't bothering anyone around them. Even in Prague, I've witnessed young adults smoking cannabis out in the open with little concern for the law. In the U.S. people can be found smoking pot at just about every rock n' roll concert with little harassment. The differences between the U.S. and most European countries, however, is that if authorities do decide to harass those smoking pot the repercussion are much more severe in the U.S.

Who Smokes Marijuana Anyway?
To assume that marijuana users are merely those on the fringes of society and reserved only for the so-called dregs of society would be a gross miscalculation. According to recent statistics provided by the federal government, nearly 80 million Americans admit having smoked marijuana. Of these, twenty million Americans smoked marijuana during the past year.[6] This many Americans can't possibly be living on the fringes of society and can't possibly all be dregs. Marijuana users come from all elements of society; from successful business and professional leaders, to average hard-working citizens, to counter-culture radicals. Even many high-level politicians and key decision makers have admitted to smoking marijuana, such as President Clinton (even though he claims he didn't inhale), New York City Mayor Michael Bloomberg

(who boasted that he enjoyed it), Supreme Court Justice Clarence Thomas, Vice-President Al Gore, New York Governor George Pataki, Conservative Newt Gingrich, Congresswoman Susan Molinar and a plethora of others. For politicians and legal professionals to continue to support such harsh punishments against those possessing or using marijuana is hypocritical and unjust.

According to the National Organization for the Reformation of Marijuana Laws (NORML), more than 700,000 Americans were arrested on marijuana charges in 2000, and more than five million Americans have been arrested for marijuana offenses in the past decade. Almost ninety percent of these arrests are for simple possession, not trafficking or sale. The Dutch perceive such rampant police activity in this area as a waste of valuable law enforcement resources that could be focused on serious and violent crime. FBI statistics indicate that one marijuana smoker is arrested every 45 seconds in America! Taken together, the total number of marijuana arrests for 2000 far exceeded the combined number of arrests for violent crimes, including murder, manslaughter, forcible rape, robbery and aggravated assault. More alarmingly, 60,000 individuals are behind bars for marijuana offenses at a cost to taxpayers of $1.2 billion per year. Taxpayers annually spend between $7.5 billion and $10 billion arresting and prosecuting individuals for marijuana violations. Almost ninety percent of these arrests are for marijuana possession only. Once again, the Dutch view this U.S. style of prohibition as *mopping the floor when the faucet is running.*

Many opponents to the toleration or legalization of soft drugs cite the health risks involved with smoking such drugs. The Dutch would agree that cannabis may not be the most healthy activity one can pursue (even though strong arguments exist for the positive health benefits), but feel it certainly can't be as bad as liquor, which is fully legal for anyone over 21 years old in America and for anyone over 18 in most developed countries. The statistics surrounding the adverse effects of alcohol such as health problems, broken families, spousal abuse, employment problems and many others are absolutely staggering. If liquors as strong as whiskey, tequila and even grain alcohol are fully legal, criminalizing marijuana use, which is benign in comparison to the previously mentioned rocket fuels, just doesn't makes much sense to the Dutch. Most fights, riots and insurrections result from alcohol abuse rather than the inhalation of soft drugs.

One of the most precarious situations in the Netherlands in the relatively recent past was during the Euro 2000 football tournament, which was held in both Belgium and the Netherlands. One weekend the English football fans trekked down to Brussels to support their home team and to start their usual football hooliganism. To no surprise there were fights, broken windows, damaged cars, the typical English football fanaticism. Much of the violence was the result, undoubtedly, of the effects of the strong Belgium beer. Hundreds of English were arrested and thrown in jail. The next weekend the games were to be held in Ajax stadium in Amsterdam and the packs of English hooligans were foaming at the mouths because they were playing their archrivals, the Germans. The entire city of Amsterdam was on edge and more cops than ever were patrolling the streets. The English packs came in by the hundreds early Saturday morning. The first item on the agenda for the English football fans was to head straight for the watering holes in order to start the inebriation process. While in the process of getting intoxicated, they took advantage of the Dutch liberal drug laws and started smoking the cannabis in typical hooligan excess. Since cannabis is a depressant, the English football fans were pacified and all ambitions for violence were depleted. So there they were, hundreds of glassy-eyed English hooligans previously ready to tear up the city, staring blankly into space throughout the hundreds of Coffeeshops in Amsterdam. Not one incident occurred and not one arrest was made.

The current global trend with regard to marijuana use is overwhelmingly to move away from the American "do drugs-do time" drug policy model to the Dutch model of tolerance and regulation. Current drug policies in many cultures simply

English Hooligans too "relaxed" to cause a ruckus

don't deter the use of marijuana, but lead to the overcrowding of prisons and to the likely violation of human rights. The Netherlands is leading the way in controlling soft drug use, a worldwide phenomenon, with pragmatic and sensible laws that ensure safety and the preservation of individual rights. Even with the Dutch liberal drug policies, there are no signs of visible decay, no overwhelming fear and no rampant crime even in the highly-populated drug areas of Amsterdam. Societal harm reduction actually results because of the presence of Coffeeshops in the Netherlands for there are no drug dealers pushing marijuana or hashish on the street corners or in schools. The Dutch have succeeded in separating the harmful hard drugs from the less disruptive soft drugs. With soft drugs off the streets, law enforcement can focus exclusively on the dangerous hard drugs and other perilous crimes.

Even with the legalization of marijuana and hashish, Dutch drug use is not prevalent. In fact, the Dutch use drugs less than most other cultures throughout the world. Despite easy availability, marijuana prevalence among 12 to 18 year olds in the Netherlands is only 13.6 percent -- well below the 38 percent use-rate for American high school seniors.[7] Furthermore, drug-related deaths are much lower in the Netherlands than in other cultures. In 1995, the most recent year for which statistics are available, there were 2.4 drug-related deaths per million inhabitants in the Netherlands, compared to 9.5 in France, 20 in Germany, and 27.1 in Spain. Moreover, Dutch drug users are the least likely in Europe to contract AIDS. Continent-wide, 39.2 percent of AIDS victims are intravenous drug users, while in the Netherlands the number is 10.5 percent.[8] The Dutch continue getting criticized by other nations for their liberal drug policies, but they merely deflect these insults in their typically Dutch calm manner and justify their policies with statistics that overwhelmingly support their efforts. The Dutch view those dictatorial drug policies throughout the world as hypocritical, serving only to *mop the floor while the faucet is still running.*

EUTHANASIA

Another deeply sensitive and controversial social issue that the Dutch confronted head on is euthanasia, or mercy killing. In typical Dutch form, this touchy subject was the center of intense discussions and every facet of the issue was scrutinized greatly. On April 1, 2002, Euthanasia became legal in the Netherlands, under specific circumstances. The Dutch practiced its customary form of *gedogen* in the twenty years preceding this world-shattering decision. Since the Dutch tolerated this practice for such a length of time, the decision to legalize euthanasia was not nearly as ground-breaking for the Dutch as it was for the rest of the world. The law put into effect in April, 2002 does not allow doctors to discriminately end persons' lives. In fact, technically speaking, there are still cases where euthanasia is still illegal in Holland, but this new law establishes criteria under which doctors will not be prosecuted for ending a life at the patient's request. Dutch doctors are supposed to report instances of euthanasia to regional committees of their peers. It used to be up to a district attorney to decide whether to prosecute doctors; now, under the new law, if the regional committee decides the doctor acted in accord with the guidelines, the prosecutor's office does not get involved.

Strict criteria exist for doctors to abide by in order to assist patients in ending their lives. Those criteria are as follows:

- A request for euthanasia must be voluntary, well considered and repeated over a period of time
- Suffering must be unbearable, with no prospect for improvement
- The doctor must have informed the patient of his or her situation and further prognosis
- The doctor and patient must have discussed the situation and reached the conclusion that there is no other reasonable solution
- The doctor must consult with one other physician, with no connection to the case, who performs an independent analysis and states in writing that the doctor has satisfied the due care criteria

As can be seen, clear and unambiguous criteria must be met in order for doctors to carry out this practice. Supporters say the law brings out into the open a practice that happens all the time in other countries, where it is hypocritically hidden from view. The consequence, they believe, is that euthanasia will actually become less common in Holland, because patients will not hide their intentions or act out of panic. Belgium, France, Britain and Australia are actively debating similar laws or legal cases. In the U.S., Dr. Jack Kevorkian, or Dr. Death as he was nicknamed by opponents, made headline news by assisting numerous patients who were terminally ill to end their lives. Dr. Death isn't practicing his own form of mercy killing these days for he is serving a 10-25 year prison term for his unabashed crusade for the rights of patients to choose their fate.

Opponents to the Dutch law draw parallels to the killing of disabled and mentally ill of Nazi Germany. Germany, incidentally, fervently opposes its neighbor's liberal policies on euthanasia. Additionally, opponents feel that having such a law in effect will desensitize society on issues relating to death creating an increase in euthanasia cases and even abortion. There were 2,123 reported cases of euthanasia in the Netherlands in 2002.[9] Proponents to legalized euthanasia state that a profuse amount of cases of euthanasia occur clandestinely around the world. Interestingly enough, World Health Organization figures indicate that the abortion rate in The Netherlands is one of the lowest in the world. In 1996, the United States had 1,365,700 induced abortions -- 22.9 for every 1,000 women between 15 and 44. In Holland, the rate was 6.5, even though the practice of euthanasia was tolerated and abortion had been legalized for many years preceding 1996.[10] It doesn't appear that the Dutch are desensitized to death. Furthermore, adversaries to the law believe that throngs of suffering foreigners will trek to the Netherlands in order to easily end their lives. The Dutch declare that such deaths will not occur because patients must have close relationship with their doctors. The Dutch constantly and unswervingly reject these despairing individuals.

The Dutch model of tolerance certainly puts the tiny country of the Netherlands on the world map. The Dutch tackle social issues head-on through an intricate process of consensus and toleration. Many of these social issues bitterly divide other nations. Even with the liberal social laws, the Dutch don't view their country as more decadent than others, just less hypocritical. They look at harm reduction as opposed to total elimination of certain behaviors in dealing with the societal dilemmas that plague countries throughout the world. Many view the Netherlands as a social laboratory for the world and as the pioneer in establishing pragmatic solutions to common societal problems. Many countries are following their lead in facing social problems once considered taboo and attempting to regulate them in order to ensure safety and to reduce the overall harm to their societies. Many countries where the Catholic Church is still a strong political entity, such as Italy and Spain, may not be as quick to accept these Dutch liberal laws and to test them out in their own countries. Regardless of where cultures stand on the Dutch form of tolerance, many issues are now being openly debated as opposed to continuing to be repressed due in a large part to the Dutch model. It will be interesting to see when and how many countries will alter their ideologies and adopt policies similar to those of the Dutch in years to come.

9. ETHNIC HOLLAND

During my initial taxi ride from Schiphol airport to my hotel in the heart of Amsterdam, my amicable taxi driver (yes, the same one who introduced me to the throat peculiarities of the Dutch and the unusual sounding word *gracht*) informed me rather proudly of the ethnic diversity found in his homeland. He stated that Amsterdam is the most ethnically diverse city in Europe and is home to approximately 185 different registered nationalities. Being simultaneously jetlagged and energized to begin my European adventure, I dismissed the ethnic diversity discourse being espoused from this tall, blonde-haired, blue-eyed, very Dutch looking person as just rhetoric and tourist-welcoming propaganda. After all, what city these days doesn't boast about its ethnic diversity? I was sure that this pleasant Dutchman was simply embellishing the very small percentage, if not just a mere handful, of ethnic diversity that existed in this small, northwestern European country. After all, I did just arrive to the legendary land of cheese, windmills, tulips and the bicycle-riding, easy-going Dutch. Such Dutch stereotypes implanted in my mind never conjured up images of ethnic or racial diversity, as being described by my hospitable taxi driver.

As I arrived to my plush hotel in the Dam Square, I was welcomed by even more pleasant and mild-mannered Dutch men and women. Nearly all of them were tall and possessed the physical characteristics that I had envisioned of the Dutch. I immediately opened all of the tourist brochures and planned out my activities over the course of the next few days prior to reporting to my first day of work. I wanted to immerse myself into Dutch culture as much as possible in the short period of time that I had in order to be Dutch-savvy by the time I started my work assignment. I didn't want to appear culturally ignorant to my future colleagues or to give the impression that I was ambivalent about assimilating into their society.

I spent the next couple of days eating in traditional Dutch restaurants, drinking in historic *bruin* (brown) cafes, practicing Dutch phrases and talking to as many Dutch people as I possibly could, mainly in the more prosperous sections of town. I became, by no means, an expert in that short period of time, but felt that I indoctrinated myself adequately enough to be at least conversant on Dutch culture and the societal norms upon starting employment with my Dutch company. Although my focus had been on traditional Dutch aspects of society, I did observe several ethnic restaurants and the small percentage of ethnic diversity, to the levels that met my expectations, but nothing quite like the proportions that the taxi driver conveyed to me.

Perhaps due to the influence of my past military training, I decided to perform a reconnaissance of the area of town where I was going to be working. I wanted to make certain that I could navigate the Dutch train system and find my work building in order to avoid any kind of logistical mishaps the morning of my first day on the job. Plus, I certainly didn't want to be late because it didn't take long to realize the Dutch propensity for timeliness and order. I also planned on exploring the restaurants, cafes and parks in the area since I was going to spending a significant amount of time in the region over the next several months.

I mapped out my journey, boarded the number 54 metro train and headed out to Amsterdam *Zuidoost* (Southeast). Being a Sunday, it was a very peaceful train ride and I enjoyed observing the Holland landscape as the train headed further away from the center of the city. I arrived to my destination approximately twenty-five minutes later and set off to find my place of employment. Of course I was disoriented as I departed the train, not knowing east from west or north from south, and not really caring since I had all Sunday afternoon to explore. I eventually picked a direction and ventured off to see what lied ahead. After all, this was also an exploratory excursion so I was looking forward to stumbling across typical Dutch neighborhoods and was curious to observe the lifestyles of the Dutch outside of the city center.

As I proceeded, I noticed that things were drastically different in the southeast section of town compared to the center of Amsterdam, several kilometers away. In fact, I didn't even feel like I was in Holland anymore. As I continued to walk, I soon realized that the people in this part of town not only didn't look, dress or act Dutch, but didn't even speak the Dutch language. In fact, the language they were speaking and the clothing they were wearing didn't even appear to be European. I could only venture to guess, based upon my initial observations of their dialects and clothing, that the masses of dark-skinned people in this southeastern section of town were from the continent of Africa. I was truly flabbergasted with the large contingent of ethnic Africans in this small northwestern country of Europe.

Soon realizing that I was lost, I picked another direction and headed out for more exploration, quite curious to see what lied ahead this time. After several minutes of trekking through these unfamiliar and rather surprising neighborhoods, I realized that I was not even close to any corporate complexes, but was in the heart of a residential area that was obviously home to hordes of immigrants, mainly from Africa or the islands of the West Indies. I approached several people to ask for directions, but the communication barriers were impenetrable. Even my futile attempts at Dutch fell on deaf ears as these immigrants spoke only their native tongues, which were very, very foreign to me.

Needless to say I meandered around these neighborhoods for quite some time trying to find my way back to the train station. To my astonishment, many of the neighborhoods were impoverished and rather rundown. My expectations of finding affluent and idyllic Dutch suburbs in this economically prosperous country certainly weren't met. After wandering around in what appeared to be continuous circles, a very friendly person of African descent approached me and asked, in very broken English, if I was lost. I'm sure that being the only person of Caucasian descent in the entire vicinity studying a map was a clear indicator that I was indeed lost! He pointed out the direction which eventually led me back to the train station. From there, I was able to gain my bearings and to locate my corporate building, which, of course, was in the exact opposite direction from the one I initially set out in.

My little venture into the outskirts of Amsterdam did indeed produce culture shock. This culture shock, however, did not occur because I was in a foreign country, but because I was in a foreign country *inside* of a foreign country! This region, commonly referred to as the Bijlmer area, is an ethnic enclave where people from foreign descent live, mingle and observe the cultural norms of their homelands. Even though I was in Holland for only a short period of time, it was quite obvious that the people of this region weren't talking, dressing or acting Dutch, but maintaining the lifestyles that they were accustomed to in their homelands, wherever that was. I now realized that the oration about ethnic diversity from that cordial taxi driver was not rhetoric at all, but, in fact, a reality.

Background on Holland's Diversity

Approximately twenty percent of the Dutch population of just over sixteen million is foreign born. The most substantial of the immigrant population in Holland includes the Turks, the Surinamese and the Moroccans, and to a lesser degree, the Antilleans, Indonesians and sub-Saharan Africans. The rest of the 185 registered nationalities that the taxi driver boasted about come from virtually all corners of the globe. Even though Holland has always been a refuge for freedom-seeking foreigners, the immigrants who have migrated to Holland over the past fifty years have been more visible as they now arrived from non-western civilizations. The increasing numbers of immigrants arriving from non-western cultures have resulted in national challenges for the Dutch, as they now had to contend with numerous and fundamentally differing cultures, religions, values and overall ways of life. With the numerous immigrants living in Holland, it's almost unfathomable that the second line of an older Dutch national anthem, preceding the current national anthem, the *Wilhelmus*, stated that *Dutch blood must be free of alien stains.*

Immigration from non-western cultures began in earnest in the 1950s as persons from the Dutch colonies started to arrive in Holland seeking better ways of life or fleeing turmoil in their homelands. Such immigrants from the Dutch colonies included the Surinamese, Antilleans and Indonesians. Since these migrants came from Dutch colonies, they were able to assimilate relatively easily, as compared with the subsequent waves of immigrants, since most of them spoke the Dutch language and were already fairly accustomed to the Dutch culture.

The early 1970s saw a drastic increase in the number of immigrants due mainly to the economic vitality and need for unskilled laborers to fill the numerous voids within the Dutch job market. The Dutch actively sought out foreign laborers, specifically young and healthy men, from parts of the world that could satisfy their labor requirements. The Dutch imported guest workers, mainly from Turkey and Morocco, and offered them relatively high-paying salaries to fulfill the required job functions in order to keep the Dutch economy flourishing. The original intent of the guest worker policy was to have the foreign laborers perform the required job functions for only short periods of time and then the foreign workers would go back to their homelands with sizable amounts of money in their pockets. As these guest laborers became accustomed to the higher standard of living in Holland, however, they chose to remain in the country as opposed to returning to their homelands where the economies weren't nearly as strong. Instead of venturing back home with fistfuls of guilders, they paid for their families to come to Europe in order to settle permanent residences in flourishing Holland. The Dutch didn't expect such events to transpire and were ill-prepared and ill-equipped for the masses of guest workers remaining in their country and the waves of immigrant families that ensued.

The increasing numbers of political asylum seekers in the late 1970s exacerbated the immigration problems in Holland. Holland, along with many other prosperous western European nations, served as a safe haven for refugees from various, tumultuous parts of the world who were fleeing political turmoil, instability and even persecution within their homelands. Most of these asylum seekers came from unstable regions of sub-Saharan Africa and the Middle East. The Dutch, with their proclivity for tolerance and freedom, welcomed these political asylum seekers and provided a safe refuge for them. As word spread about the tolerant ways of the Dutch and Holland's wealth, asylum seekers from all over the world started flooding into the country, both legally and illegally.

Many of the western European nations were experiencing similar illegal immigration issues as Holland. Hordes of refugees sought sanctuaries in any part of western Europe, and many of them did not have their sights set specifically on Holland. But as other European nations began implementing stricter immigration controls, refugees were denied sanctuary. These refugees, therefore, began bouncing from one country to the next in hopes of eventually finding a safe haven where they could settle. The migratory path of these refugees began in the southern portions of Europe, particularly Italy and Greece. As countries began refusing refugees permanent residences, the freedom-seeking migrants continued their journeys northward. The refugees eventually made their ways as far as Holland, the most northwestern portion of continental Europe. With the Dutch realizing that there was no place left for these refugees to go, they found themselves in very compromising positions. For the Dutch it was indeed a classic "Catch-22" as they cherished the ideals of an open society and individual freedom, but they were also very concerned that their small country was being inundated with illegal immigrants who weren't assimilating very well into the Dutch culture and were taxing their generous, liberal social systems.

On numerous occasions I've heard the Dutch venting about their country being the final stop and settling place for such a massive amount of refugees. They adamantly expressed their frustrations with other European nations for simply shuffling the freedom seekers from country to country, which more often than not resulted with the masses of refugees winding up in Holland. Germany was also susceptible to a multitude of political asylum seekers with its economic prosperity and high standard of living. In fact, Germany leads Europe with housing the largest number of political asylum seekers, followed by the Netherlands. As Holland possesses the largest population of Surinamese outside of the country of Surinam, the German city of Berlin possesses the largest population of Turks outside of the country of Turkey.

Large segments of the Dutch population were oblivious to the actual magnitude of such illegal immigration occurring in their country. It took an unfortunate plane accident to bring these immigration issues to the forefront in Dutch society. In 1992, an El Al Boeing plane crashed into the residential area of the Bijlmer (same place where I was wandering around aimlessly) and killed over forty people. Among the casualties were people whom the Dutch authorities could not identify as being residents of their country, although they've been living there for quite some time. This regrettable calamity placed the Bijlmer region into the spotlight and the Dutch populace saw how significant the illegal immigration issues really were. The Dutch were stunned when they realized the enormity of the illegal population residing in their country and the magnitude of the sub-cultures that resided in the Bijlmer region.

Today, the majority of the residents in the Bijlmer mini-city of approximately 100,000 are Surinamese, Africans and Antilleans. Unfortunately, an overall negative perception permeates throughout Holland about this region, for it is rampant with crime, violence, illegal drug use and high-unemployment. I certainly could have picked a better place to get lost in Holland on my first weekend in the country! Incidentally, on future bicycle excursions out to the Dutch countryside, people invariably cautioned me to steer clear of this region.

Although Bijlmer has the unfortunate reputation as an impoverished, unsafe area, this region has many attributes that make it one of the most exciting and enjoyable places for many Dutch people, even ones of European descent. Many of these Dutch people reside in the area and wouldn't trade it in for better abodes in the city center or Amsterdam-Zuid. People are attracted to the diversity of the region and feel that the area has much more character than the *popular* parts of Amsterdam. Every fruit, vegetable and type of food can be found in the markets in the Bijlmer, along with many other products from all over the world. The large, unsightly buildings, furthermore, are being taken down in order to make room for more spacious and more attractive types of housing. The annual *Kwakoe* Festival attracts numerous visitors from all parts of Holland. This festival started out as a football tournament amongst Surinamese people, and has turned into a popular multi-cultural festival with international foods, diverse music and football matches that are enjoyed by all types of ethnicities.

IMMIGRATION CONCERNS

As with the Bijlmer region, there are other ethnic enclaves dispersed throughout the Netherlands where immigrants congregate amongst themselves and have little to no integration with the Dutch mainstream culture. The Dutch being ill-prepared to manage the waves of immigrants certainly contributed to the numerous, isolated ethnic regions found throughout the country, mainly in the cities. With being segregated from the rest of Dutch society, members within these ethnic working class neighborhoods continue practicing their own rituals and abiding by their own cultures. These immigrants, therefore, aren't indoctrinated into the culture of their newly found homes, resulting in limited opportunities to truly learn and adapt the

Dutch way of life. Children born into these segregated regions continue following in the cultural footsteps of their parents and grandparents, far removed from Dutch society. Such gregarious immigrant behavior is typical and even predictable; immigrants throughout history have been settling into new areas en masse and have been establishing ethnic communities throughout the world. After all, as the old adage proclaims, *birds of a feather flock together.*

In the span of a day, one can travel throughout the New York metropolitan region and encounter Little Italy of Manhattan, the Portuguese Ironbound section of Newark, the Hasidic Jewish enclave of Brooklyn, the Polish commune of Greenpoint, the Indian community of Edison, the Hispanic neighborhood of Spanish Harlem, Chinatown of lower Manhattan, the Russian section of the East Village, the Asian section of Fort Lee, plus numerous other ethnic communes. These ethnic enclaves have remained strong throughout the years due to the intensity of ethnic groups to remain together and to preserve their cultural similarities. The ethnic regions of Holland were developed out of the same intensity of immigrants to preserve their cultures and identities. The challenge that Holland faces, as well as many other industrialized nations throughout the world, is integrating immigrant families into the mainstream Dutch culture while affording them opportunities to adhere to their cultural traditions, as long as they don't run counter to the established societal values.

With all of the ethnic and cultural segregation, Dutch society is, in many ways, reverting back to the old "pillar" system that was commonplace in Holland from the latter part of the 19th century up until shortly after World War II. Pillarization, or *Verzuiling*, was a social partitioning within Dutch society that resulted in a number of distinct groups, characterized by their own political, religious or class associations. The pillarization concept was so pervasive in Holland that people even established their own affiliations based upon their preferences for sports, arts, literature and music. The Dutch mainly congregated within their own pillars and rarely strayed outside of these social circles. Power struggles amongst the numerous pillars were widespread and the impact that the stronger pillars had on political, religious and social institutions was immense. Many of the modern-day, ethnic pillars sprouting up in Dutch society are gaining strength and momentum and are wielding their influence over such institutions in similar manners as the Dutch pillars of the past.

As many immigrants arrive to Holland, their loyalty to their homelands, and even to their national football teams, remains fervent. On one particular evening I was awoken from a sound sleep to what sounded like a riot in city streets below. I looked out the window and observed hordes of people singing in the streets and frantically waving non-Dutch flags. A continuous parade of speeding cars traversed the streets with all of the drivers incessantly honking their horns. People were hanging out of the car windows shouting at the tops of their lungs and enthusiastically waving these non-Dutch flags. Being completely ignorant as to why such ceremonious behavior was occurring, and also being perturbed that it was occurring at such a late hour of the night, I called the front desk and inquired about the unusual events taking place outside. Upon asking the Dutch receptionist about the boisterous behavior, she casually explained that the Turkish national team had won a football match and that the local Turks were celebrating the victory. She told me to get used to these late night uproars as such celebratory events by immigrant groups are common in Holland.

As I looked back down on the city streets I could observe that the flags were indeed Turkish flags that were being waved passionately. Feeling somewhat at ease that a riot wasn't taking place downstairs, I went back to sleep, well at least tried to. The ear-piercing sounds of car horns and the deafening roars of the jubilant crowds continued well into the night and early parts of the next morning. The celebrating Turks were displaying national pride in their homeland and made it known to all of Holland that their football team had won a significant match. Arriving to work that morning was rather comical as nearly everyone was tired and grouchy due to their lack of sleep because of the all night celebrations. Anti-immigrant sentiments and xenophobia were definitely running higher than normal in Holland that particular morning. The question that lingered throughout the day was, "Would the immigrants and their Dutch-born children and grandchildren show the same passion and enthusiasm if the *Dutch* team had won a significant match?"

Whereas the United States has been a bastion for immigrants from all over the world since its early beginnings as a country, the small country of Holland is still experiencing growing pains in dealing with immigration issues. The lack of control over immigration has led to Holland's welfare state being overtaxed and has resulted in increases in traffic, hospital congestion, housing waiting lists and school classroom sizes. Unemployment amongst foreign-born residents in Holland is a striking four times higher than that of Dutch citizens. These foreigners, furthermore, make significantly less in salary than the overall population, further escalating the rift between the immigrants and Dutch nationals. Undoubtedly linked to these economic gaps, crime, violence and drug use remain persistent in many of Holland's ethnic communities.

Although violence is still relatively minimal in Holland, especially when compared to other industrial nations, it has been steadily increasing in many communities. Any violent incident is still considered a tragedy for the residents of this peaceful country. Upon hearing of the escalating violence in Holland, the Dutch often like to exclaim, "What is this, the wild west of America? This stuff only happens in America." Unfortunately for the Dutch, the harsh realities of violence in overcrowded cities has hit home.

Over the past couple of years, the Dutch have been increasingly cognizant of the issues stemming from immigration. The Dutch have become outspoken with their discontent of the numerous foreigners living in Holland who have not assimilated into the Dutch culture. The Dutch are dismayed over the fact that second, and even third, generations of immigrants can't speak the Dutch language. For centuries, the most common name given to a newborn boy in Holland was Jan. The most common name given to newborn boys today is Mohammad, indicating the prevalence of migrants from the Middle East. In fact, the largest mosque in all of Europe is under construction in Rotterdam, in proximity to the Feyenoord football stadium. The Dutch have become fearful that immigration is spiraling out of control and are now speaking out on such issues after years of suppressing their concerns. Many parents, furthermore, are concerned that their children will grow up speaking the Dutch language with Turkish or other ethnic accents, due to the magnitude of foreigners in the public schools. In many schools systems, there are less than a handful of Dutch children for every ten students, with the rest being from foreign lands.

The Dutch are especially distraught over the disdain that many of the foreign-born residents display towards Dutch tradition and culture. Each year the Netherlands observes a two-minute silence in honor of its citizens who had made the ultimate sacrifice during World War II. This somber tradition precedes the following day's celebrated holiday of Liberation Day, which commemorates Holland's liberation from Nazi Germany in 1945. Prior to the two-minute silence, the Queen lays a wreath at the National War Monument located in the Dam Square in Amsterdam. During the two-minute silence, the people of Holland stand still in silence and pay tribute to the numerous casualties of war. There have been many occasions where immigrants have disrupted the two-minute silence, showing total disrespect for perhaps the most somber of ceremonies observed in Holland. Immigrant children, mainly of Muslim descent, have disrupted ceremonies throughout all parts of Holland by not adhering to the two-minute silence and even chanting malicious statements such as, "All Jews should be killed." They even destroyed and set flowers ablaze and used the commemorative wreaths that were laid in honor of the war dead as footballs in their attempts to disrupt the ceremonies.

Islamic radicalism has also started to emerge throughout Holland. Dutch authorities are now faced with rising concerns that Muslim leaders are promoting anti-European, anti-woman and anti-gay agendas. In fact, a controversial book recently emerged in Holland, *De weg van de moslim* (The Way of the Muslim) which advocates violence against women and the killing of homosexuals. The book suggests that gay people should be thrown head first off of high buildings and if they're not killed on impact, they should be stoned to death. Such radicalism certainly runs counter to the Dutch ideals of tolerance and respect for all.

RISE OF THE RIGHT — PIM FORTUYN

Bringing the immigration issues into the spotlight as never before in the Netherlands was the sociology professor turned politician, Pim Fortuyn. In 2001, Mr. Fortuyn rose to prominence in the city of Rotterdam, home to Europe's largest sea port. With Rotterdam being the largest shipping port in Europe, its population consists mainly of blue-collar dockworkers, ship workers and truck drivers – hardworking, middle-class people. Over the years, Rotterdam has transformed itself into a quintessential immigrant town, with the immigration population now comprising half of the total population. As the demographics began to shift, Rotterdam began experiencing rising crime, increasing street violence, deteriorating public schools and worsening health care benefits. The Dutch residents of this shipping town began feeling increasingly less safe in their own neighborhoods and increasingly disgruntled with the lack of control over immigration. Pim Fortuyn was the solution that these disgruntled Dutch citizens of Rotterdam were looking for.

Pim Fortuyn ran on a campaign of anti-immigrant, anti-big government, anti-welfare and pro-law and order. The working class citizens of Rotterdam welcomed this revolutionary with open arms. Liberal Holland has never seen the likes of such a conservative, fiery politician, who, parenthetically, happened to be a homosexual. Fortuyn made proclamations that the Netherlands was filled to capacity and that there was no more room left in the tiny country of 16.2 million. Furthermore, he openly criticized many segments of the immigrant population for not assimilating into Dutch society or adhering to Dutch values. He specifically lambasted the Muslim enclaves as being "backward" for being oppressive to women and homosexuals, which runs counter to the number one virtue in Dutch society – tolerance.

In May of 2002, just nine days before the Dutch election, Pim Fortuyn was brutally gunned down following a radio interview in Hilversum. A Dutch animal rights activist shot Fortuyn five times as he emerged from the radio studio. The killer's motives, as he later proclaimed, were to protect the weaker members of Dutch society. All of Holland was in shock and disbelief over such a violent incident occurring in the public spotlight. There hadn't been a political assassination in Holland for over four hundred years prior to the cold-blooded murder of Pim Fortuyn.

Amazingly, the deceased Pim Fortuyn still received more than 1.3 million votes in that election, more than fourteen percent of the total. With Holland's governmental policies of proportional representation, a vote for a particular candidate is also a vote for that candidate's party. Lijst Pim Fortuyn (LPF), the national party of Pim Fortuyn, finished second in the election with twenty six seats behind the Christian Democrats who won forty three. Even though Pim Fortuyn was deceased, his message remained clear and the people of Holland responded in great numbers in favor of that message.

The legacy of Pim Fortuyn still lives on today. Many of Mr. Fortuyn's hard-line and controversial views on immigration have made their ways into the mainstream of Dutch politics and society. The city of Rotterdam is currently a political anti-immigrant stronghold. Leefbaar Rotterdam (Livable Rotterdam) is the dominant political party in the city council. Rotterdam's city council has even proposed a five-year moratorium on new foreign residents   Leefbaar Rotterdam is commonly seen as the local party of the Lijst Pim Fortuyn (LPF). The party attracts attention and criticism for the un-political behavior of its members and its unconventional, sometimes right wing vision on immigration and tolerance.

The rise to prominence of an individual such as Pim Fortuyn could not have happened in any other country. Mr. Fortuyn was able to achieve political success in Holland mainly because he was *so Dutch* and the entire situation was *incredibly Dutch*. Mr. Fortuyn was a right-wing, moody politician with a shaved head and was very openly gay. Public reports surfaced about Pim Fortuyn's preference for young Muslim men and even his visits to gay dark rooms. Holland is the land of numerous paradoxes; the rise of Pim Fortuyn is no exception. Mr. Fortuyn's extravagant characteristics certainly weren't aligned with those who eventually supported and voted for him, mainly the hard-working, sober working class.

Pim Fortuyn appealed to more than just those people unhappy with immigration policies; he appealed to a larger segment of the Dutch population that was looking for *any* kind of change. Dutch society had been experiencing an underlying unease and discontent with the current state of affairs and with the status quo of the government. To the Dutch, everything seemed to be going wrong and general feelings of fear and distress became paramount within the social consciousness of the Dutch. Pim Fortuyn understood the unease within the Dutch social consciousness and addressed such concerns. Mr. Fortuyn was the catalyst that the unsatisfied Dutch needed in order to speak their feelings in a public forum. Once this public forum was established, the Dutch didn't hold back in addressing their concerns.

As Pim Fortuyn was delivering his radical messages on immigration control, Europe as a whole was seeing its political landscape being dramatically redrawn. A shift was occurring in the political landscape from the left to the right, due mainly to anti-immigration candidates preaching messages similar to Pim Fortuyn. As immigration was spiraling out of control throughout many parts of Europe, right-wing politicians were no longer fearful about speaking out on the once taboo issue of immigration. Also contributing to the rise of the right was the fact that European national identities were being threatened due to the European Union, the Euro standard currency and, of course, the influx of immigrants compromising national cultures. Great Britain alone received an astounding 72,000 political asylum seekers in 2001.[1]

Influential right-wing politicians began sprouting up all across Europe with anti-immigration viewpoints. Such politicians included Pita Kjaersgaard of Denmark, Jorg Haider of Austria, Edmund Stoiber of Germany, Jose Durao Barroso of Portugal, Silvio Berlusconi of Italy and Jean-Marie Le Pen of France. Many of these politicians have ascended into powerful positions in their countries and are still wielding their power and influence over national, and even European, policies.

In response to Pim Fortuyn's poignant message on the failures of Holland's immigration policies and due to the rising tide of xenophobia throughout the country, the Dutch parliament established the Blok Commission which investigated Holland's immigration policies over the past thirty years. In January, 2004 the commission produced a 2,500 page report detailing the effects of Holland's immigration policies. This report, however, was somewhat ambiguous with regard to the commission's findings. The report stated that a large number of immigrants fully or at least partially managed to fit into life in the Netherlands despite the apparent failure of government integration policies. The report didn't specifically label immigration as a failure, but stated that integration took place in Holland "in spite of" rather than "thanks to" the immigration policies of the successive governments over the past thirty years. The massive report wasn't very Dutch-like with its generalities and non-committal findings. Many of the Dutch residents would have preferred a more Dutch-like report with less pages and more direct findings and recommendations.

The report did, however, state that successive governments did not do anything worthwhile to prevent ethnic separatism. The commission found the worst mistake of the government was to encourage children to speak their native tongues instead of Dutch in the primary schools. As a result of the weak governmental policies, the thirty year experiment in tolerant multiculturalism had hardly been a success, and has resulted in poor schools, increasing violence and ethnic ghettoes. Additionally, such separatism contributed to immigrants, and even their children, eschewing intermarriage with the Dutch for marriage with members from their ancestral homelands. The majority of Dutch-born members of immigrant families import their spouses from their parents' homelands, even though they were born in Holland. Children, and even grandchildren, of immigrants importing their spouses from their ancestral homelands certainly doesn't encourage integration and assimilation into mainstream Dutch culture, but produces a continuation of ethnic separatism and sub-cultures.

DEATH OF WESTERN CIVILIZATION?

With all of the outrage and controversy surrounding immigration in Europe, one has to wonder how it spiraled so out of control and how it was possible for such large percentages of immigrants to make their ways into European cities in such a short period of time. Mass immigration began in earnest throughout Europe due mainly to the labor shortages experienced in the industrialized countries. In short, there simply weren't enough nationals to fulfill all of the job vacancies that their countries maintained. European countries had to actively import foreigners to fill these numerous job vacancies. Why did these industrialized European countries have such a sizable gap in the number of job vacancies and the number of national citizens to fill them? The population figures of European countries have been diminishing at a rapid rate due to the increasingly low birth rates over the past fifty years.

With such low birth rates, the population of these countries simply couldn't keep pace with the expanding job markets, thus resulting in the need to import foreign workers.

With the prevalence of birth control and abortion in the western world, to include Europe, the U.S. and Canada, the birth rates have been greatly reduced over the past fifty years. Additionally, people of the western world are getting married much later in life and are not having nearly as many children as previous generations. Many men and women throughout the western world are pursuing their careers first and foremost and holding off on having families until their careers are firmly established. Most families in the modern, westernized world, furthermore, no longer need to have a multitude of children to work the family farm or to run the family business as previous generations. Of the twenty nations with the lowest birthrates throughout the world, eighteen are in Europe.[2] The average fertility rate of a European woman is 1.4, and the fertility rate needed just to replace the existing population is 2.1.[3] Europe is experiencing a less-than-zero population growth rate. With the ever-shrinking western population, immigration is one way in which to fill the occupancy voids.

The United States has also seen an exploding immigration population over the last thirty-five years as well, with most of the immigrants arriving mainly from Mexico. The U.S. population is becoming increasingly Hispanic and less European. Today, eighty million Americans trace their ancestry to non-European roots; in 1960 only sixteen million Americans did not trace their ancestry back to Europe.[4] America, as with industrialized European nations, has experienced drastic demographic shifts over the past few decades and is continuing to experience these drastic shifts in population. Such shifts are occurring to supplement the shrinking populations and to fill the numerous voids in the unskilled labor markets.

Between the years 2000 and 2050, the world population will grow by more than three billion to over nine billion, and fifty percent of this increase in global population will come entirely in Asia, Africa and Latin America.[5] As populations in these parts of the world increase substantially, one hundred million people of European ancestry, meanwhile, will vanish from the earth during the same time period due to the less-than-zero population growth-rate.[6] In 1960, people of European ancestry comprised 1/4th of the world population. In 2000, it was 1/6th of the world population and in 2050, it is projected that people of European descent will comprise a mere 1/10th of the world population.[7]

European global representation getting even smaller

With these shrinking population reserves in the western world, industrialized countries have been relying on immigration to keep their economies running strongly. Many of the immigrants are coming from parts of the world where they have a glut of population reserves. These countries have much higher birth rates than in the western countries. Abortion and birth control certainly aren't as prevalent in these non-industrial countries as in the western world. Additionally, due the higher mortality rates at birth in these countries, people are more apt to produce more offspring to ensure survival. Furthermore, the economies aren't nearly as strong in these countries; thus, people aren't as concerned about establishing their careers prior to raising families. Women are giving birth at much younger ages than in Europe, allowing them to produce much more offspring throughout their child-bearing years.

While Holland and many other countries of the western world are experiencing less-than-zero population growth rates, non-industrialized countries are experiencing significant population increases. Western nations have been leveraging these population reserves in support of their strong economies and to fill their numerous job vacancies. Unfortunately, immigration has risen to levels not previously expected due to a myriad of reasons. Furthermore, the rise of illegal immigrants and political asylum seekers has overburdened many of Europe's generous social programs and led to decaying, crime-ridden ethnic enclaves. Holland and it European neighbors are now making sweeping reforms of their immigration policies and taking proactive stances in efforts to gain control of their immigration problems.

Dutch Revolutionary Solutions...Once Again

With persistent immigration issues and the conclusion that the immigration policies over the past thirty years have been failures, the Dutch authorities are now taking these issues head-on and leading the European Union in progressive, and even controversial, immigration policies and reforms. Freedom seeking migrants have been settling in the Netherlands at an alarming rate, both legally and illegally, in order to reap the benefits of an open and tolerant society. The Dutch are now taking active measures to control the tremendous waves of asylum seeking immigrants. The government recently announced that approximately twenty-six thousand asylum seekers currently residing in the Netherlands will be deported back to their homelands over the course of the next three years. The law applies to asylum seekers who arrived to the Netherlands before April 1, 2001, and have exhausted all of their appeals for asylum. Many of these soon to be deported asylum seekers have been residing in Holland awaiting approval of their applications for well over five years. This drastic deportation plan is proving to be quite disconcerting for both the asylum seekers and human rights advocates throughout the world. Although twenty-six thousand is certainly a significant number, it's rather pale in comparison to the eight-to-twelve million illegal immigrants currently residing in the United States.

Many opponents to the plan feel that such a mass expulsion of asylum seeking people from around the world, mainly Iraq, Somalia, Chechnya and Afghanistan, is too extreme a measure, especially with the political turmoil that many of these countries are still experiencing. Many of these asylum seekers have been holding full-time jobs in Holland for several years and have been raising their children in Dutch society. The Dutch authorities feel, however, that such proactive measures are necessary in order to bring immigration under control. The Dutch government will provide free flights home for those being deported and will also provide repatriation cash bonuses. Those refusing such incentives will be considered illegal residents and will have no rights to any of Holland's substantial social benefits.

Such aggressive immigration control policies greatly disturb the liberal, left wing contingent, who feel that Holland's reputation as a welcoming, open society will be forever tarnished. The Dutch have been world-renown for their pioneering efforts in the field of human rights. The liberal left feels that mass expulsion of immigrants will offset the great strides that have been made in the protection of these human rights. They feel that such a drastic policy of depriving immigrants of their legal status will only force them into the criminal underworld. They also feel that the deportation of people, especially children, back into hostile territories is a breach of international law that may produce a domino effect throughout Europe. The Dutch blue-collar, working class citizens, meanwhile, welcome such aggressive immigration-control proposals for they are the ones living in those areas that are most affected by the failed immigration policies. Additionally, those people living outside of these areas also welcome the aggressive immigration-control policies because they don't want to see their neighborhoods becoming adversely affected as did many of the working class areas of Holland.

The Dutch government is cognizant that it is nearly impossible to deport all illegal aliens and rejected asylum seekers with one clean sweep. As people refuse deportation and remain in Holland illegally, they will have a much more difficult time in finding loopholes in the system. Dutch authorities are cracking down on illegal immigrants and are also creating stiffer penalties for those who aid and abet illegal immigration. The Dutch are substantially increasing the capacity of their deportation centers and intensifying the efforts of their police forces to curb illegal immigration. Additionally, employers will be penalized with stiffer fines for employing illegal workers. These fines will be nearly quadrupled the current fines for employing illegal aliens. Furthermore, employers will be forced to pay retroactive social security premiums and taxes if they are found to have employed illegal immigrants for at least six months. Dutch authorities will also be targeting landlords who rent homes or apartments to illegal immigrants. Rental contracts will be dissolved and in the case of illegal subletting, landlords could even lose their homes.

In addition to many third-generation residents residing in Holland not being able to speak the Dutch language, many of them possess dual nationalities and maintain citizenship with their ancestral homelands. The Dutch believe that third-generation citizens of Holland maintaining dual nationalities shows unwillingness to integrate into Dutch society. Plans are currently in development by the Dutch government to terminate the law that allows for dual citizenship for third-generation citizens. The Dutch maintain that third-generation citizens have firmly entrenched roots in Holland and that they should actively choose Holland as their primary homeland. The Dutch government is hopeful that third-generations maintaining just Dutch citizenship will integrate more easily into the Dutch culture.

In efforts to curb Islamic extremism in Holland, the Dutch government is proposing new legislation to outlaw all activities that undermine democracy and societal values. Under this proposal, Islamic religious leaders could be held criminally accountable for any actions that are deemed dangerous and run counter to the Dutch ideals of tolerance. Such actions include the preaching of gay people to be murdered or violent subjugation of women.

Even though the Dutch are cracking down ardently on most immigration, they are actually encouraging specialized immigrants from around the world to migrate to the Netherlands. With the Dutch shrinking population and the need to fill job vacancies, especially high-skilled ones, the Dutch government is encouraging the immigration of highly-skilled laborers. These "knowledge migrants" will find it much easier to gain access into the Netherlands and less bureaucracy in establishing residence. Knowledge migrants must possess a sought after skill for the job force and must earn a minimum gross income to be considered for employment in the Netherlands. The Dutch are now being much more particular on who they allow into their country.

Even with the proposed mass expulsion of twenty-six thousand asylum seeking immigrants and the stricter immigration laws, Holland will still possess a very large ethnic contingent and the integration issues won't immediately go away. For this reason, the Dutch government will be establishing integration examinations that immigrants will be required to complete and will hold immigrants accountable for passing these tests. Both newcomers and settled immigrants will be required to successfully pass the integration exams in order to prove that they have fully integrated or are fully capable of integrating into Dutch society. The law is primarily aimed at non-European Union immigrants. Immigrants seeking entrance into the Netherlands will be required to complete a basic integration test in their countries of origin before embarking upon the Netherlands. The Dutch are world pioneers by establishing such integration exams and even requiring immigrants to complete pre-arrival integration courses. The Dutch have experienced enough integration and assimilation problems that they are now taking proactive measures to ensure that such problems never occur again.

Once again the Dutch are leading the way with progressive, yet controversial, policies that are being studied and scrutinized throughout much of the world. As with other Dutch social policies, such as the ones relating to drugs, prostitution, euthanasia and same-sex marriages, the proposed immigration policies are proving to be initially contentious on the world arena. Although a touchy subject, the Dutch are exhibiting leadership in taking immigration issues head-on and devising solutions to alleviate many of the problems that have been plaguing their country for decades due to the lack of strong assimilation and control policies. Although the Dutch policies on immigration may appear to be extreme, many European countries are already following in the footsteps of the Dutch and devising similar strategies in dealing with their immigration issues. As with the other social policies of the Dutch, at first they may appear to be excessive and unviable, but once the proverbial dust settles after all of the debating takes place, many countries throughout the world start investigating similar policies, even though at first they adamantly opposed them. Similar events will undoubtedly transpire throughout Europe once the Dutch lead the way in implementing their highly-planned out immigration assimilation and control policies.

10. CONCLUSION

As time marches on, the Dutch will continue to perplex and astonish people throughout the world, although, paradoxically, they will carry on their cultural ideologies of *striving to be just average* and *acting normal because that's weird enough*. People from all parts of the world will continue to envision Holland as this idyllic place full of fairy-tale images, tulips, windmills, cheese, picturesque landscapes and happy-go-lucky inhabitants. People will continue to envision the capital city, Amsterdam, as this insidious place where everyone is high on drugs, engaging in licentious street prostitution and killing their unborn and elderly. People will also continue viewing the Netherlands as a bastion of liberalism where traditionalism is rejected and where socialistic policies are undermining capitalism and helping to steer the world towards communism. And people will continue to envision the Dutch as these strange people who still walk around in those legendary wooden shoes. The Dutch have been misunderstood since the beginning of their existence; some things just don't ever change.

In fact, the longest-running primetime animated series in history, *The Simpsons*, recently perpetuated the wooden shoe stereotype of the Dutch. In a recent episode, Moe the bartender proclaimed to his friends that he was Dutch and then awkwardly walked out of the bar wearing cumbersome, Dutch prototypical wooden shoes. Although somewhat disconcerting to many Dutch, the wooden shoe typecast, along with the many other Dutch stereotypes, isn't going away anytime soon, especially with preeminent television sitcoms propagating such images on a global scale. Even with such categorizations, the Dutch, as they've done for centuries, will continue to focus on just doing their own thing and continue marching to the beat of their own drum, without ever skipping a beat.

People can say what they want about the Dutch with their intriguing ways, controversial policies and inimitable country, but world reports have consistently ranked the Netherlands as possessing one of the best qualities of life in the entire world. In the United Nations Human Development Report of 2004, the Netherlands was ranked fifth in the world and second in the European Union (EU) in terms of health and life expectancy, education and earnings. The report stated that the Netherlands had an average life expectancy of 78.3 years, among the highest in the world. The top ten countries listed in the UN's Human Development Report of 2004 are as follows:

1. Norway
2. Sweden
3. Australia
4. Canada
5. The Netherlands
6. Belgium
7. Iceland
8. United States
9. Japan
10. Ireland

The liberal and socialistic policies of the Dutch and their unique customs and mannerisms certainly don't seem to be having an adverse effect on their country, as many people from around the world would like to believe.

As in the patriotic song, *De Zilvervloot*, where the Dutch honor the naval hero Piet Hein by proclaiming *your name is small but your deeds are great*, the tiny country of the Netherlands has achieved, and continues to achieve, monumental accomplishments. The Dutch astonishingly survived raging waters and reclaimed the majority of their country through the use of ingenuity and cooperation. Because of this monumental feat, the Dutch are fond of stating, *"God may have made the earth, but the Dutch made Holland."* They further went on to build one of the mightiest economic empires that the world had ever seen. The Dutch continue to be one of the most industrialized nations in the world and are leaders in the field of social justice. For the modern-day Dutch, as their country is throttling full steam ahead, it's simply business as usual.

What started out as a small trading association between a handful of countries, The European Union (EU) is now the driving force in European politics and economics. European integration and cooperation is paramount in order for the EU to continue building upon its successes. Many European nations find such cooperation and acceptance of other cultures daunting, but for the small trading nation of Holland, such foreign cooperation and interaction is simply business as usual. The Dutch built their robust economic infrastructure through international commerce, cooperation and acceptance of other cultures. The Dutch are active participants in attempts at further solidifying the European Union and claim to be willing to forfeit some of their national identity and sovereignty in order to assist with this comprehensive objective. As they recently abandoned their precious guilder with little resistance or remorse, the Dutch are progressively looking forward and cooperating with their neighbors in working towards European integration that, they feel, will enhance the qualities of life for all of its members. Even with such altruistic efforts of sacrificing national sovereignty for the advancement of the EU, the Dutch will, undoubtedly, never forfeit their *Dutchness* and will continue being *so Dutch*, as they have throughout their existence. The great transformations occurring in Europe in the context of culture, politics, economics, sociology and even psychology, cannot alter the persevering nature of the Dutch in preserving their deeply ingrained Dutch ideologies and attributes.

The Dutch will continue to balance the fine line between capitalism and socialism. As a small trading nation with deeply established mercantile roots, the Dutch strive for profitability; but with egalitarianism also deeply rooted, the Dutch won't leave even their frailest of citizens isolated or neglected in the fast-paced, money driven world in which they operate. The Dutch will continue relying on pragmatism in dealing with universal problems and will continue to alleviate them with practical, very *Dutch-like* solutions. The Dutch perceive such problems as seeds of opportunity. As they seize these opportunities, the Dutch will continue to be pioneers in the world with breakthrough, revolutionary solutions, which, undoubtedly, may be just too radical for some cultures to accept. The Dutch have been confronted with intense global scrutiny over many of their revolutionary social policies. The Dutch merely shrug off such scrutiny and like to proclaim, rather superciliously, that *"the world will come around to our way of thinking eventually."* With many nations throughout the world following in their footsteps by exploring, and even implementing, similar social policies, the Dutch haughty proclamation holds merit.

With globalization and an ever-shrinking world, the preservation of cultures is becoming an arduous and painful task for many nations around the globe. Many cultures are fighting incessantly the increasing trends of global corporate hegemony, which they feel are leading to social inequality and pervasive consumerism. General Douglas MacArthur dramatically stated in his farewell address to congress after his abrupt dismissal during the Korean conflict, *"Old soldiers never die, they just fade away."* As with the old soldiers, many cultures are increasingly fearful that their traditions, customs and values will just fade away as corporate consumerism gains even more momentum and proceeds to obliterate the cherished, age-old cultural attributes that stood the test of time.

The Dutch, meanwhile, are disinclined to expend needless energy on things they cannot change, but focus mainly on those areas of life where they can make positive impacts. The Dutch have the uncanny ability of succeeding in the principle of doing less and accomplishing more. By accepting people, situations, circumstances and events as they occur, and by focusing in those areas of life that truly matter, the Dutch will continue surprising the world with remarkable achievements and imaginative solutions to the world's worst problems, in spite of their modest and humble cultural attributes. In the process, their deeply ingrained *Dutchness* will remain steadfast as it has for thousands of years. Political subjugation, religious oppression, military assaults and global ideological transformations were even unsuccessful at deposing this unwavering institution of *Dutchness.*

The Dutch will continue in their never ending pursuit for *gezelligheid*, or Dutch coziness. They will eschew the temptations of greed, riches and fame for that inviting, small, dusty café, that simple garden in the backyard or that quiet time in the den with a pipe and good tobacco. Not that the Dutch don't engage in stimulating events or exciting worldwide travel, but their priorities will always remain on the simple, yet pleasurable aspects of life. The classic children's story, *The Cow who Fell in the Canal*, explores the theme of Dutch culture in a creative, yet amazingly accurate way. In the story, Hendrika the cow is bored with spending her long days grazing on a Dutch pasture. She was experiencing the *Wanderlust* that so many of the Dutch possess. One day she fell in a canal and pulled herself onto a raft that was floating by and eventually drifted all the way into the big city. Hendrika was enamored with the city, amazed with all of the sights and had one amazing adventure after another. After spending some time frolicking around the city, Hendrika's owner discovered her and brought her back to the pasture. Back at the pasture, Hendrika was no longer bored or anxious to leave her home, but was happy and content just eating grass in her pleasant little meadow. She had wonderful memories of the city and even now donned a sporty city hat, which were all that she needed. Hendrika appreciated and relished in her state of *gezelligheid.*

The uniqueness of the Dutch has led to much ambiguity, and even frustration, as people try to figure out these *Dutch-like* ways and mannerisms. Annoyed with this *Dutchness*, Napoleon Bonaparte dismissed Holland as *"a smoke-room full of obese cheese-mongers and devious bank cashiers."*[1] The foreign oppressors who lived in Holland and keenly observed the intriguing ways of the Dutch, however, saw a deeper, underlying reason for this *Dutchness*. Frenchman Joseph Garat attempted to explain the inexplicable to Napoleon and members of the French Senate in a memorandum espousing the underlying virtues of the Dutch people, who, at the time, lived under the regime of the Batavian Republic.

> *"The Batave is much more Dutch than the Englander is English, the Frenchman French or any other people in the world anything. It is not exactly their patriotism which gives the Bataves this quality of eternal fixity of character; but rather their land, their climate, their whole manner of being and living, all of which resemble nothing else that can be seen on the face of the earth...He who has built his dwelling with his own hands will never leave it; the Dutch built Holland and they have the air of forever saying "What we have done is good,"...their dazzling but odorless flowers grown beneath the fogs of Haarlem; the wreaths of smoke from their tobacco delight their senses far more than the most exquisite perfume under the most perfect skies...They believe that if this is taken from them they will simply cease to be Bataves; for them it is not just a matter of losing their name, it would be to lose their very lives."* [2]

These sentiments certainly lay claim to the proposition that the Dutch are the most unique people in the world. What's next for the Dutch and for Holland? How will these Gentle Giants in this intriguing land perplex the world in future years? One can only anxiously wait, for the Dutch are in no rush for anything. For the time being, people will continue to visit Holland and continue to observe the peculiar ways of the Dutch and the mystifying makeup of the land. Whether it's the leaning buildings, the scantily-clad ladies in windows, the aromas emanating from the numerous hash houses, the nonchalance of the Dutch, the spectacular museums and cultural exhibits, the controversial social policies, the capricious weather, the fervent cyclists, the intriguing canals, the ingenious windmills, the towering heights of the Dutch, the overarching conformity, the resilient individuality, or any of the other oddities that transpire within the Dutch borders, people will continue to be in awe and will often find themselves shaking their heads and muttering to themselves, "Only in Holland, Only the Dutch."

Chapter Notes

Chapter 1   Introduction to this Intriguing place
             called Holland

1. Dodge, Mary Maples, *Hans Brinker or the Silver Skates* (New York, Charles Scribner's Sons, 1899), p29.
2. Geo Hive, Global Statistics, http://www.xist.org/global/pop_data2.php.
3. White, Colin and Boucke, Laurie, *The UnDutchables* (Colorado, White-Boucke, 2001), p2.
4. Driesum, Rob van and Hall, Nikki, *Amsterdam* (Australia, Lonely Planet, 2002), p10.
5. Fin Facts.ie, *Worldwide 2004 Quality of Life City Rankings*, http://www.finfacts.ie/qualityoflife.htm.
6. van Driesum, Rob and Hall, Nikki, *Amsterdam* (Australia, Lonely Planet, 2002), p26.
7. Amsterdam Heritage, Department for Monuments and Archaeology of Amsterdam, http://www.bmz.amsterdam.nl/adam/uk/intro/intro.html.
8. Driesum, Rob van and Hall, Nikki, *Amsterdam* (Australia, Lonely Planet, 2002), p24.
9. Dodge, Mary Maples, Hans Brinker or the Silver Skates (New York, Charles Scribner's Sons, 1899), p34.
10. Simply Amsterdam, *The Eight Windmills of Amsterdam*, http://simplyamsterdam.nl/windmills/windmills.php.
11 Driesum, Rob and Hall, Nikki, *Amsterdam* (Australia, Lonely Planet, 2002), p7.

12. Driesum, Rob van and Hall, Nikki, *Amsterdam* (Australia, Lonely Planet, 2002), p26.
13. Lonely Planet, Western European Phrasebook, (Australia, Lonely Planet Publications, 1997), p 28.
14. Wikipedia, *Frisian Language*, http://en.wikipedia.org/wiki/Frisian_language.
15. World Climate, http://ww.w.worldclimate.com/.
16. Dutch News Digest, *The People's Queen Juliana Passes Away*, March 22, 2004, http://www.dnd.nl/.
17. New Jersey Herald, *People's Top 10 Cover Stories*, April 10, 2004.
18. Henri Willig, *The History of Gouda Cheese*, http://www.henriwillig.com/Cheese_History.htm.
19. Henri Willig, *The History of Gouda Cheese*, http://www.henriwillig.com/Cheese_History.htm.
20 White, Colin and Boucke, Laurie, *The UnDutchables* (Colorado, White-Boucke, 2001), p121.
21. XS4ALL, *Amsterdam as a Business City*, http://www.xs4all.nl/~wdb/business.html.
22. Starbucks, Store Locator, http://www.starbucks.com/retail/locator/default.aspx.

CHAPTER 2   BRIEF HISTORY OF THE NETHERLANDS

1. Mak, Geert, *Amsterdam* (Massachusetts, Harvard University Press, 1994), p76.
2. Schama, Simon, *Patriots and Liberators* (London, Collins, 1977), p94-95.
3. Schama, Simon, *Patriots and Liberators* (London, Collins, 1977), p105.
4. Schama, Simon, *Patriots and Liberators* (London, Collins, 1977), p139.
5. Rietbergen, P.J.A.N., *A Short History of the Netherlands* (Amersfoort, Bekking Publishers, 2002), p121.

CHAPTER 3   DUTCH WORLDLY IMPACT

1. Mak, Geert, *Amsterdam* (Massachusetts, Harvard University Press, 1994), p120.
2. Mak, Geert, *Amsterdam* (Massachusetts, Harvard University Press, 1994), p120.
3. The Netherlands Embassy, *U.S. Towns and Cities with Dutch Names*, http://www.netherlands-embassy.org/article.asp?arti cleref=AR00000382EN.
4. Driesum, Rob van and Hall, Nikki, *Amsterdam* (Australia, Lonely Planet, 2002), p14.
5. Mak, Geert, Amsterdam (Massachusetts, Harvard University Press, 1994), p117.
6. Barreveld, Dirk J., *From Amsterdam to New York* (Nebraska, Writers Club Press, 2001), p60.

CHAPTER 4   THE LAND OF THE GENTLE GIANTS

1. Schama, Simon, *The Embarrassment of Riches* (New York, Vintage Books, 1987), p262.
2. Schama, Simon, *The Embarrassment of Riches* (New York, Vintage Books, 1987), p263.
3. Winner, David, *Brilliant Orange* (Great Britain, Bloomsbury, 2000), p111.
4. Winner, David, *Brilliant Orange* (Great Britain, Bloomsbury, 2000), p111.
5. Winner, David, *Brilliant Orange* (Great Britain, Bloomsbury, 2000), p111.
6. Winner, David, *Brilliant Orange* (Great Britain, Bloomsbury, 2000), p219.
7. Winner, David, *Brilliant Orange* (Great Britain, Bloomsbury, 2000), p17.
8. Ajax USA, *Ajax, de Joden, Nederland,* http://www.ajax-usa.com/history/kuper/.

9. Ajax USA, *Yells inside the Stadium*, http://www.ajax-usa.com/history/kuper/we-re-hunting-the-jews.html.
10. Free Republic.com, *Increased Anti-semitism In Europe Noticeable In The Netherlands At Soccermatch*, April, 2002, http://www.freerepublic.com/focus/news/670149/posts.

CHAPTER 5   DUTCH INDIVIDUALISM: FIRST AND FOREMAST

1. USA Today, *European Gay Union Trends Influence U.S. Debate*, July 14, 2004.
2. Nuffic, *The Holland Handbook* (The Netherlands, X-PAT Media, 2002), p31.
3. Driesum, Rob van and Hall, Nikki, *Amsterdam* (Australia, Lonely Planet, 2002), p29.
4. Winner, David, *Brilliant Orange* (Great Britain, Bloomsbury, 2000), p205.
5. Football Culture.net, *Why Fans Fight*, http://www.footballculture.net/fans/feat_fanviolence.html.
6. Winner, David, *Brilliant Orange* (Great Britain, Bloomsbury, 2000), p149.
7. Mak, Geert, *Amsterdam* (Massachusetts, Harvard University Press, 1994), p267.
8. van Driesum, Rob and Hall, Nikki, *Amsterdam* (Australia, Lonely Planet, 2002), p19.

CHAPTER 6   SOCIETAL ORDER AND CONFORMITY

1. Barreveld, Dirk J., *From Amsterdam to New York* (Nebraska, Writers Club Press, 2001), p169.
2. Schama, Simon, *The Embarrassment of Riches* (New York, Vintage Books, 1987), p192.
3. Coach K The official website of coach Mike Krzyzewski, *K Quotes, http://www.coachk.com/quotes.htm*
4. Schama, Simon, *The Embarrassment of Riches* (New York, Vintage Books, 1987), p188.
5. Schama, Simon, *The Embarrassment of Riches* (New York, Vintage Books, 1987), p198.

6. Schama, Simon, *The Embarrassment of Riches* (New York, Vintage Books, 1987), p188.

CHAPTER 7   DUTCH CONSENSUS BUILDING AND
                       COMPROMISE

1. Winner, David, *Brilliant Orange* (Great Britain, Bloomsbury, 2000), p83.
2. Nees, Greg, *Germany, Unraveling an Enigma* (Maine, Intercultural Press, 2000), p106.

CHAPTER 8   DUTCH TOLERANCE

1. van Selm, Joanne, *The Netherlands: Tolerance Under Pressure*, Migration Policy Institute, August, 2002, http://www.migrati oninformation.org/Feature/display.cfm?ID=43.
2. Cowan, Roberta, *A Century of Sex Work*, Expatica.com, June 2002, http://expatica.com/.
3. Lowe, Kevin, *Pride and Prejudice*, http://www.expatica.com/ source/site_article.asp?channel_id=1&story_id=1752.
4. Allen, John L., *The Dutch Way: Tolerance Fuels Social Experiment*, National Catholic Reporter, October 19, 2001, http://www.natcath.com/NCR_Online/archives/101901/ 101901a.htm.
5. Allen, John L., *The Dutch Way: Tolerance Fuels Social Experiment*, National Catholic Reporter, October 19, 2001, http://www.natcath.com/NCR_Online/archives/101901/ 101901a.htm.
6. The National Organization for the Reform of Marijuana Laws, http://www.norml.com.
7. Allen, John L., *The Dutch Way: Tolerance Fuels Social Experiment*, National Catholic Reporter, October 19, 2001, http://www.natcath.com/NCR_Online/archives/101901/ 101901a.htm.
8. Allen, John L., The Dutch Way: Tolerance Fuels Social Experiment, National Catholic Reporter, October 19, 2001. http://www.natcath.com/NCR_Online/archives/101901/ 101901a.htm.

9. New York Times, *Dutch Legalize Euthanasia, The First Such National Law*, April 1, 2002.
10. Allen, John L., *The Dutch Way: Tolerance Fuels Social Experiment*, National Catholic Reporter, October 19, 2001, http://www.natcath.com/NCR_Online/archives/101901/101901a.htm.

CHAPTER 9   ETHNIC HOLLAND

1. Cowell, Alan, *Europe Rubbing its Eyes at the Ascent of the Right*, New York Times, May 18, 2002.
2. Buchanan, Patrick J., *The Death of the West* (New York, St. Martin's Press, 2002), p13.
3. Buchanan, Patrick J., *The Death of the West* (New York, St. Martin's Press, 2002), p13.
4. Buchanan, Patrick J., *The Death of the West* (New York, St. Martin's Press, 2002) p3.
5. Buchanan, Patrick J., *The Death of the West* (New York, St. Martin's Press, 2002), p12.
6. Buchanan, Patrick J., *The Death of the West* (New York, St. Martin's Press, 2002), p12.
7. Buchanan, Patrick J., *The Death of the West* (New York, St. Martin's Press, 2002), p12.

CHAPTER 10   CONCLUSION

1. Schama, Simon, *Patriots and Liberators* (London, Collins, 1977), p655.
2. Schama, Simon, *Patriots and Liberators* (London, Collins, 1977), p655.

BIBLIOGRAPHY

Ajax USA, *Ajax, de Joden, Nederland,* http://www.ajax-usa.com/
history/kuper/.

Ajax USA, *Yells inside the Stadium,* http://www.ajax-usa.com/
history/kuper/we-re-hunting-the-jews.html.

Allen, John L., *The Dutch Way: Tolerance Fuels Social Experiment,*
National Catholic Reporter, October 19, 2001, http:
//www.natcath.com/NCR_Online/archives/101901/
101901a.htm.

American Woman's Club of the Hague, *At Home in Holland*
(Delft, Uitgeverij Eburon, 1988).

Amsterdam Heritage, *Department for Monuments and Archaeology
of Amsterdam,* http://www.bmz.amsterdam.nl/adam/uk/
intro/intro.html.

Amsterdam Heritage, Municipal Department for Monuments and
Archaeology of Amsterdam, http://www.bmz.amsterdam.nl/
adam/index_e.html.

Barreveld, Dirk J., *From Amsterdam to New York* (Nebraska,
Writers Club Press, 2001).

Buchanan, Patrick J., *The Death of the West* (New York, St. Martin's
Press, 2002).

Cowan, Roberta, *A Century of Sex Work,* Expatica.com, June 2002,
http://expatica.com/.

Cowell, Alan, *Europe Rubbing its Eyes at the Ascent of the Right,*
New York Times, May 18, 2002.

Dodge, Mary Maples, *Hans Brinker or the Silver Skates* (New York,
Charles Scribner's Sons, 1899).

Bibliography

Driesum, Rob van and Hall, Nikki, *Amsterdam* (Australia, Lonely Planet, 2002).

Dutch News Digest, *The People's Queen Juliana Passes Away*, March 22, 2004, http://www.dnd.nl/.

Expatica.com, *The Story behind Prinsjesdag*, http://www.expatica.com/source/site_article.asp?subchannel_id=6&story_id=1742.

Fin Facts.ie, *Worldwide 2004 Quality of Life City Rankings*, http://www.finfacts.ie/qualityoflife.htm.

Football Culture.net, *Why Fans Fight*, http://www.footballculture.net/fans/feat_fanviolence.html.

Free Republic.com, *Increased Anti-semitism In Europe Noticeable In The Netherlands At Soccermatch*, April, 2002, http://www.freerepublic.com/focus/news/670149/posts.

Geo Hive, Global Statistics, http://www.xist.org/global/pop_data2.php.

Gosling, Patricia and Nation, Fitzroy, *Ethnic Amsterdam* (Amsterdam, Uitgeverij Vassallucci, 2001).

Harris, Bruce and Bird Michelle, *Closed Curtain lives of de wallen* (Colorado, White-Boucke, 2001).

Hoge, Warren, *Britain to Stop Arresting Most Private Users of Marijuana*, New York Times, July 11, 2002.

Horst, Han van der , *The Low Sky, Understanding the Dutch* (The Netherlands, Scriptum Publishers, 2001).

Irving, Washington, *A Knickerbocker's History of New York* (Louisiana, Firebird Press Book, 2001).

Jensma, Folkert, *A Dutch Radical's Message to Europe*, New York Times, May 14, 2002.

Krasilovsky, Phyllis, *The Cow Who Fell in the Canal* (USA, Scholastic Book Services, 1969).

Lonely Planet, Western European Phrasebook, (Australia, Lonely Planet Publications, 1997), p 28.

Lowe, Kevin, *Pride and Prejudice*, http://www.expatica.com/source/site_article.asp?channel_id=1&story_id=1752

Majoor, Mariska, *When Sex becomes Work* (Amsterdam, Stichting Prostitutie Informatie Centrum (PIC), 2002).

Mak, Geert, *Amsterdam* (Massachusetts, Harvard University Press, 1994).

McNeil, Donald G., *Not Only in America: Gun Killings Shake the Europeans*, New York Times, May 11, 2002.

The National Organization for the Reform of Marijuana Laws, http://www.norml.com

Nees, Greg, *Germany, Unraveling an Enigma* (Maine, Intercultural Press, 2000).

The Netherlands Embassy, *U.S. Towns and Cities with Dutch Names*, http://www.nethcrlands-embassy.org/article.asp?arti cleref=AR00000382EN.

New Jersey Herald, *People's Top 10 Cover Stories*, April 10, 2004.

New York Times, *Dutch Legalize Euthanasia, The First Such National Law*, April 1, 2002.

New York Times, The Netherlands: A Million Votes for Dead Man, May 22, 2002.

Nuffic, *The Holland Handbook* (The Netherlands, X-PAT Media, 2002).

Pauker, Joe, *GET LOST The Cool Guide to Amsterdam* (The Netherlands, Get Lost Publishing, 2001).

Rietbergen, P.J.A.N., *A Short History of the Netherlands* (Amersfoort, Bekking Publishers, 2002).

Robinowitz, Christina Johansson and Carr, Lisa Werner, *Modern Day Vikings* (Maine, Intercultural Press, Inc., 2001).

Schama, Simon, *Patriots and Liberators* (London, Collins, 1977).

Schama, Simon, *The Embarrassment of Riches* (New York, Vintage Books, 1987).

Selm, Joanne van, *The Netherlands: Tolerance Under Pressure*, Migration Policy Institute, August, 2002, http://www.migrati oninformation.org/Feature/display.cfm?ID=43.

Shipman, Hugh, *The Serious Drinker's Amsterdam Beer Café Guide* (U.K., Bierlijn Publications, 1999).

Simons, Marlise, *Proudly Gay, and Marching the Dutch to the Right*, New York Times, March 22, 2002.

Simply Amsterdam, http://simplyamsterdam.nl/.

Starbucks, Store Locator, http://www.starbucks.com/retail/locator/default.aspx.

Stevens, Harm and Pers, Walburg, *Dutch Enterprise and the VOC* (Amsterdam, Stichting Rijksmuseum Amsterdam, 1998).

Tagliabue, John, *In Rotterdam, Even a Politician's Foes Pays Respects*, May 7, 2002.

The National Organization for the Reform of Marijuana Laws, http://www.norml.com/.

The Netherlands Embassy, *U.S. Towns and Cities with Dutch Names*, January 1, 2003 http://www.netherlands-embassy.org/article.asp?articleref=AR00000382EN.

USA Today, *European Gay Union Trends Influence U.S. Debate*, July 14, 2004.

Vossestein, Jacob, *Dealing with the Dutch* (Amsterdam, KIT Publishers, 2001).

White, Colin and Boucke, Laurie, *The UnDutchables* (Colorado, White-Boucke, 2001).

Wikipedia, *Frisian Language*, http://en.wikipedia.org/wiki/Frisian_language.

Henri Willig, *The History of Gouda Cheese*, http://www.henriwillig.com/Cheese_History.htm.

Winner, David, *Brilliant Orange* (Great Britain, Bloomsbury, 2000).

World Climate, http://ww.w.worldclimate.com/.

XS4ALL, *Amsterdam as a Business City*, http://www.xs4all.nl/~wdb/business.html.

About the Author

Marc Resch is a graduate of the United States Military Academy at West Point and served as an Army Officer in Europe and the U.S. He received a Masters in Business Administration (MBA) from the University of North Carolina and received a Masters in Science (MS) from Stevens Institute of Technology in New Jersey. Marc is President of Resch Consulting Group (RCG), specializing in intercultural affairs, project leadership and business consulting. He possesses the Project Management Professional (PMP) certification and is active in the New York and New Jersey chapters of the Project Management Institute (PMI). Marc is also an active member of the Foreign Policy Association (FPA). Marc currently resides in New Jersey.